THE YEAR IN MUSIC 1979

THE YEAR IN MUSIC 1979

Judith Glassman

A Gladstone Book   COLUMBIA HOUSE, New York

Cover photographs:
Mick Jagger by Charlyn Zlotnik
Kenny Rogers courtesy Ken Kragen
Donna Summer by Chuck Pulin
Anne Murray by Frank Edwards/Fotos International
The Village People by Lynn Goldsmith, Inc., © 1979
The Bee Gees by Waring Abbott
Rod Stewart by Charlyn Zlotnik
Willie Nelson by Charlyn Zlotnik
The Blues Brothers by Lynn Goldsmith, Inc., © 1979
Linda Ronstadt by Arthur D'Amario, III/Retna
Barry Manilow by Robin Platzer, Images
Olivia Newton-John by Robin Platzer, Images

This book prepared and produced by Gladstone Books, Inc.
ISBN 0-930748-12-3

Editorial Director: Ford Hovis
Art Director: Allan Mogel
Associate Art Director: Eric Marshall
Photo Editor: Judith Glassman
Photo Research: Lester Glassner, Neal Peters
Contributing Editor: Toby Goldstein
Editorial Assistants: Grair Glassman, Jeanne McClow
Indexer: Lonnie Danchik

for Columbia House:
Paul A. Harris, *Vice President, Editorial Services*
Kathleen Nevils, *Director, Editorial Services*
Joanne Loria, *Manager, Editorial Services*
Frank Gesualdi, *Production Director*
Robert J. Kasbar, *Production Manager*
Alyce Kuchera, *Editorial Assistant*
Copy Staff: Sylvia Hare, Alva J. Horton, Harris Poor,
Guy Crandell Waid.

Contents

Dedication

The world of music lost three masters and one of its most promising voices in 1979. Arthur Fiedler, Stan Kenton, and Charlie Mingus were visionary artists whose bold experiments over the years continually thrust music into the future; Minnie Riperton was a gracious and lovely lady, whose soaring songs touched everyone who heard them.

Fiedler's symphonic pop, Kenton's wall of brass, Mingus's explorations of the jazz bass, and Riperton's supple expressiveness cheered and inspired millions of people. With gratitude for the gifts they so openly gave, *The Year in Music, 1979* is dedicated to them.

Introduction

In 1978 two monster albums, *Saturday Night Fever* and *Grease,* both high-priced, two-record sets, sold a total of some 40 million copies. Following nearly twenty-five years of consistent music-industry growth, these gorillas were viewed by eager record-company owners as signs of the times. Ignoring the equally significant portent of 1978's lackluster summer concert scene, record companies finished 1978 riding high on a fairy-tale boom. They beefed up their staffs and offered top artists sky-high guarantees and royalties to lure them from other labels. More dangerous, however, they pressed millions of copies of end-of-the-year disks by top artists, plastered distributors and retailers with these instant golds and platinums, and sat back, expecting the traditional Christmas sales rush. When it didn't materialize and retailers returned records in droves, record companies were caught with their economic pants down and their warehouses crammed full of rejected vinyl. Continually rising production costs with correspondingly higher retail prices discouraged buyers and further eroded first- and second-quarter profits of major companies. Home taping and record counterfeiters also took their toll on record-company income, which dipped substantially in the first half of 1979.

As the year went on there was no *Saturday Night Fever* and no *Grease* to pull the recording industry out of the hole. By the beginning of September there was as yet no titanic album from Fleetwood Mac or the Eagles or Stevie Wonder or Linda Ronstadt. Several superstar entries were disappointments, producing no hit singles to boost their sales into the anticipated multimillions. With concert tickets higher and potential concertgoers sticking close to home because of gasoline unavailability, some major concert attractions failed to sell out giant arenas, and concert promoters began to feel the pinch.

As the bad news emerged, record companies reacted, paring expenses to the bone and laying off large numbers of employees. Several major record company executives croaked gloom and doom, and the media, sniffing blood, almost triumphantly trumpeted front-page stories about the death of music, painting a dismal canvas of an industry teetering on the brink of collapse.

The media, however, revealed only part of the picture. As any music lover knew, there was a far more cheerful aspect bouncing off record turntables and out of radio speakers. Reports of music's demise were grossly exaggerated. The music was not only compelling—it was selling. Rod Stewart, even though Warner Brothers may have put the lid on $40,000-promotional parties, had the biggest hit of his career with the single "Do Ya Think I'm Sexy," and the 4-million-selling album *Blondes Have More Fun*. Supertramp's *Breakfast in America* sold 3 million copies; the Doobie Brothers' *Minute by Minute* was a 4-million-seller; Donna Summer enjoyed multimillion sales of her scintillating album *Bad Girls*; Kenny Rogers's *The Gambler* was a 2.5-million-seller; and the Bee Gees, snapping back from the failure of their *Sgt. Pepper* soundtrack, sold 4.5 million copies of *Spirits Having Flown*. Although RSO Records president Al Coury reported to *People* magazine that this figure was a disappointment, even he realized that his statement was a measure of the music industry's overblown expectations. Before 1978's massive sellers, an album that sold one million copies was regarded as a stellar success; a year that had produced such emphatic million-selling debuts as the Knack's *Get the Knack*, Dire Straits' and Rickie Lee Jones's self-titled premieres, and the Blues Brothers' *Briefcase Full of Blues* as well as such newly emergent million-sellers as Cheap Trick, the Cars, and Blondie, would have been looked on as a bonanza. There was a rich exuberance of new artists; in April of 1979 half the top-fifty albums on *Billboard*'s chart were by new performers. There was vigor and vitality in dance music, with disco inspiring hoofers from mainland China to Studio 54 and producing such stars as Donna Summer, Chic, Gloria Gaynor, and the Village People.

Profits may have been down, but the business was in no way moribund. There was also a healthy speed to record companies' reactions to the slump, not only cutting expenses and tightening credit, but signing economical new-wave bands who showed, as producer Mike Chapman demonstrated with the Knack, that albums could be cut for tens of thousands rather than hundreds of thousands of dollars. The Recording Industry Association of America discouraged initial overshipments by ruling that albums could not be certified as gold or platinum until four months after their release, when all returns would have been made. Responding to consumer resistance to high disk costs, many labels slashed the list price of catalog albums. Other positive signs included the development of the videodisc, with its enormous potential, the opening of the vast Asian and Chinese markets, and a new internationalism in marketing top performers. Columbia Records sent its top names to Cuba for Havana Jam, the first American concert in Cuba since the Castro takeover. Japan's leading pop duo, Pink Lady, appeared on United States television. Russia welcomed both Elton John and B.B. King and began to pay performance royalties for American music played in the Soviet Union.

Best of all, on the heels of late summer's gloomy prognostications, the shiny new albums from top stars began to emerge, and retailers across the country began to smile again. The music was there. *Slow Train Coming*, Bob Dylan's 1979 album, is perhaps the best of his career; Led Zeppelin's *In Through the Out Door* charged out of the gate with strong sales; long-awaited new product exploded from such stars as Bruce Springsteen, Fleetwood Mac, Stevie Wonder, the Eagles, Barbra Streisand, the Village People, Foreigner, Chic, the Rolling Stones, the Bee Gees, Cheap Trick, Neil Diamond, the Jefferson Starship, Waylon Jennings, Willie Nelson, Aerosmith, Boz Scaggs, Barry Manilow, Toto, and Steve Martin.

People continued to sing, to dance, to call their friends breathlessly, turn up their radios, and shout, "You've got to hear this!"

The music was there and the world was listening.

Preceding page: *Leif Garrett fans.* Clockwise from
upper left: *Disco's irresistible pulse swept the country
in 1979. The Bee Gees scored with "Tragedy." An
exuberant Rod Stewart at Madison Square Garden.
Peaches and Herb shake it up. Chic livened up
1979 with "Good Times." The tongue-in-cheek macho
of the Village People added bounce to 1979.
Donna Summer's "Hot Stuff" was a pop and disco smash.*

Frank Edwards, Fotos International

Chuck Pulin

Waring Abbott

Charlyn Zlotnik

Richard Creamer

Waring Abbott

THE YEAR IN M

Rock

In 1954 a clean-cut singing group called the Crew Cuts recorded a cover version of the Chords' song "Sh-Boom," which swept to the top of the pop charts. It was quickly followed by Bill Haley and the Comets' "Rock Around the Clock," and, springing from roots in black blues, rhythm and blues, and white country, rock and roll was born, sweeping sentimental crooners and big bands from the airwaves with a brand-new sound—an uninhibited, slam-bang, dead-ahead music. Every adolescent adored it instantly, and every right-thinking adult proclaimed, "That's not music. It sounds like noise to me."

In 1979, a quarter century later, the pulse that every pundit had predicted was a short-lived fad had become the basic idiom of pop music. Since the mid-1950s multimillion-dollar careers have soared in time to the throb of that backbeat, and the once dispensable has become gospel. In 1980, for the first time, four Grammy awards will be given for rock performances. The revolutionary has become respectable.

Inevitably, as rock and roll matured into rock, it became sophisticated and lost some of its initial frenzy. Its power rush of guitar, bass, and drums was slowed down and softened by electronic wizardry, complexity, and wistful longings for high art.

In 1979, however, another musical revolution is brewing, fomented by a generation that craves the lean and hungry sounds of those dirt-spare first records. And their hunger is being satisfied by an explosion of new-wave rockers that, with low production costs and heavy word-of-mouth support, are winning the hearts, souls, and dancing feet of this new breed of music lovers.

In 1979 the charts became a battleground. The top rock LPs of late 1978 and 1979 included the predictable: the soundtrack of *Grease*, the Who's *Who Are You*, Boston's *Don't Look Back*, the Rolling Stones' *Some Girls*, Foreigner's *Double Vision*, Billy Joel's *52nd Street*, Rod Stewart's *Blondes Have More Fun*, the Bee Gees' *Spirits Having Flown*, the Doobie Brothers' *Minute by Minute*, Bad Company's *Desolation Angels*, Supertramp's *Breakfast in America*, the Electric Light Orchestra's *Discovery*. But unexpectedly challenging these traditional rockers was a group of new bands with a clean, fresh sound: there were *Dire Straits* and *Communiqué* by Dire Straits, *Cheap Trick Live at Budokan* by Cheap Trick, *Parallel Lines* by Blondie, *Get the Knack* by the Knack, and *The Cars* and *Candy-O* by the Cars.

On the singles charts the same battle raged. There were the predictable smashes by the established rock titans: Boston's "Don't Look Back"; Little River Band's "Reminiscing"; Foreigner's "Double Vision"; the Bee Gees' "Too Much Heaven," "Tragedy," and "Love You Inside Out"; Billy Joel's "My Life"; Rod Stewart's "Do Ya Think I'm Sexy"; the Doobie Brothers' "What a Fool Believes"; and Wings' "Goodnight Tonight." But there was also a troupe of new names; some of them had a long performing history but no previous American hit, such as Exile, who scored with "Kiss You All Over," Nick Gilder with "Hot Child in the City," Suzi Quatro and Chris Norman with "Stumblin' In," John Stewart with "Gold." And there was a group of brash performers whose pared-down sound was as refreshingly energetic as "Blue Suede Shoes" had been in the 1950s. These included Blondie with "Heart of Glass" and "One Way or Another," Cheap Trick with "Surrender" and "I Want You to Want Me," the Knack with "My Sharona," and Joe Jackson with "Is She Really Going Out with Him."

Although their dominance of the pop charts was not as total as it had been in 1978, the Bee Gees were leaders once again; their 1979 achievements

Top: *As the New Barbarians, Ron Wood and Keith Richards toured in 1979 to promote Wood's album,* Gimme Some Neck. *Bottom:* Foreigner, *caught in action in London in November 1978, before Rick Willis replaced Ed Gagliardi on bass.* Head Games *was their 1979 sizzler.*

Ebet Roberts

Chris Walter/Retna

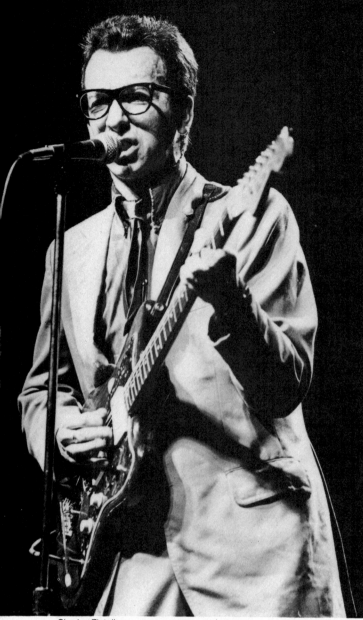

Charlyn Zlotnik

included gathering together a dazzling roster of pop performers for their ninety-minute television special "A Gift of Song—The Music for UNICEF Concert," aired on NBC January 10 and simulcast on more than 250 FM radio stations, the largest such broadcast ever. This star-studded gala featured ABBA, Rita Coolidge, John Denver, Earth, Wind & Fire, Andy Gibb, Elton John, Kris Kristofferson, Olivia Newton-John and Rod Stewart, each of whom donated their services to the event and perpetual rights to one song to UNICEF.

In 1979 The Bee Gees had six number-one singles in a row, tying the Beatles who had a string of six number-one hits in 1965 – 66. "Too Much Heaven," "Tragedy," and "Love You Inside Out," from their number-one multimillion-selling album *Spirits Having Flown*, gave them a career total of nine number-one singles, winning them fourth place on the all-time list. Their American tour, their first in two years, included fifty-eight concerts between June 28 and October 6 and was a slick, sold-out sensation.

During 1979 a host of major rock bands crisscrossed America. Queen brought a dazzling light show to accompany their power-packed end-of-1978 tour, playing thirty-four performances between October 28 and December 20 and requiring a near-military operation to carry twenty tons of equipment (including more than five hundred lights) from city to city. The Doobie Brothers sparkled as they recapped their nine years as a band in arenas across the country including a memorable set at New York's Palladium on December 9. In July they sang at Los Angeles's Universal Amphitheatre in a show that featured new members Cornelius Bumpus on saxophone, Chet McCracken on drums and vibes, and John McFee on guitar and violin.

Rock and roll in 1979 was Rod Stewart, forever a rocker despite his monster disco hit, "Do Ya Think I'm Sexy." On his mammoth, three-month tour, backed by his tight five-man band, Rod delighted his audiences, strutting onstage to the tune of "The Stripper," changing costumes midshow, his husky, unmistakable voice in fine form. Rock in 1979 was Yes, who won platinum at the end of 1978 with the LP *Tormato*. Visually, their show was quiet and unadorned, but it was a two-and-a-half-hour blast for the ears, joined for the final few electric numbers by Rick Wakeman. Also quiet visually were progressive rockers Supertramp, who scored with their number-one album *Breakfast in America* and with tasteful, pop-flavored songs, such as their number-one "The Logical Song."

Kiss was on the road again for the first time in more than a year, their heavy metal blitz matched by their outrageous stage spectacle, complete with fireworks, levitation, an exploding guitar, new 1979 costumes and the old familiar make-up, which was also sported by many members of the audience.

Ebet Roberts

Rock in 1979 was Boston, out on the road with Sammy Hagar. Although the beloved band had no new songs for its fans, the familiar opening chords of "Peace of Mind" and "More than a Feeling," raised ecstatic shrieks.

ABBA began its long-promised tour of the United States in September, arriving on their terms—as headliners, without ever having to play small clubs or to appear as an opening act.

Rock in 1979 was the Marshall Tucker Band, their expertise charging audiences to stomping and yelling. Van Halen displayed its dramatic, heavy metal din in the setting of a highly polished, seemingly chaotic stage show, featuring the aggressive athletics of lead singer David Lee Roth. Toto. Leif Garrett, Billy Joel, Kansas, Heart, Foreigner, Peter Frampton, Eddie Money, Ted Nugent, Jethro Tull. Poco. and Santana also wowed audiences.

Ebet Roberts

Charlyn Zlotnik

Opposite, top: *Punk mainstay Elvis Costello's spare music inspired a new generation of rough-and-ready rockers.* Bottom: *Their fans waited eagerly throughout 1979 for Boston's third album.*
Above, top: *Cheap Trick didn't achieve their staggering success until they went to Japan, but* Live at Budokan *opened America's eyes to their driving rock.* Bottom: *Meat Loaf's* Bad for Good *was an explosive followup to the dynamic* Bat Out of Hell.

In a fall tour called Back in the USSA, Elton John performed to sold-out houses, bringing the same manic enthusiasm with which he had earlier whipped usually staid Russian audiences into frenzies. The four concerts he gave in Leningrad between May 21 and May 23 and the four in Moscow between May 27 and May 30 were completely sold out. Elton suffered a mysterious collapse late in 1978, attributed to exhaustion and overwork; but in 1979 he showed his international fans that he was more than ready for the rigors of the road. His Russian jaunt was the climax of an overwhelmingly successful four-month tour of Europe and prelude to an equally smashing two months in the United States. Bad Company, touring in support of its million-selling album, *Desolation Angels*, gave a series of searing concerts, marred only by excessive fireworks set off by fans in some venues, notably Madison Square Garden. Although nobody was hurt, such episodes raise the question of how to restrain potential violence among rock crowds.

There were a number of incidents during the year: Aerosmith's lead singer, Stephen Tyler, was cut on the face when a fan threw a bottle from the balcony of Philadelphia's Spectrum. Although Tyler was not seriously injured, the band cut the show short. Led Zeppelin fans rioted at the Drake Theatre in Queens, New York, when the theater manager refused to turn up the volume on Zep's film, *The Song Remains the Same*. Angry Wisconsin fans smashed chairs, windows, and vending machines in the Milwaukee Arena on April 29 when promised "nationally known surprise acts" failed to appear at a New Barbarians concert. At Wichita's Herman Hill Park a riot occurred during an Easter Sunday concert causing damages of $100,000; more than sixty persons were hurt and eighty-eight arrested in the disturbance, blamed on overcrowding. The first World Series Rock Concert, held July 28 at Cleveland's Lakefront Stadium, was marred by preconcert violence: There were two deaths, five shootings, and a number of robberies, car thefts, and drug dealings. Much of the tension was caused by the presence of more than 65,000 white fans in the predominantly black neighborhood. In Boston, fighting after a Parliament-Funkadelic show at the North Shore Coliseum led to vows that rock concerts would never again be held in that facility. Because crowds of teenagers prevented firemen from putting out fires near a 1978 rock concert, the city of Philadelphia sponsored no free rock concerts during the summer of 1979. Even London's Roundhouse, a long-time rock showcase, had to agree to restrict the number of annual concerts and to reduce the noise level.

In what was perhaps the worst blow to rock concerts of all, plans for two mammoth festivals in New York State, one to be called the Hamlet of Hurleyville Music Festival and the other to be called Woodstock II, were cancelled when no community was willing to host the concerts. Contingency plans for a similar festival, to be called Second Gathering, also fell through, and ten years after the original Woodstock tribe came together for its weekend of love, peace, and celestial harmony a second such event did not happen.

Other rockers from the sixties were in evidence, however. The Who's movie *The Kids Are Alright* was a loving look at their career, its concert footage capturing some of the band's splendid onstage moments. *Tommy*, their rock opera, was staged in London as a major West End musical; their *Quadrophenia* was filmed, and in September, with new member Kenny Jones on drums and John (Rabbit) Bundrick on keyboards, the band appeared before massive crowds during a week of performances at New York's Madison Square Garden. They brought with them new energy and inspiration, as Peter Townshend told the *New York Times*'s John Rockwell, "Right now I feel very fired up and stimulated."

A reunited Allman Brothers scored with both their gold-winning album *Enlightened Rogues* and dynamic stage performances. The Byrds enjoyed a partial reunion as Roger McGuinn, Gene Clark, and Chris Hillman, three charter members of that influential 1960s quartet, cut an album together called *McGuinn, Clark and Hillman* and toured the country with their often imitated but never equalled sound. Joe Cocker, complete with gravel voice and stage contortions, made sporadic appearances to always full houses, his performances embracing such classics as "The Letter," "With a Little Help From My Friends," "You Are So Beautiful," and "Delta Lady." Jan Berry and Dean Torrance, known to 1960s fans as Jan and Dean, performed with uncontrolled vitality, moving audiences to standing ovations as they enthusiastically tore into such hits as "Surf City," "Linda," "Sidewalk Surfin'," and "Drag City." The Beach Boys, too, continued their endless summer with sold-out concerts throughout the year, often appearing before fans who were in diapers when the band first formed. Mitch Ryder released a new album, *How I Spent My Summer Vacation*, and toured for the first time in six years. The Seeds and Stems label, co-owned by Mitch and his manager Tom Connor, released *Michigan Rocks, Vol. I* in 1978, a collection of 1960s performances by such Detroit bands as Ryder and the Detroit Wheels, the MC5, and SRC.

The 1960s superheavy band Blue Cheer returned with bass player Dicky Peterson the only original member. And Elektra Records released *American Prayer*, an album featuring the late Jim Morrison's poetry backed by new instrumental tracks from the original Doors, John Densmore, Robby Krieger, and

The beloved Doobie Brothers, one of America's veteran bands, performs a stunning set at New York's Palladium in November 1978. During 1979 they changed personnel, replacing John Hartman and Jeff Baxter with John McFee, Cornelius Bumpus, and Chet McCracken.

Ray Manzarek. It also contained several Doors songs. some new and some old.

Some other sixties rockers who never went away were back on the road with new strength. Stephen Stills sizzled at his performances. sounding much harder than the folk-rock of Crosby. Stills. and Nash. His piercing guitar work drew comparisons with that of another ace guitarist, Eric Clapton, who toured forty-seven cities beginning March 28, accompanied by blues master Muddy Waters. Audiences at Clapton's April 19 show at Atlanta's Great Southeast Music Hall were treated to a thirty-minute jam with B.B. King.

The San Francisco contingent also brought its audiences highs. The Grateful Dead had audiences across the country dancing from their first notes. even though *Shakedown Street* did not become the smash album they have never had. The Jefferson Starship gave a surprise free concert in Golden Gate Park, erecting the stage under cover of darkness as the Parks and Recreation Department. while granting other bands permission to play, continued to deny the Starship that privilege. Their album *Gold* was a gold-seller, and the band continued to charge into the future even without Grace Slick and Marty Balin.

The Rolling Stones did not tour but still remained in the news. Mick was busy trying to work out his divorce with Bianca; a suicide in the home of Keith Richards made headlines while Richards was touring America with his band, the New Barbarians. Richards, Jagger, and Charlie Watts, along with Ian McLagan and Mick Fleetwood, guested on Ron Wood's LP *Gimme Some Neck.*

And then there were the Beatles, who were in the news more than ever this year. Southern California college newspaper editors voted them the favorite album rock artists of the past fifteen years, with *The White Album* tying Fleetwood Mac's *Rumours* as all-time favorite album. The Beatles were the subject of an informal course given at Princeton University. Capitol Records introduced a $160 package of thirteen Beatle albums, including one special disk containing 45s that were never before available on an album. Individual members of the band were in the news as well. John Lennon and Yoko Ono took a full-page ad in both the Los Angeles and New York *Times* at the end of May, a slightly murky missive that revealed John and Yoko's domestic tranquility and belief in magic. Mention of three angels looking over their shoulder were interpreted by many as an indication that there were no longer any hard feelings toward the other three Beatles. Paul McCartney rode high, winning a multimillion-dollar contract with Columbia Records and releasing *Back to the Egg*, a

hard-rocking album, and "Goodnight Tonight," a single that didn't appear on the album. In addition, Paul's publishing company, MPL Communications, continued to acquire the rights to old, successful songs, including the entire Buddy Holly catalog. George Harrison recorded *George Harrison* and the single "Blow Away," a top easy-listening hit. George and Ringo attended the reopening of the Star Club in Hamburg, Germany, appearing at the request of Tony Sheridan, the performer who had originally hired the embryonic Beatles, then called the Beat Brothers, to back him in 1960. And on May 19, Paul, Ringo, and George sang and played on a makeshift outdoor stage at the wedding reception of Eric Clapton and Patti Boyd, formerly Mrs. George Harrison. Perhaps the rock event of the year, the partial reunion was seen and heard by some two hundred wedding guests, including many top American and British stars.

Other 1960s rockers made their presence felt. Led Zeppelin, after two years of not touring, made two appearances at England's Knebworth Festival, first appearing at Copenhagen's intimate Falkoner Theatre for a special run-through. New Yorkers who wanted to see their British shows could buy tickets through Ticketron, the first time that tickets for rock concerts abroad have been made available to American audiences. And, although Bob Dylan finished his American tour late in 1978, he was represented by a dynamic live album, *Bob Dylan at Budokan,* which contained many updates of his classics, and by *Slow Train Coming*, an album recorded in Muscle Shoals with two members of the band Dire Straits. Black Sabbath celebrated its tenth anniversary together. Repeatedly delayed albums by Fleetwood Mac, Pink Floyd, and the Eagles were eagerly awaited.

Both the artists and the music of the 1950s were back with renewed vigor in 1979. Sha Na Na celebrated its tenth anniversary with two nights at New York's Radio City Music Hall on February 3 and 4; the wildly successful Sixth Rock 'n' Roll Record Meet and Film Festival took place in New York's Hotel Diplomat on March 31 and April 1, drawing rock-and-roll fans and fanatics from all over the country. A 1950s music room, the Golden Rock, opened to SRO business in Phoenix, Arizona. The lounge features Elvis mementos, early rock-and-roll memorabilia, waitresses dressed as high school cheerleaders, and bands that re-create 1950s hits.

Many performer/songwriters who formerly rejected material by others are looking to the fifties for songs that have already proven their power in the marketplace. Such classics as "Up on the Roof," "On Broadway," "Will You Love Me Tomorrow," "Cryin' in the Rain," and "Locomotion" have been given new life by contemporary singers.

In 1979 there was a flurry of activity to commemorate the twentieth anniversary of Buddy Holly's death. On February 3, the anniversary of Holly's final concert at Clear Lake, Iowa's Surf Ballroom, a memorial concert was held at the Surf, featuring Jimmy Clanton, Del Shannon, Flash Cadillac and the Continental Kids and MCed by Wolfman Jack. In New York, WBAI-FM deejay Peter Bochan put together a ninety-minute radio show called "Not Fade Away," including interviews with Holly by Alan Freed, Ed Sullivan, Dick Clark, and others, as well as live recordings of Holly, original

Richard Creamer

Robin Platzer

Opposite page, top: *Kiss's Gene Simmons wins the upper hand in an arm wrestling contest with Sha Na Na's Bowser at a 1978 Kissmas party. Bottom: Pounding piano man Billy Joel's* 52nd Street *was a top album in 1979. Clockwise from below: Ted Nugent and Rick Derringer jam in New York City. Dickey Betts and Gregg Allman starred in the reunion of the year. Bob Dylan's* Slow Train Coming *was either adored or despised, the master musician finding himself in the eye of the hurricane once again.*

Chuck Pulin

Ebet Roberts

Merry Alpern/Lynn Goldsmith, Inc © 1979

cuts, and several cover versions of Holly's songs cut by other artists. The program was aired in New York, Dallas, Denver, Tampa, Boston, and several smaller markets. In addition, a small San Francisco record company called Solid Smoke pressed some Buddy Holly cuts on hand-tinted picture disks and sold them through the mail.

In 1979 Elvis fever continued to run high. An open call by Pete Bennett to audition Elvis imitators for his forthcoming film biography of Presley, *The King of Rock 'n' Roll*, drew more than 150 aspirants to New York's Barbizon Theatre. Many events marked August 16, the second anniversary of Elvis's death. The biggest was the unveiling of the Elvis Presley Memorial Chapel in Tupelo, Mississippi, his birthplace. The chapel was built by donations from Elvis's fans, and its stained-glass windows show the mythic entertainer in different stages of his career. Paying homage at his grave on that day were thousands of fans from all over the world.

Some seminal 1950s rockers were very much alive in 1979. Jerry Lee Lewis cut a new self-titled album for Elektra Records, his first label change after twenty years on Mercury. He also made a rare New York City appearance for the grand opening of Club Lorelei, easily displaying how he won the nickname Killer by pounding out quicksilver rock and roll on his piano and wittily inventing new lyrics for old songs whenever the spirit moved him.

The legendary Chuck Berry was sentenced to four months at the Lompoc California prison farm after which he was ordered to give one thousand hours of community service, including benefit concerts, for income tax evasion. His last series of concerts, held at Los Angeles's Roxy, were no-holds-barred rockers, thrilling performances by Berry and his muscular four-piece band, preceded by some tunes from daughter Ingrid.

And it is, after all, dancing that rock and roll is all about. Rock lovers who want to dance but who disdain disco have inspired a rush of discos that boast the ambience of regular discos but play only rock, many of them featuring live acts in addition to records, most of them relying heavily on new-wave acts. New York is the rock disco leader, with the vast, comfortable space of Hurrah, as well as the Mudd Club, Club 57, and Studio 10. Even the Copacabana and the Cotton Club occasionally feature rock groups. In southern New Jersey the Ivystone Inn, a vast room in Pennsauken, became a mammoth rock club. In Chicago, Mother's on the near northside is a militantly antidisco rock club, and in Boston the Space became that city's first rock-and-roll disco.

Because some of 1979's best-selling rock music came from such groups as Blondie, Cheap Trick, the Cars, and the Knack, major record labels, burdened with hundreds of thousands of dollars of studio costs

Richard Creamer

Clockwise from above: *A California audience responds feverishly to the futuristic minimalism of Devo. The Knack blasted to pop stardom with the infectious stutter of "My Sharona." Dire Straits, another band that sprang from nowhere to overnight success; their music shimmered with the haunting guitar work of Mark Knopfler. With a number of television specials Leif Garrett grew in popularity as a teen idol in 1979. Playing the trumpet for her fans at New York's rock club Hurrah, Debbie Harry's onstage vitality provides a powerful visual focus for top pop rockers Blondie.*

21

for their top recording groups, eagerly signed on new-wave bands. These companies agreed with ace producer Mike Chapman, who produced Exile's "Kiss You All Over," Nick Gilder's "Hot Child in the City." and Blondie's *Parallel Lines* and brought in the Knack's *Get the Knack* for a total production cost of only $18,000. Chapman pointed out to *Billboard*'s Jim McCullaugh, "If the songs are really there. there's no need to spend endless hours and money in the studio."

CBS Records signed to distribute records by Stiff, the notorious English new-wave label; A & M signed with the International Record Syndicate, a company that represents a group of British new-wave labels. Other deals included Elektra's agreement to distribute both Polydor and Radar and Atlantic's signing on Virgin. Ariola, noted for its disco hits, has also moved heavily into rock, signing a number of new-wave groups.

Seething just beneath the lofty pop pinnacles scaled by 1979's new-wave winners were a group of performers secure in their record labels and their moderately successful recordings and/or growing reputations. Spearheaded by British bands, as was the booming rock revival of the mid-sixties, these include the Boomtown Rats, Elvis Costello, the Police, Devo, Marshall Chapman and Jaded Virgin, the Ramones, Talking Heads, Mink DeVille, the Clash (who toured America with Bo Diddley), the Tubes, the very 1950s yet 1980s B-52s, the Shirts, Nick Lowe, Joe Jackson, Rachel Sweet, Graham Parker and the Rumour, Bram Tchaikovsky, Tom Robinson, Ian Dury, Lene Lovich, and M. Standing apart from the typical new-wave crowd with his topflight versions of early American rock and roll is George Thorogood, the Louisiana-born singer/guitarist whose albums smashed onto the charts almost totally through word of mouth.

And just below *these* already established bands was an incredible number of struggling punk, new-wave, and exotic, unclassifiable groups, getting ready to erupt. They include such aggressively minimal, often ominous but sometimes spontaneously joyful bands as the Plasmatics, Quincy, Ruby and the Rednecks, the Buzzcocks, the Cramps, the Gang of Four, the The, Suicide, Birdland, Neon Leon, Pearl Harbor and the Explosions, the Blowdriers, Dead Kennedys, the Nervebreakers, Suspect, the Pink Section, the Mutants, and the theatrical, extravagantly costumed Mystic Knights of the Oingo Boingo.

These bands are supported by appearances in such small clubs as New York's CBGB and San Francisco's Mabuhay Gardens, where members of the audience with half blond, half brunette crewcuts, bright blue curls, or twenty-first century costumes draw as much attention as the performers. These musicians are promoted by such intelligent and

influential journals as *New York Rocker* and by such record stores as Long Beach California's Zed Records, which imports nearly 10,000 European new-wave singles each month. Even before they are signed by a record company these new bands get airplay on such radio programs as New York's WPIX-FM's "No Major Record Show," which plays only demos by unsigned bands, and on San Francisco's KSAN-FM's "The Heretics," which seeks out the newest records by the most outrageous new bands.

The bands are fed by such pioneering record companies as Greg Shaw's determinedly independent Bomp Records. The Los Angeles company, long a specialist in new-wave singles, has recently expanded to cutting and distributing albums as well. Although Shaw has signed with Decca for distribution in England, he is building his own American distribution network.

For the most part, the music of the new wave is fresh, accessible rock and roll, the kind of music that makes you jump up to turn up the volume and stay up to dance. If the sound is reminiscent of the fifties, so are some of the comments it evokes. About one of these bands, the highly mechanized Devo, one young Paul McCartney fan, her nose wrinkled with revulsion, said, "I don't like them. It just sounds like noise. It doesn't sound like music to me."

Chuck Pulin

Above: *Boston band the Cars rocketed to success with their self-titled debut album, followed by Candy-O, another winner.* Opposite, top: *When John Travolta made a surprise appearance at the Bee Gees' Houston concert their audience's mere pandemonium turned to roaring chaos.* Bottom: *Wed in April, Rod and Alana Stewart were 1979's most radiant couple.*

Rhythm and Blues

Rhythm and blues 1979 was a dynamic collection of showstoppers; a staggering range of expression and styles blasted out in venues both predictable and unexpected. At New York's Palace Theatre Nick Ashford and Valerie Simpson sizzled their way through an evening of their biggest hits; Aretha Franklin soared at Harrah's in Lake Tahoe with a show combining soul, jazz, pop, and MOR; Natalie Cole at the MGM Grand in Las Vegas moved audiences with a powerful version of her father's hit "Mona Lisa"; Earth, Wind & Fire at Honolulu's Blaisdell Arena crackled in a taut, energetic set; Patti Labelle exploded at New York's Beacon Theatre, lifting her audience from their seats with her dramatic voice and irresistible enthusiasm; Peter Tosh hypnotized a crowd at New York's Wollman Rink in Central Park with his majestic stage presence and unrelenting reggae; Funkadelic, gimmick-free except for guitarist Gary Shider's eye-catching diaper, set the normally seat-bound audience at New York's Palladium dancing in the aisles; the Pointer Sisters leaped into the pop stratosphere at the Santa Monica Civic with a completely new image, including firecracker rock, R & B, and even a few of their 1940s retreads, throbbing to a new beat. Diana Ross dazzled her fans at Buffalo's Memorial Auditorium with a deliciously flashy show, holding the audience in the palm of her hand. Stephanie Mills was the opening act at a Carnegie Hall concert, but her powerful voice left almost no room in the audience's heart for the headliner. Teddy Pendergrass tenderly seduced his 85 percent female audience at Madison Square Garden before offering his single "Turn Off the Lights" as America's energy-conservation theme song. The outrageous Rick James fronted his Stone City Band with abandon at New York's Felt Forum, only slightly upstaged by powerhouse opening act

Sister Sledge. Millie Jackson's funky set at New York's elegant Avery Fisher Hall bubbled with her usual raunchy stage patter, which delighted the audience as much as her songs.

In 1979 black performers reached out. With rhythm and blues as a rock-steady base they commandeered disco, moved easily into rock and pop, and rediscovered their past. For black artists and their music, 1979 was a particularly significant year, as it saw the beginning of the long-planned Black Music Association, organized to perpetuate, preserve, and protect black music. In congratulating the infant organization, President Carter declared, "Black music is also the root of contemporary American rock and disco music." He proclaimed June Black Music Month and held a buffet dinner at the White House in honor of the association. Headed by Kenneth Gamble, the organization held its first official meeting in early June, a session sparked by a dynamic thirty-two-minute film featuring the entire spectrum of black stars, from Miles Davis and Herbie Hancock to Isaac Hayes, the Jacksons, Donna Summer, Stevie Wonder, Barry White, Natalie Cole, Peabo Bryson, George Benson, Marvin Gaye, James Brown, and Teddy Pendergrass.

The association must have been heartened in its first few months of existence to hear positive news for the world of black music. At the end of 1978, Clive Davis, president of Arista Records, called on Larkin Arnold, former head of Capitol's soul division and a recognized authority in the field, to work for Arista, emphasizing the importance of black music to Arista's development. A & M announced a number of marketing innovations to help promote its black acts; EMI-America/United Artists Records formed an R & B division, as did RSO. The second annual "Rhythm and Blues Awards," hosted by Patti Labelle and Isaac

24

Opposite: *Ace bluesman B. B. King and his guitar Lucille won a warm welcome from Russian audiences on a 1979 Soviet Union jaunt.*

Hayes, was a shining presentation aired on ABC-TV. The Kool Jazz Festival sponsored a day of Soul on the Green at The Oakland Stadium on May 27, featuring the Emotions, the Bar-Kays, Chic, Peabo Bryson, Rose Royce, and B.B. King. On May 26, 61,000 funk fans screamed and boogied at the World's Greatest Funk Festival at the Los Angeles Coliseum. Concertgoers were amused, outraged, and totally warmed up by the cream of the funkified groups, including Bootsy Collins, Rick James, Con Funk Shun, Parlet and the Brides of Funkenstein, and the headliners, the inimitable Parliament/Funkadelic, who filled the stage with masterful illusions and filled the air with monstrously good, loud funk. The show was enormously successful, and with twenty-five cents

1979's top R & B performers sparkled with audacity and wit. Below: Earth, Wind & Fire flashed their ebullient optimism at every performance. Opposite, top: Rick James is as aggressive as his hit album, Bustin' Out of L Seven. *Bottom: Parliament's Gary Shider showed off outrageously in a diaper.*

Michael Putland/Retna

Top: *Ashford and Simpson, Quincy Jones and wife Peggy Lipton share a celebrative dinner.*
Above: *The Blues Brothers, better known to television audiences as Dan Aykroyd and John Belushi,gave up "Saturday Night Live" to film* The Blues Brothers.

from each concert ticket going to the United Negro College Fund, filled a black community function as well. As Renny Roker, head of R & B Productions, who produced the concert, told *Billboard's* Jean Williams, "Through our concerts we try to build community awareness, instill black pride, and prove to parents that we care about their kids."

The new organization, however, immediately found itself challenged by another new group, United Black Concert Promoters, with a slightly different set of priorities. Hosea Williams, a member of the Georgia State Legislature and a supporter of black promoters, in a letter to the Black Music Association urged that black acts be put off limits to white promoters as long as white acts rejected black promoters. The militant Williams called for picketing and boycotting the shows of any black act that would not cooperate.

The Black Music Association retained its more moderate stance. They saw that in addition to the problems facing black promoters there were other issues as well, concerning radio programming, job security, and the poor treatment given to small black-music dealers. As Kenneth Gamble put it, "We're not about picketing. We don't want to force anybody to do anything. We want to see how smart we are, see if we can figure out this puzzle." And at the organization's first Founders' Conference at Philadelphia's Sheraton Hotel feelings ran high as these problems were vigorously discussed.

The newly formed BMA will undoubtedly inspire renewed interest in the roots of black music, a movement that has already begun. One of these rich sources, blues legend B.B. King, began a startlingly successful four-week tour of Russia on February 28. The beloved black artist, his guitar Lucille, and a ten-piece American band communicated easily with friendly Russian audiences. Although no official jams took place, in Leningrad, King and his fellow American musicians met with the members of the Leningrad Dixieland Jazz Band. In the Russian state of Tbilisi, King was honored by local fans and Russian jazzmen who showed a film called *Tbilisi—78*, shot at the local annual jazz festival. Back in the United States, blues legend Billie Holliday was honored in a tribute called Ladies Sing the Blues. Held on August 12 at the Hollywood Bowl, it featured Nina Simone, Maxine Weldon, Morgana King, Carmen McRae, and Esther Phillips. During the summer of 1979 blues also began a strong resurgence in New York City, with such stars as Blind John Davis, Otis Rush, Eddie Kirkland, Abdullah Ibrahim, Lightning Hopkins and Ken McGorry. Johnny Winter and Louisiana Red, and John Lee Hooker appearing in such unlikely places as Tramps, the avant-garde Squat Theatre, and the Lone Star Café, formerly a strictly country venue.

Preceding page: *Singer/songwriter
Neil Diamond scored in 1979
with a Barbra Streisand duet.*
Opposite: *Willie Nelson
teamed with Leon Russell for
their winning album* One
for the Road. Above: *The
enthusiasm generated by
Sister Sledge onstage helped
sell a million copies of
their album.* Right: *The disco
throb of "Shake Your Groove
Thing" put Peaches and Herb
back in the spotlight.*

Below: *Although it was the long disco song "Love to Love You" that won Donna Summer her first fame, her growth as a performer is pushing her beyond the limits of disco. In her cover interview in* Penthouse *she revealed a sharp mind and a shrewd self-knowledge. Opposite: The warm, sensual vocals of Barry White is just one of the performer/composer/businessman's many talents. In addition to creating such platinum-winners as* The Man, *he runs his own record label.*

Chuck Pulin

Roz Levin Perlmutter

Opposite: *Felipé Rose and his Indian costume were the inspirations for the Village People.* Above: *Vivacious performer Alfa Anderson added her dynamic stage presence to Chic, 1979's disco unbeatables.* Following page: *One of rock and roll's living legends, Chuck Berry was sentenced to four months in prison and one thousand hours of community service for income-tax evasion.*

On November 29 jazz singer/composer Jon Hendricks brought his stunning musical-theater piece "Evolution of the Blues" to Los Angeles's Westwood Playhouse. Originally performed more than ten years ago at the Monterey Jazz Festival, the show, a brilliant and moving history of blacks from preslavery to today, has played for the past four years at San Francisco's Broadway Theatre.

At the beginning of 1979, Motown released *From the Vaults*, a collection of ten never-before-released cuts by some of Motown's top 1960s acts, including Gladys Knight and the Pips, the Supremes (with Diana Ross), the Temptations, Martha and the Vandellas, Marvin Gaye, the Spinners, the Marvellettes, Mary Wells, and Smokey Robinson and the Miracles. Robinson himself saw a renewed interest in his song catalog, with four of his classic songs on the charts at the end of 1978: Linda Ronstadt's version of "Ooh Baby Baby," Peter Tosh's handling of "You Gotta Walk and Don't Look Back," Eddie Money's performance of "You Really Got a Hold on Me," and Robinson's own "Shoe Soul."

James Brown, long known as the godfather of soul, made a surprise appearance on a street corner in a black Los Angeles neighborhood, soon gathering a huge crowd of autograph seekers, much to the consternation of his record-label escort. A bus driver even stopped his busload of passengers to get Brown's autograph. Brown, said the record company later, simply wanted to meet some fans. Brown also spread out into new directions, emerging with a disco record, selecting Neil Diamond as his new producer and songwriter, and appearing at Nashville's Grand Ole Opry on March 10.

Memphis blues also got a boost this year from a most unlikely and surprising source. "Saturday Night Live" stars John Belushi and Dan Aykroyd, calling themselves the Blues brothers, performed a stinging version of Isaac Hayes and David Porter's "Soul Man," boosting original performers Sam and Dave to a new popularity. Amii Stewart successfully revived Eddie Floyd's "Knock on Wood," backing it with a supercharged disco beat.

Disco did not live up to some expectations, but it did help several black performers. At the beginning of 1979, record-company executives forecast that rhythm and blues songs would become big disco hits and would then cross to the pop charts. This didn't happen. Instead, traditional R & B and black ballads were frequently ignored in the rush to disco. Several black disco records, such as Chuck Brown's "Bustin' Loose" and James Brown's "It's Too Funky in Here," were rejected by disco radio stations as being too ethnic. However, black disco producers did well and disco songs thrust such black performers as Donna Summer, Chic, Peaches and Herb, Gloria Gaynor, Anita Ward, Evelyn "Champagne" King, and McFadden and Whitehead to stardom.

Despite its problems, R & B remained vital and exciting and enormously optimistic, the top albums of the year included *Is It Still Good to Ya* by Ashford and Simpson; *One Nation Under a Groove* by Funkadelic; *Blam* by the Brothers Johnson; *Togetherness, Devotion* by L.T.D.; *Come Get It* and *Bustin' Out of L Seven* by Rick James; *The Man* by Barry White; *Live and More* and *Bad Girls* by Donna Summer; *Chaka* by Chaka Kahn; *C'est Chic* and *Risqué* by Chic; the *Best of Earth, Wind & Fire, Volume 1* and *I Am,* by Earth, Wind & Fire; *Motor Booty Affair* by Parliament; *Cheryl Lynn* by Cheryl Lynn; *Wanted* by Richard Pryor; *Crosswinds* by Peabo Bryson; *Here, My Dear* by Marvin Gaye; *2 Hot* by Peaches and Herb; *Love Tracks* by Gloria Gaynor; *Cruisin'* by the Village People; *Destiny* by the Jacksons; *We Are Family* by Sister Sledge; *Funk* by Instant Funk; *Livin' Inside Your Love* by George Benson; *Disco Nights* by G. Q.; *Rock On* by Raydio; *Inspiration* by Maze; *Songs of Love* by Anita Ward; *Winner Takes All* by the Isley Brothers; *Teddy* by Teddy Pendergrass; *Street Life* by the Crusaders; and the self-titled albums *Rose Royce Strikes Again, Chuck Brown and the Soul Searchers,* and *McFadden and Whitehead.*

Songs that reached the top five of the soul charts included Funkadelic's "One Nation Under a Groove"; Ashford and Simpson's "It Seems to Hang On"; the Jacksons' "Blame it on the Boogie" and "Shake Your Body"; Earth, Wind & Fire's "Got to Get You Out of My Life," "September," and "After the Love Has Gone"; Sylvester's "Dance"; Barry White's "Your Sweetness Is My Weakness"; Chaka Kahn's "I'm Every Woman"; Rick James's "Mary Jane"; Chic's "Le Freak," "I Want Your Love," and "Good Times"; Cheryl Lynn's "Got to Be Real"; Rose Royce's "Love Don't Live Here Any More"; Gene Chandler's "Get Down"; Peabo Bryson's "I'm So Into You"; Parliament's "Aqua Boogie"; Lakeside's "It's All the Way Live"; Chuck Brown and the Soul Searchers' "Bustin' Loose"; Tavares' "Never Had a Love Like This Before"; Peaches and Herb's "Shake Your Groove Thing" and "Reunited"; Instant Funk's "I Got My Mind Made Up"; Gloria Gaynor's "I Will Survive"; Sister Sledge's "He's the Greatest Dancer" and "We Are Family"; Rod Stewart's "Do Ya Think I'm Sexy"; G.Q.'s "Disco Nights"; George Benson's "Love Ballad"; Foxy's "Hot Number"; Raydio's "You Can't Change That"; the Isley Brothers' "I Wanna Be With You"; McFadden and Whitehead's "Ain't No Stoppin' Us Now"; Donna Summer's "Hot Stuff" and "Bad Girls"; Gap Band's "Shake"; Anita Ward's "Ring My Bell"; Earth, Wind & Fire and the Emotion's "Boogie Wonderland"; Con Funk Shun's "Chase Me"; the Jones Girls' "You Gonna Make Me Love Somebody Else"; and Teddy Pendergrass's "Turn Off the Lights."

Country and Western

In 1979 top country artists moved confidently onto the pop, easy-listening, and even disco charts. Kenny Rogers, whose platinum album *The Gambler* was an immovable number one on the country charts for six months, scored on the easy-listening charts with the title song and with "She Believes in Me." Lovely Anne Murray, whose gold LPs *Let's Keep It That Way* and *New Kind of Feeling* spent months in the top five of the country charts, scored on the country, easy-listening, and pop charts with "You Needed Me" at the end of 1978 and on the country and easy-listening charts with "I Just Fall in Love Again" and "Shadows in the Moonlight" in 1979. Eddie Rabbitt's "Suspicions" was a number-one country single and a top-twenty pop single. Dolly Parton had a surprising disco hit with her country number-one, "I Really Got the Feeling/Baby I'm Burning."

In 1979 other country artists whose records sold more than half a million copies to win coveted gold disks were Willie Nelson with *Willie and Family Live*, Tanya Tucker with *TNT*, Waylon Jennings with his *Greatest Hits*.

Country festivals and concerts also thrived. On April 14 to 16, London's eleventh International Festival of Country Music at the Wembley Arena drew more than 31,000 fans. The performers included such country sensations as Ronnie Milsap, Tammy Wynette, Crystal Gayle, Conway Twitty, Bobby Bare, Marty Robbins, Billie Joe Spears, and a host of others, all of whom turned in crackling performances.

The two annual July 4 country celebrations, the Statler Brothers' Happy Birthday U.S.A. Celebration (their tenth) and Willie Nelson's July 4 Picnic (his seventh), were huge successes, the Statler's drawing 52,000 of their fans to Staunton, Virginia for an all-day festival and concert, while Nelson gathered 17,000 outlaw fans to hear him, Leon Russell, Ernest Tubb,

Bobby Bare, Johnny Paycheck, and the Geezinslaw Brothers. The Princeton Country Music Festival, held at Palmer Stadium in Princeton, New Jersey, showcased the Oak Ridge Boys, Larry Gatlin, Roy Clark, the Earl Scruggs Revue, Con Hunley, Janie Fricke, Hoyt Axton, Mary K. Miller, Rex Allen, Jr., and Kelly Warren, all of whom performed with gusto before a crowd of more than 50,000. And, although Broadway Opry '79, an ambitious lineup of country talent playing in a legitimate Broadway theater, folded early, Waylon Jennings packed in a full house of New Yorkers who came to see him play his special brand of outlaw country, first with the Crickets, his first band, and then with the Waylors.

In 1979 Nashville was busting out all over. The Country Music Association's 1979 radio survey showed that for the first time more than 2,000 radio stations in the United States program some country music, with the number of full-time country stations leaping from 1,119 in 1978 to 1,424 in 1979. According to Arbitron, the leading radio survey, country dominates more individual radio markets than any other format.

In 1979 a burgeoning Tennessee motion picture industry began to blossom, sparked by the success of Clint Eastwood's *Every Which Way But Loose*, which featured top country songs by Eddie Rabbitt, Charlie Rich, and Mel Tillis. That movie, and such other country winners as *Smokey and the Bandit*, *W. W. and the Dixie Dance Kings*, and 1978's *Harper Valley P.T.A.*, showed that moviegoers were interested in country settings and people. Scheduled for release in 1980 are a spate of movies with a country theme and/or country stars, including the spectacular $8.5-million *Coal Miner's Daughter*, taken from Loretta Lynn's best-selling autobiography and starring Sissy Spacek, Tommy Lee Jones, and Levon Helm; the $12-

Opposite: Mel Tillis wins audiences with his engaging personality and such wry country songs as 1979's "Coca Cola Cowboy."

Clockwise from right: *Crystal Gayle, voted best female vocalist 1978 by the Country Music Association and Barbara Mandrell, the top female vocalist according to the Academy of Country Music. Young Tanya Tucker projected a tough, sexy image in 1979.*

Chuck Pulin

Charlyn Zlotnik

Charlyn Zlotnik

million *Urban Cowboy*, starring John Travolta, and *Middle-Aged Crazy*, based on the Jerry Lewis song hit and starring Bruce Dern and Ann-Margret. There were plans for *Red-Headed Stranger*, based on a song of Willie Nelson's, *The Electric Horseman*, starring Willie in a nonsinging role, and for sequels to *Smokey and the Bandit* and *Every Which Way But Loose*.

Country's familiar twang exploded around the country and the world. For the first time, Switzerland's Montreux International Jazz Festival included country music, featuring Roy Clark, the Oak Ridge Boys, Barbara Mandrell, and Buck Trent. According to Tree International, a leading Nashville publisher, its country songs are being played in more than one hundred countries around the world.

In New York City, two radio stations played western music and a new part-time country music club, the Club Lorelei, joined Gotham's other country venues, the Lone Star Café, O'Lunney's, and City Limits. Eddie Rabbitt delighted New Yorkers when he performed at a $1,000-a-ticket benefit for the handicapped held at New York's trendy department store Bloomingdales.

Wherever you looked in 1979 the Nashville sound was flourishing. "The Academy of Country Music Awards Show" on May 2 was the first to be carried live over national television in prime viewing time. Manager Jim Halsey's Tulsa '78 International Music Festival, held at the beginning of November 1978, drew 20,000 fans during two days to see the Oak Ridge Boys, Tammy Wynette, Roy Clark, Ray Price, Don Williams, Joe Stampley, Freddy Fender, Rick Nelson, and other artists. In June in northern California, the traditionally jazz-oriented Russian River Music Festival became the First Annual Russian River Country Music Festival, featuring Ronnie Milsap, Doug Kershaw, Con Hunley, Johnny Duncan, and Moe Bandy.

Nashville's famed annual festival that brings stars and fans into close contact, jammed Music City with country addicts from all over the United States who came to see, hear, and meet such country greats as Barbara Mandrell, Moe Bandy, Crystal Gayle, Ronnie Milsap, Loretta Lynn, Johnny Paycheck, and Margo Smith. In 1978 the Country Music Foundation's Hall of Fame and Museum attracted more than 500,000 visitors for the first time in its eleven-year history, with 1979 figures looking even better.

But all this expansion led to dislocation and questions. As country stars grow in international popularity and reach out more aggressively for larger and wider audiences, many Nashville purists feel country music is threatened. Such pop acts as the Bee Gees, Linda Ronstadt, and Barbra Streisand and Neil Diamond made inroads on the country charts, which were also studded with new versions of old

pop, rock, and R & B songs. Because studio time in Nashville costs less than in L.A. or New York and because many Nashville studios have spanking new, state-of-the-art facilities, those studios were booked by growing numbers of pop, rock, R & B, and disco acts; only 44 percent of 1978's studio sessions were used to record country music.

Even though crossover records brought such country artists as Dolly Parton, Kenny Rogers, Barbara Mandrell, Crystal Gayle, Dr. Hook, Eddie Rabbitt, Ronnie Milsap, and Waylon Jennings to the attention of the entire pop world, influential Nashville voices complained bitterly that the net effect was to dilute country music and weaken Nashville. In an angry *Billboard* editorial, Wesley Rose, a past president of the Country Music Association and currently one of its directors, lashed out at the crossover concept, particularly at country stations that program what he calls pop music. "If country music had started with crossovers, there wouldn't be a country-music industry today," Rose pointed out.

His letter evidently hit a nerve; *Billboard* printed a cross section of answers, some supporting Rose and others attacking him for a narrow point of view. Ray Ross, program director of WKOP-AM, a "modern-country" radio station in Binghamton, New York, maintained that when he added a small percentage of crossover records to his format the station doubled its ratings; he further claimed that his judicious use of crossover has introduced pure country to new listeners.

Most observers agree that there is a new breed of performer who calls himself a country artist but doesn't create a traditional country sound, but most also agree that this doesn't endanger country's identity. Instead, parts of the country idiom become incorporated into rock, pop, perhaps even R & B and disco, while elements of those sounds merge with country music. There will always be an audience for hard-core country and there will always be sterling-pure country performers like Conway Twitty, Loretta Lynn, Mel Tillis, George Jones, the Statler Brothers, the Oak Ridge Boys, and many others.

Perhaps because Nashville has traditionally been an isolated, self-contained music community, its growing pains have been particularly sharp. As such major country artists as Dolly Parton, Kenny Rogers, Ronnie Milsap, Tanya Tucker, and Kris Kristofferson have gone after the pop market, they have also turned to firms outside of Nashville for management, a trend Nashville managers vowed to reverse in 1979.

However, despite industry-wide concern over the possible effects of a recession, Nashville divisions of major record companies continued to be a steady source of reliable income. Because Nashville had not participated heavily in overspending on promotional frills, their layoffs were not as severe and their

Clockwise from upper right: *Kenny Rogers, Academy of Country Music's entertainer of the year. Willie Nelson presents President Carter with a crystal bowl on behalf of the Country Music Association. Veteran Johnny Cash and superstar Dolly Parton. Eddie Rabbitt, New Jersey's favorite son. Opposite, top:* The Oak Ridge Boys, CMA and Academy of Country Music's vocal group of the year. *Bottom:* Don Williams scored in 1979 with "Tulsa Time."

Paul Canty/Retna

Chuck Pulin

Wide World Photos

Wide World Photos

cutbacks not as noticeable as in the pop divisions. And, in 1979, Nashville's music was undeniably potent. The top country singles from the last two months of 1978 and into 1979 were "Tear Time" and "Golden Tears" by Dave and Sugar, "Let's Take the Long Way Around the World," "Back on My Mind Again/Santa Barbara," and "Nobody Likes Sad Songs" by Ronnie Milsap, "Anyone Who Isn't Me Tonight" and "All I Ever Need Is You" by Kenny Rogers and Dottie West, "Sleeping Single in a Double Bed" and "(If Loving You Is Wrong) I Don't Want to Be Right" by Barbara Mandrell, "Sweet Desire/Old Fashioned Love" by the Kendalls, "Little Things Mean a Lot" by Margo Smith, "Every Which Way But Loose" and "I Just Want to Love You" by Eddie Rabbitt, "On My Knees" by Charlie Rich with Janie Fricke, "The Gambler" and "She Believes in Me" by Kenny Rogers, "Burgers and Fries" and "Where Do I Put Her Memory" by Charley Pride, "All of Me" by Willie Nelson, "Tulsa Time" and "Lay Down Beside Me" by Don Williams, "Don't You Think This Outlaw Bit's Done Got Out of Hand/Girl I Can Tell" and "Amanda" by Waylon Jennings, "I Really Got the Feeling/Baby I'm Burning" and "You're the Only One" by Dolly Parton, "Lady Lay Down" and "Backside of Thirty" by John Conlee, "Your Love Has Taken Me That High" and "Don't Take It Away" by Conway Twitty, "Why Have You Left the One You Left Me For" by Crystal Gayle, "Come On In" and "Sail Away" by the Oak Ridge Boys, "I'll Wake You Up When I Get Home" by Charlie Rich, "Send Me Down to Tucson/Charlie's Angels" and "Coca Cola Cowboy" by Mel Tillis, "I Just Fall in Love Again" by Anne Murray, "It's a Cheating Situation" by Moe Bandy, "If I Said You Had a Beautiful Body Would You Hold It Against Me" by the Bellamy Brothers, "Lying in Love With You" by Jim Ed Brown and Helen Cornelius, "I Can't Feel You Any More" by Loretta Lynn, "(Ghost) Riders in the Sky" by Johnny Cash, "The Devil Went Down to Georgia" by the Charlie Daniels Band, "Heartbreak Hotel" by Willie Nelson and Leon Russell, and "Pick the Wildwood Flower" by Gene Watson.

Top-selling country albums were *Heartbreaker* and *Great Balls of Fire* by Dolly Parton; *Stardust* by Willie Nelson; *I've Always Been Crazy* by Waylon Jennings; *Living in the U.S.A.* by Linda Ronstadt; *Expressions* by Don Williams; *Every Which Way But Loose* soundtrack with Mel Tillis, Eddie Rabbitt, and Charlie Rich; *Classics* by Kenny Rogers and Dottie West; *Blue Kentucky Girl* by Emmylou Harris; *One for the Road* by Willie Nelson and Leon Russell; *Loveline* by Eddie Rabbitt; *Images* by Ronnie Milsap; and *Million Mile Reflections* by the Charlie Daniels Band.

Wide World Photos

Charlyn Zlotnik

Disco

Hundreds of lights ripple and pulse, stab and strobe, flashing off mirrored surfaces. Women in bare, slinky dresses with thigh-high slits or shiny, clinging jeans and backless mules weave and whirl. Their partners, in sleek three-piece white suits, pull them in and twirl them out. Bare-chested men in balloon-topped trousers, pegged at the ankles, thrust and shake to 112 beats per minute, the relentless rhythm track pounding through layers of synthesizers, horns, and sexually provocative lyrics. In some twenty thousand pleasure palaces across the United States, every night is party night. And with disco music now played in soundproofed cars on several of Belgian Railways trans-European routes, with disco deejays replacing on-strike steel bands at Trinidad's annual carnival, with a disco planned for Shanghai, and with costly disco equipment in the bedrooms of Arabian sheiks, disco in 1979 was on its way to becoming the first truly global social phenomenon. Critics may dismiss most of the music as mindless, monotonous, and mediocre, but disco is more than just music. In the dark, anonymous, superheated, suggestive disco environment, dancers can forget their cares and, mesmerized by lights and music, let their hair down.

In 1979 more than 36 million people flocked to discos of all kinds; in addition to dancing, they enjoyed drinks, sometimes food, occasional live entertainment, and play areas containing pinball machines and backgammon games. They danced in San Francisco's glass-enclosed Oz, that city's plushest private club, floating thirty-two stories above a breathtaking view of the glittering city. They cavorted in Los Angeles's strictly gay Studio One, or at Phazes, Atlanta's $1.5-million disco. Or, if they were one of the favored, they could enter the decade's hottest, most chic club, New York's Studio 54, where owner Steve Rubell oversees a dance floor and notorious balcony crowded with the likes of Halston, Truman Capote, Bianca Jagger, Andy Warhol, Margaret Trudeau, and other glamorous or notorious sybarites.

Throughout the country, teenagers had their own alcohol-free discos. Roller disco was a burgeoning part of the 1979 scene, as a growing percentage of the nation's 28 million roller skaters learned to dance on skates, either confidently bopping down the street with headphones or in a roller rink with a state-of-the-art sound system. Discos supported a thriving audio and lights industry. The uninhibited theatrical disco look influenced fashion designers, cosmetic companies, and interior designers, the entire scene a celebration of twentieth-century urban lifestyle.

Today's discos have their roots in discotheques of the 1960s that played largely rock, featuring both recorded music and live performers. In the early seventies disco became a major part of the black, Latin, and gay subcultures. It wasn't until the release of *Saturday Night Fever,* the film in which John Travolta crystallized the image of disco as fantasy fulfillment—a way that even the most ordinary person could become a star—that disco exploded.

In 1979 disco won some of music's highest honors, with Paul Jabara winning a Grammy for "Last Dance" as best R & B song and Donna Summer winning a Grammy for best R & B vocal performance by a female for her rendering of that song. "Last Dance" also won an Academy award as best original song. Other disco grammy-winners were the Bee Gees for album of the year and best vocal performance by a duo, group, or chorus for *Saturday Night Fever*. The Bee Gees also won for best arrangement for voices for "Stayin' Alive." Disco band A Taste of Honey was voted best new artist of the year; Barry Manilow won a

Opposite: *In 1979 the dynamic Donna Summer was an unstoppable force, every one of her songs a firecracker, from "Hot Stuff" to "Bad Girls" to her smooth September winner "Dim All the Lights."*

The sound of 1979 was the inescapable throb of disco. Clockwise, from right: Amii Stewart, who turned an update of "Knock on Wood" into a two-million-seller. Anita Ward's "Ring My Bell" dripped from every street radio throughout the summer. Chér's comeback winner was "Take Me Home." Chic could do no wrong, scoring with "Good Times."

© 1979 Charlyn Zlotnik

Lauman Abbott

Darlene Hammond/Retna

46

Courtesy T.K. Productions

Grammy for best male vocal performance for his disco song "Copacabana (At the Copa)." In 1980, the National Academy of Recording Arts and Sciences will for the first time award a disco Grammy.

Some of the best-selling music of late 1978 and 1979 was made by disco stars. Showing powerful growth as a singer and performer, Donna Summer was unquestionably the leading disco star of the year, soaring to the stratosphere of both disco and pop charts with her versions of "MacArthur Park," "Hot Stuff," and "Bad Girls." Chic scored similarly with "Le Freak" and "Good Times"; the Village People with "Y.M.C.A." and "In the Navy"; Peaches and Herb with "Shake Your Groove Thing"; Alicia Bridges with "I Love the Night Life"; Gloria Gaynor with the titanic "I Will Survive"; Amii Stewart with "Knock on Wood"; Sister Sledge with "We Are Family"; Anita Ward with "Ring My Bell." But disco artists weren't the only ones to shine with disco songs. Rod Stewart enjoyed the biggest single of his career with "Do Ya Think I'm Sexy." The Bee Gees continued their career-rejuvenating disco successes with "Tragedy." Cher scored with "Take Me Home"; Blondie with "Heart of Glass"; Wings with "Goodnight Tonight"; the Doobie Brothers with "What A Fool Believes"; the Pointer Sisters with "Fire"; Barbra Streisand with "Main Event/ Fight"; and Herb Alpert with "Rise." Deniece Williams's career got a new boost with her discofied "I've Got the Next Dance," and Diana Ross's "The Boss" was a pulsing disco and pop hit.

Other artists jumped on the disco bandwagon as well, including Herbie Hancock, the Beach Boys, Joe Tex, jazzman David "Fathead" Newman, Ethel Merman, Count Basie, and Frank Zappa with a genial parody, "Dancin' Fool." Ann-Margret, directed by *Grease* soundtrack producer Louis St. Louis, danced and sang disco to a fevered and enthusiastic crowd at Billboard's Disco Forum VI. Music queens Barbra Streisand and Donna Summer paired on a disco single from Barbra's album *Wet*. Arthur Fiedler's last record was called *Saturday Night Fiedler*. And in the first eight months of 1979, eleven of the sixteen number-one pop songs were disco.

In 1979 radio stations across the country began switching to disco. They were following the lead of New York's WKTU-FM, which, after years of limping along in the ratings basement with the mellow sound, became a disco station overnight and leaped to the number-one spot in the number-one market in the country, topping even WABC-AM, long New York's radio leader. Of the two hundred all-disco stations in the United States, 90 percent have good ratings.

Television joined the disco chase. "Midnight Special," although still programming occasional rock acts, switched from pop rock to disco for a trial run. When "The Merv Griffin Show" televised a disco dance contest, the show won its highest ratings. So

Merv Griffin Productions and 20th Century-Fox began "Dance Fever," a half-hour weekly dance contest that joined other such disco shows as "Kicks," "Soap Factory," "Disco Magic," and "Hot City." Movie companies caught on fast; Allan Carr began producing the Village People movie, and there were plans for at least two more disco films, *Roller Boogie* and *Nocturnal*. Although Broadway's *Got tu Go Disco* was a monumental failure, several producers, including *Beatlemania*'s Leber and Krebs, have Broadway disco projects in the works.

Surprisingly laggard in recognizing the importance of disco were major record companies, who watched from the sidelines while such labels as Casablanca, TK, and Salsoul cut hit disco records that went gold and platinum. It wasn't until mid-1979 that the major labels committed themselves to signing and developing disco product. Part of the difficulty may have been that record companies were not equipped: the longer cuts desirable for dancing didn't fit on a traditional seven-inch forty-five. Disco mixer Tom Moulton and engineer José Rodriguez solved the problem by creating the twelve-inch disk.

The twelve-inch singles created other problems, however. Expensive to produce, they at first were made only for promotional play in discos and on radio. But fans were angered at not being able to buy their favorite disco songs, so record companies began to cut twelve-inch singles for retail sale. Although these records generally contained only one song or a suite of songs and listed for $4.98 by late 1979, they enjoyed brisk sales.

Of course, discoland has not been nirvana. Health problems abound, the most frequently mentioned being the danger of deafness developing from long exposure to high-volume music. Club patrons who fear hearing loss can purchase any of a number of ear protectors that allow them to hear clearly while reducing the decibel level that reaches the inner ear. The Bureau of Radiological Health, a federal agency, warns that lasers can be damaging. Podiatrists are worried that women who wear stiletto heels for dancing will permanently damage their feet. Disco roller rinks are scenes of frequent accidents. But disco patrons dismiss these threats and are more than willing to dare disco going.

Disco's popularity has produced violent backlash, primarily from rock fans. This feeling exploded on July 12 at Comiskey Park when 10,000 disco records were blown up between games at a White Sox/Tigers doubleheader. Seven thousand disco haters spilled onto the playing field, smashed records, burned banners, ripped up the sod, and caused a cancellation of the second game. The riot grew out of an antidisco campaign spearheaded by Steve Dahl, a deejay at Chicago rock station WLUP-FM. Dahl, who had been pushed out of his previous job when

Courtesy Warner Brothers

the station switched to disco, arranged for fans to be admitted to the stadium for ninety-eight cents (WLUP is at 98 on the FM band) if they surrendered a disco record at the gate. As a result of the stunt, Dahl won a contract with Ovation Records, for whom he cut a Rod Stewart parody called "Do Ya Think I'm Disco," and WLUP got a boost in the ratings. Dave Herman, deejay for New York's progressive rock station WNEW-FM, suffered a taste of disco backlash when he aired Donna Summer's "Hot Stuff." He was flooded with rabid antidisco letters and phone calls. Mother's, a rock disco in Chicago, prints T-shirts that read "Death to the Bee Gees."

A potentially far more serious problem that disco faces is the relative scarcity of real stars. Because the songs are frequently conceived by record producers and cut using studio musicians, there are very few acts with real star potential who can succeed in public appearances and whose performances can sustain an entire LP. Despite the explosion of disco groups, there has been no corresponding increase in album sales, due partly to

Waring Abbott

48

the lack of strong, identifiable performers.

Of course, the record producer is a new class of star. Not only does he create the concept of the song, but as recording technology becomes increasingly sophisticated and much of the disco sound can be created in the studio, the producer becomes crucial in creating a record that gives disco dancers the novelty and the beat they want. Producers/songwriters/performers Nile Rodgers and Bernard Edwards of Chic brought success not only to their own band, they also turned the trick for Sister Sledge. Giorgio Moroder and Pete Bellotte masterminded the records of Donna Summer and Jacques Morali did the same for the Village People.

Another powerful figure to emerge is the disco deejay, who completely controls the mood of a crowd, blending songs to create new compositions, programming tempo, volume, and mood to swell, peak, subside, and then build again. Ruling from his booth above the dance floor, he is the disco deity who makes a night on the dance floor come alive and who makes every dancer shine like a star.

Charlyn Zlotnik

Far left: *Barbra Streisand wrapped her bountiful voice around "Main Event/Fight" from her movie,* Main Event. *Center: No one had ever seen a band like the Village People before Jacques Morali created them. Left, top: Rod Stewart's disco song, "Do Ya Think I'm Sexy" was the biggest hit of his career. Bottom: Roller rink operators and their patrons discovered that disco and roller skates were made for each other.*

49

Robin Platzer, Images/Neal Peters

Jazz

For jazz, 1979 was a year when classic performers shone, festivals flourished, and signs of expansion could be heard everywhere. One of America's best-loved musical forms continued to shed its reputation as cult music and to be accepted by a far vaster audience. Leading concert promoters across the United States confirm that jazz is attracting larger audiences. Such traditionally poprock promoters as Los Angeles's Wolf & Rissmiller, San Francisco's Bill Graham, and Denver's Feyline Productions report that just as such crossover artists as Chuck Mangione, George Benson, and Spyro Gyra are turning jazz albums to gold and platinum, so contemporary jazz personalities are attracting concert audiences three times as large as before.

At the beginning of 1979 the jazz world lost one of its titans when Charles Mingus, the colorful, innovative composer and jazz bass genius finally succumbed to Gehrig's disease at the age of fifty-six. The beloved musician was honored formally in two Carnegie Hall concerts on June 1 and 2, featuring his own compositions performed by such musicians as Dexter Gordon, Woody Shaw, Gerry Mulligan, and the Mingus Dynasty Band. Losing one major jazz figure made many Americans realize what unequalled and irreplaceable natural resources are our aging but vigorous jazz greats.

Because of these dynamic artists, jazz festivals in 1979 were spectacular, the most dazzling the ten-day, thirty-seven event Newport Jazz Festival, the twenty-sixth edition of George Wein's annual extravaganza.

New York City jazz buffs eagerly trekked from such predictable venues as Carnegie Hall, Radio City, Roseland, and the Saratoga Performing Arts Center in Saratoga Springs, New York, to more exotic locales, including the Staten Island Ferry, where Wallace Davenport's New Orleans Jazz Band and Wild Bill Davidson sent musical strains soaring over New York harbor. The festival also included a jazz mass, composed by Keikki Sarmanto, and such classic performers as Benny Goodman in concert with Marion McPartland; Count Basie and his big band, including guest appearances by such noted alumni as Eddie "Lockjaw" Davis, Harry Edison, Joe Newman, and singer Joe Williams; Muddy Waters as guest of honor at a Radio City Music Hall concert that also featured James Cotton and his band and B. B. King with his men; Lionel Hampton performing a dynamite show at Avery Fisher Hall; and Dizzy Gillespie, surrounded by a thundering mix of drummers, opening the festival. Such younger stars as Pat Metheny, Weather Report's Jaco Pastorius, Earl Klugh, Freddie Hubbard, Grover Washington, Jr., and Ramsey Lewis, among others, sparkled. The avant-garde was represented by such provocative bands as the Oliver Lake Trio, the Leroy Jenkins Trio, and the Anthony Braxton Quartet. And Mel Tormé and Gerry Mulligan repeated their excellent Celebration of the American Song, featuring George Shearing and Jackie and Roy.

Other jazz festivals in 1979 were equally inspired. The *Boston Globe* Jazz Festival, held between March 9 and March 18, included more than two hundred musicians in the biggest jazz festival the *Globe* ever sponsored. Included were the Brecker Brothers, Larry Coryell, Sonny Rollins, Jimmy Maxwell, and a Jazz Latino show featuring the Tito Puente Orchestra and Machito's Afro-Cuban Jazz Band, with guest soloists Sonny Stitt and Willie Bobo. Eubie Blake, more youthful than ever at ninety-six, was the star of the Dixieland Bash. Other Boston concerts included bass player Ron Carter with Zoot Sims and Al Cohn, Woody Herman and his Young Thundering Herd, and

50

Opposite: *Grammy-winning Chuck Mangione's grin is as well known as the distinctive sound of his flugelhorn, whose caressing tones propelled* Feels So Good *to million-plus sales and made* An Evening of Magic *a pop and jazz chart climber.*

the New Dave Brubeck Quartet.

Kool sponsored a series of touring jazz concerts, including three nights starring Sarah Vaughan, Count Basie, Gerry Mulligan, Mel Tormé, Betty Carter, and Eddie Jefferson. On March 25, at Florida's West Palm Beach Auditorium, George Wein sponsored an eight-hour jazz marathon that included Herbie Hancock, Eubie Blake, Muddy Waters, Stan Getz, and Charlie Byrd. Although rain dampened the tenth annual New Orleans Jazz and Heritage Festival, cutting an anticipated 300,000 attendance to 175,000 and causing the cancellation of several outdoor events, the nine evening concerts were almost entirely sold out. They included Ella Fitzgerald and the New Orleans Philharmonic Symphony Orchestra, Alberta Hunter, Eubie Blake and Earl "Fatha" Hines, the Staple Singers, Roy Ayers, Allen Toussaint, Lionel Hampton, and the Dizzy Gillespie Quintet. Although the festival lost about $75,000, public relations director Anna Zimmerman was not disturbed, as 1978's festival had earned a surplus.

George Wein masterminded New Orleans and also oversaw the 1979 Playboy Jazz Festival at the Hollywood Bowl on June 15 and 16. Six years ago in traditionally jazzless Los Angeles a Hollywood Bowl jazz festival wound up $50,000 in the red. According to Hugh Hefner, however, this year's festival was so successful that he may repeat it annually. The festival, which starred Joni Mitchell, Benny Goodman, Count Basie, Sarah Vaughan, Flora Purim, Willie Bobo, Weather Report, Chick Corea and Herbie Hancock, Lionel Hampton, closed with an all-star jam session featuring Art Blakey, Ray Brown, Stan Getz, Dizzy Gillespie, Dexter Gordon, Freddie Hubbard, Airto, and Gerry Mulligan.

April 20 through 22 saw Wichita swinging with the most exciting jazz festival in the eight-year history of that event, featuring both local groups and major stars and closing with scintillating performances by Count Basie, Sarah Vaughan, the Dexter Gordon Quartet, and the Jerry Hahn Group. In May, the 13th Annual U.C. Berkeley Jazz Festival glistened with John Klemmer, Betty Carter, the Tony Williams Band, Weather Report, Sonny Rollins, and a special tribute to Charles Mingus starring Joni Mitchell, Herbie Hancock, Tony Williams, and Dizzy Gillespie.

Memorial Day weekend saw 80,000 people jamming the sixth Old Sacramento Dixieland Jubilee, which featured such big dixieland names as Johnny Guarnieri, Wild Bill Davison, Eddie Miller, Nick Fatool, Bob Havens, Pud Brown, and Barrett Deems, in addition to some sixty lesser-known but equally dynamic bands.

On July 6, 7, and 8 at Atlantic City, New Jersey, fans witnessed performances by Nancy Wilson, Roy Ayers, Freddie Hubbard, Les McCann, Herbie Mann, Stanley Turrentine, Sarah Vaughan, Art Blakey, Bobby Caldwell, Hugh Masekela, Buddy Rich, Lonnie Liston Smith, and the Ray Charles Show in the Garden State's biggest outdoor jazz festival.

Between July 6 and July 23, the city of Montreux, Switzerland, glittered with the sights and sounds of the 13th Montreux International Jazz Festival, which this year expanded to include country music, reggae, and Brazilian music in addition to the expected blues and jazz lineups. More than 50,000 people flocked to Montreux, breaking attendance records for the festival. In addition, the fourth Northsea Jazz Festival, held in The Hague, Netherlands, attracted 23,000 people between July 13 and 15 to see Ella Fitzgerald, Count Basie, and a host of other jazz greats.

In 1979 the top jazz albums were *Children of Sanchez* and *Live at the Hollywood Bowl* by Chuck Mangione, *Reed Seed* and *Paradise* by Grover Washington, Jr., *Mr. Gone* by Weather Report, *All Fly Home* by Al Jarreau, *Flame* by Ronnie Laws, *Touchdown* by Bob James, *New Chautauqua* by Pat Metheny, *Carmel* by Joe Sample, *Livin' Inside Your Love* by George Benson, *Feets Don't Fail Me Now* by Herbie Hancock, *Morning Dance* by Spyro Gyra, *Heart String* by Earl Klugh, *Street Life* by the Crusaders, and *Mingus*, Joni Mitchell's tribute to the late genius.

In attempts to spur growth even further, one record company suggested that contemporary jazz be called jazzz to help radio stations identify it as a new form of music with appeal to mass-market audiences. Although most radio stations agreed that a new term was necessary, none reported that their use of jazzz had increased the size of their listening audience. With the vitality of jazz performers—young crossover artists as well as seasoned purists—there is no doubt that jazz will continue to flourish no matter how it's spelled.

Clockwise from upper left: *Spyro Gyra's jazz fusion sound rocked* Morning Dance *to the top of the jazz charts. During 1979 Grover Washington scored with* Reed Seed *and* Paradise. *Ebullient Count Basie at Newport. Grammy-winner Al Jarreau.*

Classical

Sales of classical records are popping, attendance at concerts is booming, live and taped operas on television are attracting millions of viewers—and, as the median age of Americans keeps rising, classical's growth is likely to continue explosively into the 1980s.

Record companies are learning to market their classical stars the way they've always marketed pop stars. In addition to stressing the musical excellence of their classical performers, the labels are presenting them as the colorful personalities they are. Such sparkling artists as Luciano Pavarotti, Beverly Sills, Vladimir Horowitz, and Joan Sutherland inspired today's interest in classical. Also adding to the surge were the classical jazz crossover of Claude Bolling, whose *Suite for Violin and Jazz Piano* and *Suite for Flute and Jazz Piano* were enormously successful on record, and the pop crossover of flutist James Galway, whose recording of John Denver's "Annie's Song" sold nearly half a million copies and reached the top of Great Britain's pop charts.

Even though the prices of classical records continue to rise, classical fans keep buying records. In California, several large record chains are establishing separate classical sections that are isolated from the sound of pop rock that reverberates through the rest of the store. When one of the largest, Los Angeles's Tower Records, devoted a separate 1700-square-foot annex to classical music, business in classical doubled. The Los Angeles Licorice Pizza chain reports that during the last six months of 1978 sales of classical records jumped from 1 percent of total sales to almost 6 percent.

Classical music blossomed in New York City. According to New York police, on August 8 more than 200,000 people carried blankets, babies, balloons, and assorted picnic fare to Central Park's Sheep Meadow. Once there, they sprawled out to enjoy the New York Philharmonic conducted by Andre Kostelanetz playing such crowd-pleasers as Rimsky-Korsakov's *Scheherazade*, the Second Suite from Stravinsky's *The Firebird*, and four rousing Sousa marches. Throughout New York City attendance was up at every major classical event, from Lincoln Center's Mostly Mozart series to the Metropolitan Opera's opening night performance of Verdi's *Otello*, presented September 24 but sold out by the first week in August. And, although sophisticated critics sometimes took the Met to task for not living up to its past, that long financially troubled opera company finished its third straight season comfortably in the black. Thanks to PBS's glittering "Live from the Met" series, more people than ever before saw and heard the true grandeur of great opera. The most serious and dedicated classical radio station in America, Chicago's WFMT, flouts every rule of commercial radio (they reject commercial jingles they feel would break the mood of a Beethoven symphony, for example) and yet is one of the country's most successful classical stations.

Perhaps the biggest classical news of the year was the Boston Symphony Orchestra's trip to mainland China during the month of March; they were greeted with wild enthusiasm by the Chinese, particularly when Seiji Ozawa merged the Boston with the Peking Central Philharmonic Orchestra for a massive version of Beethoven's Fifth Symphony. Chinese pianist Liu Shih-Kun performed the Liszt Piano Concerto no. 1 and Liu Teh-Hai played the pipa, a Chinese lutelike instrument, in a concerto composed by a committee of three.

In 1979 there was an increased interest in avant-garde classical music, led by the trance music of Philip Glass, whose opera *Einstein on the Beach*

easily sold out a first pressing of 10,000 copies and sailed into a second pressing of 10,000 despite a thirty-dollar list price. Other avant-garde composers began breaking away from the rigid, unemotional tonal clusters and random programming of electronic sounds that opened chasms between them and their audience in the past ten years. The latest compositions by such composers as William Schuman, Samuel Barber, Jacob Druckman, Andrew Imbrie, and Krzysztof Penderecki expressed a new romanticism, showing that classical composers are once again willing to take the chance of writing for a mass audience, ensuring that today's serious contemporary music will be the classical music of tomorrow.

The most popular albums during the last two months of 1978 and through 1979 were *Bravo Pavarotti, Hits from Lincoln Center,* and *The World's Favorite Tenor Arias* by Luciano Pavarotti; the Paillard Chamber Orchestra's performance of the Pachelbel: *Kanon: Two Suites,* and Fasch: *Two Symphonies;* Vladimir Horowitz and the New York Philharmonic performing the *Rachmaninoff Piano Concerto #3, Nyiregyházi Plays Liszt;* Verdi's *Otello,* performed by Placido Domingo, Renata Scotto, and the Metropolitan Opera Company conducted by James Levine; Donizetti's *Don Pasquale,* featuring Beverly Sills; *Up in Central Park,* with performances by Beverly Sills; Mascagni's *Cavalleria Rusticana* and Leoncavallo's *Pagliacci,* featuring Luciano Pavarotti and the National Philharmonic Orchestra; Claude Bolling's *Suite for Violin and Jazz Piano,* performed by Bolling and Pinchas Zuckerman; the soundtrack to the movie *Manhattan,* with music by George Gershwin; Schumann's *Kreisleriana;* and Itzhak Perlman's collection called *Virtuoso Violinist.*

Clockwise from upper left: *The enchanted flute of James Galway made a British pop hit out of John Denver's "Annie's Song." Grammy-winner Luciano Pavarotti pulled in that honor for his performance on* Hits from Lincoln Center. *The entire music world was saddened by the loss of Arthur Fiedler, whose joyful music was loved by millions.*

Easy Listening

Easy Listening 1979 was one surprise after another. It was Linda Ronstadt with her torchy rendition of "Ooh Baby Baby"; or Billy Joel with the aggressive "My Life"; or Nicolette Larson thrusting her voice into hyperspace on "Lotta Love"; it was Olivia Newton-John sizzling her way through "A Little More Love" and "Deeper Than the Night"; it was England Dan and John Ford Coley pounding out "Love Is the Answer"; and Elton John with the bouncy "Mama Can't Buy You Love." In fact, these easy-listening hits were pop or rock hits as well, and some, such as Maxine Nightingale's "Lead Me On" and Barbra Streisand's "Main Event/Fight," were even disco hits.

Of course, as always, the easy-listening charts were full of the softer staples, such as Anne Murray caressing such songs as "You Needed Me," "I Just Fall in Love Again," or "Shadows in the Moonlight." For pure romanticism there was Engelbert's "This Moment in Time"; Randy Vanwarmer's "Just When I Needed You Most"; and Neil Diamond's "Forever in Blue Jeans." However, in 1979 faster moving and harder rocking songs made more inroads on the easy-listening charts than ever before, as many easy-listening, or middle-of-the-road (MOR), radio stations programmed more hard-edged music. In the middle of 1979 *Billboard* even changed the heading of its easy-listening charts to "Adult Contemporary," indicating the change that was brewing.

John Davidson, one of a group of easy-listening performers who remain top stars through personal appearances rather than record sales, established a private camp for singers who haven't quite made it. Called John Davidson's Singers' Summer Camp, it is located in a posh private cove on California's Santa Catalina Island. For $1600 John will take a fledgling singer for four weeks, teach him the rudiments of acting, dancing, and comedy, hone his voice, and transform him into a total entertainer. Davidson is helped by such impressive guest lecturers as Kenny Rogers and Tony Orlando.

Other easy-listening stars who were appreciated in live performances rather than on vinyl in 1979 were Johnny Mathis, who appeared at the end of June at the Dick Clark Westchester Theater in Tarrytown, New York, in a series of shows that showcased the polished performer at his best. At the beginning of November 1978, Neil Sedaka gave SRO audiences at Las Vegas's Riviera Hotel a warmly emotional evening, blending such ballads as "The Hungry Years" with a medley of his old songs, including "Oh Carol," "Happy Birthday Sweet Sixteen," and "Calendar Girl." Winning with nostalgia was 4 Girls 4: Rosemary Clooney, Rose Marie, Helen O'Connell, and Margaret Whiting, who continued taking their delightful show of standards, show tunes, and ballads around the country.

Other easy-listening winners in 1979 included Kenny Loggins with "Whenever I Call You Friend"; Al Stewart with "Time Passages"; Neil Diamond with his Barbra Streisand duet "You Don't Bring Me Flowers" and his solo "Say Maybe"; Andy Gibb, who climbed the charts twice with "Our Love, Don't Throw It Away"; the Bee Gees with their warm ballad "Too Much Heaven"; Kenny Rogers with "The Gambler" and "She Believes in Me"; Barry Manilow with "Somewhere in the Night"; Poco with "Crazy Love"; Frank Mills with "Music Box Dancer"; George Harrison with "Blow Away"; Orsa Lia with "I Never Said I Love You"; and Peaches and Herb with "Reunited."

In addition to soft ballads, easy listening rocked in 1979. Opposite: Olivia Newton-John sizzled with Totally Hot.

Clockwise from right: *Some of the top easy-listening stars of the year 1979 were Nicolette Larsen, John Denver, Frank Mills, and Andy Gibb.*

Tracy Frankel/Neal Peters

Waring Abbott

Lynn Goldsmith

59

Robin Platzer

Stage, Screen, and Television

The big Broadway winner of 1979 was, of course, *Sweeney Todd.* Subtitled "The Demon Barber of Fleet Street," this twentieth-century version of nineteenth-century British *grand guignol* was set to music by Stephen Sondheim, impeccably directed by Harold Prince, slickly produced, and handsomely mounted. The graphically gruesome musical not only swept off with eight of the nine Tony awards for which it was nominated—best musical, best score, best book of a musical, best actress, best actor, best direction, best scenic design, and best costumes—but also spawned a best-selling album and was a box-office smash.

Audiences ate up this unlikely candidate for a hit. No matter that its hero is a wrathful barber, vengeful after returning from an unjust imprisonment, whose razor slices into more than his enemies' beards. He neatly disposes of their remains with the help of the manager of a London pie shop, who obligingly minces them fine and blends them into her famous meat pies. Somehow the brilliant Sondheim music and lyrics, Prince's direction,and outstanding acting and singing by Tony-winners Len Cariou as the barber and Angela Lansbury as his baking ally transform the grim plot into an evening of spine-tingling theater.

They're Playing Our Song, which played for eight weeks at Los Angeles's Ahmanson Theatre at the end of 1978 before opening on Broadway on February 11, was written by Neil Simon with music and lyrics by Marvin Hamlisch and Carol Bayer Sager. Comic Robert Klein and performer Lucie Arnaz, daughter of Desi Arnaz and Lucille Ball, play a famous composer and a struggling lyricist who fall in love during the course of a musical collaboration. Based on the real-life experiences of Hamlisch and Sager, the musical featured top performances by Klein and Arnaz, strong songs from Hamlisch and Sager, and sometimes

inspired but often tired comedy from Simon. Despite critical whacks at the Simon book, the play chugged along to respectable business thanks to its musical verve and appealing costars.

Whoopee, a fifty-year-old musical, returned to Broadway on February 14 by way of Connecticut's Goodspeed Opera House, which first mounted the successful revival in the summer of 1978. Charles Repole starred in this breezy show about an unlikely ladies' man. Studded with instant nostalgia in such songs as "My Baby Just Cares for Me," "Yes, Sir, That's My Baby," "Love Me or Leave Me," and the title song, the show ran until August.

On September 6 Sandy Duncan flew into New York's Lunt-Fontanne Theater in a soaring revival of *Peter Pan* that had reviewers crowing about her confident flight and authentic portrayal of James M. Barrie's eternal little boy.

A number of one-performer shows were successful. Singer/songwriter Peter Allen triumphed in an elegant tour de force that opened May 23 for a limited engagement at New York's Biltmore and was held over by popular demand. Allen, who has written such hits as "I Honestly Love You" and "Don't Cry Out Loud," packed twenty-five of his handsome songs into an evening that combined his outrageous camp presence with appealing if not exactly deft dancing. His breezy patter captured the audience as surely as if he were in a more intimate cabaret setting. With assured musical direction provided by nineteen-year-old whiz kid Marc Shaiman, Allen shone.

In March veteran performer Geraldine Fitzgerald brought her one-woman musical revue, *Streetsong,* from New York's cabaret Reno Sweeney to the off-Broadway Roundabout Stage One Theatre. Her rough-and-ready voice and commanding stage presence created a vibrant evening of such songs as "Poor

Opposite, above: *Angela Lansbury and Len Cariou in Stephen Sondheim's Tony champ,* Sweeney Todd. Right: *Handsome Christopher Reeve was a perfect Superman to John Williams's soaring score.* Far right: *Cheryl Tiegs was one of the beauties on "John Denver and the Ladies."*

Martha Swope   The Lester Glassner Collection   The Lester Glassner Collection

Top: *Robert Klein and Lucie Arnaz try to work out their problems in Neil Simon's* They're Playing Our Song. *Above:* The Bee Gees performed with their usual polish on "A Gift of Song."

People of Paris," "Danny Boy," and "Theme from the Three Penny Opera."

On June 13, Phyllis Newman opened in the loosely autobiographical *The Madwoman of Central Park West,* in which she sang, danced, and acted out a catalog of the problems facing a woman who tries to juggle home, husband, children, and career in theater while maintaining her sanity. Music by such contemporary masters as Stephen Sondheim, Leonard Bernstein, Peter Allen, and Joe Raposo created a warm and funny entertainment, with the lovely and charming Miss Newman by turns valiant, slightly crazed, shrewd, and vulnerable.

For the last few weeks in July New York's Winter Garden box office was thronged by lines of ticket buyers who needed no critics to preview the performance of one of their darlings, "Saturday Night Live's" Gilda Radner, who opened in *Gilda Radner— Live from New York* on August 2. Although even the kindest of Miss Radner's critics complained that the show was merely a pastiche of her "Saturday Night Live" routines, evidently all her fans wanted were such Radner creatures as Rosanne Rosannadanna, the unabashedly earthy television newswoman; Emily Litella, the spinster schoolteacher; Judy Miller, the wacky moppet with dreams of stardom; and Lisa Loopner, the adenoidal high schooler. Originally scheduled to run only through September 1, the show was extended for an additional three weeks.

Evita, the Robert Stigwood-produced musical based on the life of Eva Péron, sailed into Los Angeles's Dorothy Chandler Pavilion on the wings of a smash British run. After nine weeks in Los Angeles and seven in San Francisco, the show moved to Broadway in September with its strong cast of Patti LuPone as Eva Peron, Mandy Patinkin as Ché Guevara, and Bob Gunton as Péron in the story of Eva's rise from the streets to the president's palace. With lyrics by Tim Rice and music by Andrew Lloyd Webber, the splashy musical featured the international winner "Don't Cry for Me Argentina," which has already been recorded by a varied group of recording artists, from Olivia Newton-John to Stan Getz to the Carpenters.

But these shows and such previous Broadway smashes as *Annie, Ain't Misbehavin', The Best Little Whorehouse in Texas, A Chorus Line,* and late 1978's *Eubie* were the bright exceptions in a season studded with musical theater pratfalls. Some $13 million, much of it from starry-eyed first-time investors, was lost on such unmitigated flops as *Alice, King of Hearts, Platinum, A Broadway Musical, Oh, Kay, Back Country, The Grand Tour, Carmelina, Home Again, Home Again, The Utter Glory of Morrissey Hall, Ballroom, Saravá,* and perhaps most disappointing to theatergoers, *I Remember Mama.* When the Richard Rodgers musical based on John van Druten's stage play moved into New York's Majestic Theater on May 31, it already had a long and troubled out-of-town history, with replacements and last-minute assistants for the director, lyricist, choreographer, and several performers. Most critics agreed that, while the Rodgers score was pleasant, it was far from sensational. Thomas Meehan's book did not make the family alive or meaningful; and both Martin Charnin's and Raymond Jesse's lyrics were weak. The main attraction of the play, and no doubt what kept it running for its 108 performances despite barely respectful reviews, was the luminous Liv Ullmann, who, unchallenged by the vapid role, did not draw the expected crowds to the box office.

The most overhyped and overspent (an estimated $2 to $4 million) production, that thudded most resoundingly, was the critically crushed and audience-avoided *Got tu Go Disco*. Despite the involvement of such respected pop composers as Ashford & Simpson, Kenny Lehman, and Nat Adderley, Jr., the show failed on every count, from story line to staging to its basic concept of making disco a spectator sport, which it emphatically is not.

Many factors contributed to Broadway's problems, primarily today's enormous theatrical expenses. These include not only getting a Broadway musical onstage, but the extra greenery required to keep it on the boards long enough to develop word of mouth and overcome negative or lukewarm reviews. Other factors were inexperienced or unsupportive producers, particularly movie companies merely looking for a film property.

Despite the lackluster season, Broadway buzzed with record labels, with RCA the largest investor in *Sweeney Todd*, MCA footing half the bill for *I Remember Mama*, and cast albums from seven major companies. Although theater is rarely a sure investment and never offers a quick financial return, it is regarded by such heavily involved firms as Columbia Records as a cultural commitment.

Summer theater 1979 included Don Stewart and newcomer Mary D'Arcy in Meredith Wilson's perennially fresh *The Music Man* at the Jones Beach State Theater. Carol Lawrence and Howard Keel starred in *I Do, I Do* at Long Island's Westbury Music Fair.

Theater on the West Coast included a ten-week engagement for Gene Persson's updated production of *You're a Good Man, Charlie Brown*. Based on the Charles Schulz comic strip and billed as "The Ultimate Family Musical," it opened in San Francisco on April 24.

Perhaps the most eagerly anticipated theatrical event of 1979 was the revival of *Oklahoma*, the first major production of that show in twenty years. The current production of the thirty-five-year-old masterpiece opened on May 1 at Los Angeles's

Pantages Theatre. William Hammerstein, Oscar's son, supervised the show. Agnes de Mille's exuberant choreography was lovingly reproduced by Gemze de Lappe, and a spirited cast winningly re-created the roles of Curly, Laurie, Jud, Ado Annie, and the rest of the feuding farmers and cowmen.

After 1978's musical movie bonanzas, 1979 was a fairly quiet year for music on the screen. There were only two full-fledged movie musicals; one grew out of a children's television show while the other was a reproduction of a 1960s Broadway musical. Both, however, were 24-karat sparklers, critically adored box-office smashes.

Released in March, the bountiful musical *Hair* was faithful to the Rado and Ragnie lyrics and Galt McDermott score. The cast list glittered with such impressive newcomers as Treat Williams, John Savage, Beverly D'Angelo, Annie Golden of the rock band the Shirts, and Don Dacus of Chicago. The true star, however, was Milos Forman; his direction provided not simply a re-creation of the 1967 play but a powerful cinematic transformation, using every filmic opportunity to enlarge the story to mythic proportions. The unforgettable songs—"Aquarius," "Easy to Be Hard," "I Got Life," "Let the Sunshine In," and of course, "Hair"—shimmered in the New York City settings and provided a rich background for Twyla Tharp's irrepressible choreography.

Kermit the Frog and Miss Piggy starred in *The Muppet Movie*, based on Jim Henson's loveable television characters. Both starring and bit player Muppets are even sweeter on the screen than on the home tube, easily lifting the show from such otherwise scene-stealing human beings as the late Edgar Bergen, Milton Berle, Mel Brooks, Madeline Kahn, Carol Kane, Telly Savalas, Orson Welles, and even droll Paul Williams, who, with Kenny Ascher, created the music. Only Steve Martin's daffiness kept him, too, from being upstaged by the Muppets' charm. Perhaps he has Muppet blood in his veins.

There were several rock movies, including *Rock 'n' Roll High School,* the 1979 version of teens versus adults over rock 'n' roll. Featuring the cheerful, rousing rock of the Ramones as well as musical moments by Nick Lowe, Alice Cooper, Devo, and Brownsville Station, the flimsy plot takes place at Vince Lombardi High School and revolves around the attempts of teenage Ramones fan Riff Randell (played by P. J. Soles) to get the band to play at the school despite school officials, whose idea of fun is burning rock-and-roll records.

The Kids Are Alright, a documentary containing footage of the Who's early concerts and interviews, as well as some promotional and private films, was an energetic and affectionate look at one of rock's great bands. Jeff Stein, whose love for the Who beams out of every frame, spent four years unearthing and editing hard-to-get footage, creating a breathless classic.

Despite the somewhat strained fantasy in which Neil Young embedded the concert footage of *Rust Never Sleeps,* the murky documentary of his performances, the film captures the singer/songwriter/guitarist's often moving if lugubrious music.

Released during the summer, *More American Graffiti,* George Lucas's sequel to the unequalled *American Graffiti,* featured many cast members from the original, including Candy Clark, MacKenzie Phillips, Ron Howard, and Cindy Williams. Despite their presence, however, and the music by such 1960s artists as Bob Dylan, Martha and the Vandellas, the Byrds, Donovan, Country Joe and the Fish, and Cream, the new film did not rise to the heights of its model. In honor of its tenth anniversary, *Woodstock,* the movie that celebrated the 1969 festival, reappeared on local screens. And for those unfortunate youngsters who weren't allowed to see the R-rated *Saturday Night Fever* the first time around, an edited PG version made the rounds during the summer of 1979, teamed with *Grease* for an unbeatable Travolta orgy.

The avid movie music fan could also catch snatches of pop, rock, country, and disco in such films as the Clint Eastwood smash *Every Which Way But Loose,* which featured Eddie Rabbitt singing the hit title song and performances by Charlie Rich and Mel Tillis. *When You Comin' Back Red Ryder,* the Marjoe Gortner flop, featured Tammy Wynette and Freddy Fender. *Moment by Moment,* the John Travolta embarrassment, included music by Yvonne Elliman, Stephen Bishop, 10cc, Dan Hill, Charles Lloyd, Michael Franks, and John Klemmer. The riot-inspiring *The Warriors* featured Desmond Child and Rouge, while American International's *California Dreaming* included the title single performed by America. *Americathon,* an interminable comedy, was not saved by the brief appearances of Elvis Costello and Meat Loaf.

Three memorable movie scores appeared: John Williams's emotional, teasingly familiar yet appropriately spectacular music for *Superman,* the same composer's brilliantly romantic score for the Frank Langella *Dracula,* and the New York Philharmonic's stirring performance of George Gershwin's music for Woody Allen's *Manhattan.*

Federico Fellini's controversial *Orchestra Rehearsal,* the first film in three years from that master director, contained more politics than music, presenting a trenchant and frightening statement about contemporary society.

Between music specials, award presentations—the Grammy awards, the Academy awards, the Academy of Country Music awards, and the Country Music Association awards—and such venerated series as "American Bandstand," "Midnight Special," "Don Kirshner's Rock Concert," "Soul Train," "In Concert," "Austin City Limits," "Lawrence Welk," "Hee Haw," (which celebrated its tenth anniversary in 1979), and even the music-oriented "WKRP in Cincinnati," there was more music than ever on the home screen in 1979.

Part of this music was on disco dance programs that proliferated rapidly, including "The Soap Factory Disco," "Disco Magic," "Dance Fever," and "Kicks." Even "Midnight Special" went disco and PBS offered "Disco Dancing," eight half-hour programs of disco dance lessons, as well as interviews with deejays, disco owners, top dancers, musicians, record-company spokesmen, and podiatrists.

The most publicized 1979 special was the Bee Gees' "A Gift of Song," telecast January 10 on NBC and featuring ABBA, Rita Coolidge and Kris Kristofferson, John Denver, Earth, Wind & Fire, Andy Gibb, Olivia Newton-John, Rod Stewart, and Donna Summer, with hosts David Frost, Gilda Radner, Henry Fonda, and Henry Winkler. Performed in the General Assembly of the United Nations, with royalties of each of the songs performed donated to UNICEF, the show unfortunately did not add up to a terribly exciting evening.

In another charitable effort, Don Kirshner persuaded such top pop music names as Donna Summer, Gloria Gaynor, and the Village People to perform for Easter Seals in a March telethon that raised a record-breaking $12.5 million.

The medium was used far more effectively by ABC when it broadcast "Heroes of Rock 'n' Roll" on Friday, February 9. Pulling a 34 share of the viewing audience, the Malcolm Leo and Andrew Solt production was slick, comprehensive, and brilliantly paced. It slammed out jolts of excitement with every quick cut and in scenes of the embryonic Beatles at their beginnings in Liverpool's Cavern, very early Presley, Phil Spector with the Crystals, Otis Redding's last performance, and other memorable moments from the first quarter-century of rock and roll.

Other exciting specials included "Playboy's 25th Anniversary Celebration." The May 7 program, less revealing than some viewers might have hoped, was short on originality but long on Hugh Hefner, who endeared himself to nonsingers everywhere with his attempts at song. On March 27, CBS Reports showed "The Boston Goes to China," a report on the orchestra's Chinese tour. On April 9, Pam Dawber and Bernadette Peters decorated the "Perry Como Springtime Special" on ABC, and on May 13, ABC presented "A Little Bit of Country, A Little Bit of Rock 'n' Roll Festival," which starred Loretta Lynn, Chuck Berry, Chubby Checker, Wolfman Jack, and Donny and Marie Osmond. NBC debuted the mini-series "Presenting Susan Anton" on May 3.

A made-for-TV musical, "Sooner or Later," featured Denise Miller as a thirteen-year-old whose first love is a

seventeen-year-old rock singer and guitar instructor. Rex Smith played the soft-rocking hero, displaying a pleasant voice in a number of tuneful songs.

Major pop stars appeared on television specials in 1979. They incuded ABC's "The Third Barry Manilow Special," with a mellow Manilow joined by John Denver for a popping medley of Everly Brothers tunes. The program also contained such Manilow chestnuts as "Ready to Take a Chance Again" and "I Write the Songs," in addition to a rendition of 1978's smash, "Copacabana." John Denver himself turned up on February 28 on ABC on "John Denver and the Ladies," which featured Denver and a bevy of top women music stars. "Carol and Dolly in Nashville," a Valentine's day gift from CBS-TV, showcased the contrasting looks and talents of Carol Burnett and Dolly Parton, while the Doobie Brothers were guests of honor on Dinah Shore's July 30 tribute "The Doobie Brothers and their Friends."

On Friday, March 16, CBS telecast "Wings Over the World," a Paul McCartney special, and the rest of the Beatles were the subjects of NBC's "How the Beatles Changed the World," which featured Richie Havens, Melanie, Blood, Sweat and Tears, Frankie Valli, and Melissa Manchester singing their favorite Beatles songs.

"Elvis!" drew 43 million viewers to ABC-TV on February 11, outdrawing such gargantuan television offerings as *One Flew Over the Cuckoo's Nest* and *Gone With the Wind*. "Elvis: Love Him Tender," hosted by Joel Siegel on August 19, commemorated the second anniversary of the King's death.

Other musical stars who enjoyed their own specials included Cheryl Ladd, Chér, Leif Garrett, and Glen Campbell on Home Box Office. And although Ann-Margret didn't have one special all to herself, she starred in both "Las Vegas Palace of Stars" and "Rockette, a Salute to Radio City Music Hall." Two country stars made their acting debuts, Tanya Tucker in NBC's "Amateur Night," shown Monday, January 8, and Loretta Lynn in an episode of the CBS series "The Dukes of Hazzard," called "Find Loretta Lynn," about the kidnapping of a country star.

On March 18 PBS presented a behind-the-scenes portrait of the late Arthur Fiedler, celebrating his nearly half-century as conductor of the Boston Pops Orchestra.

Top: *Animal, one of the irresistible stars of* The Muppet Movie, *towers over a house after eating too many growth pills.* Above: *Leif Garrett, "inteviewed" by Flip Wilson on "The Leif Garrett Special."*

65

Trends

With disco undeniably 1979's most popular musical form, mass music may have been escapist, but the hearts and minds of a growing number of musicians were moving toward   political activism. Punk and new-wave bands made strong statements with their music and life-styles. Northern Ireland's strife led Elton John to write "Madness," his first political song. Steaming mad about long lines at the gas pumps, Phoenix producer and songwriter Brent Burns invested his last $1,800 to record a country rocker called "Cheaper Crude or No More Food" that called on America to raise the price of grain exports as OPEC raises the price of oil. Recorded by Phoenix deejay Bobby Butler under the name Bobby Sofine, the song was greeted positively by listeners and by such deejays as Bo Weaver of Trenton, New Jersey's WTTM-AM, who played it nonstop for almost eleven hours.

In addition to such tactics, a group of 1979's leading performers began to donate time, artistry, and a percentage of their profits to political causes. UNICEF declared 1979 The Year of the Child, a theme that inspired many events. The Bee Gees led off the year when they gathered a glittering array of 1979's stellar musical talents for "A Gift of Song," the January 10 televised UNICEF benefit. Each of the artists who donated his time and talents to the benefit also turned over royalties for the song performed to UNICEF, earning for the world's children the proceeds of such 1979 winners as "Too Much Heaven" by the Bee Gees, "Do Ya Think I'm Sexy" by Rod Stewart, "Rhymes and Reasons" by John Denver, and "That's the Way of the World" by Earth, Wind & Fire. It was estimated that royalties from "Too Much Heaven" alone would amount to more than $500,000. In addition, record retailers in the Washington/Baltimore area donated a dime from the profits of each copy of *Spirits Having Flown,* the Bee Gee's 1979 album, to UNICEF. Part of the income earned at the June 17 Tokyo Music Festival was donated to UNICEF. Also inspired by UNICEF's Year of the Child, the International Children's Appeal and national disco operators held a nationwide Perfect Couple Contest to raise money for that organization.

On January 19, Melissa Manchester was among the impressive roster of stars hosting a benefit called A World Without Hunger. Held at California's Pasadena Civic Auditorium, the proceeds went to the Southern California U.N. International Year of the Child Commission, the Pasadena Hunger Projects Committee, and the International Cooperation Council.

The nuclear accident at Pennsylvania's Three Mile Island fueled a number of highly successful anti-nuclear-power concerts. On June 10, more than 18,000 foes of the Diablo Canyon, California, nuclear plant jammed the Hollywood Bowl for Survival Sunday II, cheering pointed songs by Peter Yarrow, Jackson Browne, Graham Nash, John Sebastian, John Hayward, John Hall, Joan Baez, Melissa Manchester, Gil Scott-Heron, Sha Na Na's Jocko Marcellino, and Peter, Paul and Mary. A group of musicians called Musicians United for Safe Energy (MUSE) organized four concerts held at New York's Madison Square Garden on September 19, 20, 21, and 22. Featuring such headline names as Jackson Browne, Graham Nash, John Hall, James Taylor, Bonnie Raitt, Carly Simon, the Doobie Brothers, Bruce Springsteen, and Chaka Khan, the concerts sold out swiftly and raised three quarters of a million dollars for the anti-nuclear cause.

Other new charitable efforts by performers included a March 16 concert organized by Todd Rundgren that raised $30,000 for the International Rescue Committee to aid the Vietnamese boat people. Performers included Rundgren, Patti Smith, Blue Öyster Cult, and the David Johansen Group.

On March 24 and 25, Jack Klugman and Don Kirshner cohosted the 1979 Easter Seals Telethon. Even the Ramones did a benefit on April 10 to raise money for bulletproof vests for New York City police.

Paul Kantner of the Jefferson Starship, which as the Jefferson Airplane was the 1960s first and foremost political band, summed it up when he told Ira Mayer of the *New York Post,* "There are certain things wrong now in our lives that we have to change and be aware of and make better. . . . Going into the eighties it's time to stand up again."

A related but different response to world tensions was 1979's burgeoning of gospel music. It is significant that Bob Dylan's landmark 1979 album, *Slow Train Coming,* his best in years, prominently features a cross on the cover. With his usual clairvoyance, Dylan presents us with a stunning born-again vision in 1979. Such powerful songs as "Gotta Serve Somebody" and "Precious Angel," with its firmly spiritual "shine a light" refrain, underscore the expansion of traditional gospel music into the pop marketplace. On October 6, 1978, Andrae Crouch and the Disciples, a leading gospel group, became the first gospel act ever to perform at Los Angeles's Greek Theatre. Singer/musician/composer Crouch was signed by Warner Brothers Records in 1979. MCA, while dismissing thirty employees in its pop division, invested heavily in Songbird, a new religious label. Gospel singer Dan Peek's "All Things Are Possible," produced by writer/producer Chris Christian for Pat Boone's Lamb and Lion Records, was the first religious song ever to rise to the top twenty-five on *Billboard's* easy-listening chart (now called Adult Contemporary). As Pat Boone exulted to *Billboard* reporter Gerry Wood, "My biggest desire for ten years has been to get Jesus music into the secular marketplace." One of the most prominent gospel companies, Word, Inc., which comprises fourteen labels and publishing companies, has doubled its sales volume in the past five years, its aggressive and dedicated sales people combining selling with spreading the word.

Gospel is blossoming not only because religious music always prospers in times of crisis, but because the sound of gospel itself has become more contemporary. As Andrae Crouch explains it, "Jesus rock is Christian contemporary country-rock, with a sound much like the Eagles. It's going back into almost a folk type of music. Contemporary gospel is like pop/MOR, away from the hymns and southern quartets and not down-and-out sad."

Another 1979 trend was the increasing number of young performers, not yet signed with major record companies, who are choosing to cut and distribute their own records. The most successful example was the fusion band Spyro Gyra, whose self-titled first album sold so well that it led to a record contract and *Morning Dance,* a top-selling jazz disk.

Picture disks, which were so popular at the end of 1978, dropped off sharply after a December peak. The first batch included a new pressing of the Beatles' *Sgt. Pepper's Lonely Hearts Club Band,* Rod Stewart's *Blondes Have More Fun,* Willie Nelson's *Stardust,* and Toto's "Hold the Line," the first 45-RPM picture disk.

In 1979 mere colored vinyl and picture disks were old-fashioned, as records in different shapes began emerging, the first a heart-shaped record by jazz and R & B singer/guitarist Bobby Caldwell, *What You Won't Do for Love,* distributed by TK. Toto led the way again

with an octagonal-shaped picture 45 of their April single, "Georgy Porgy." In June, A & M released Police's "Roxanne" on a 45 shaped like a police badge, while in August, Wayne Newton released Barry, Robin, and Maurice Gibb's song "You Stepped into my Life" on a star-shaped disk. And, as if that weren't enough, Laserdisc Records, part of the Lasergram Company of Burbank, released the first LP ever with a photo made by a laser process that creates the illusion of three dimensions.

Chuck Pulin

Chuck Pulin

Waring Abbott

In 1979 major pop stars donated time and talent to political causes. Clockwise from lower left: Donna Summer sings to a young member of the audience at "A Gift of Song." Rod Stewart and Kris Kristofferson mug during rehearsals. Patty Smith at Todd Rundgren's benefit for the boat people.

CONCERTS, EVENTS, AND TOURS

Concerts and Events

October 1978

On October 6 Bob Dylan drew nearly 19,000 fans to a sold-out performance at Philadelphia's Spectrum, the biggest venue he played during the last leg of his 1978 tour. For New Yorkers on October 6 and 7 the big one was the Nassau Coliseum appearance of Steve Martin and Steve Goodman, who lit up crowds totaling 35,000 on those two nights. Meanwhile, in the Los Angeles Forum on October 5 and 6, Yes entertained more than 33,000 fans.

Other acts drawing sell-out crowds throughout October 1978 were Aerosmith and Exile, who blasted out fierce heavy metal music to a crowd of 17,500 at the St. Paul Civic Center on October 14, and Neil Young and Crazy Horse, who packed 15,000 into that same venue on October 15. The Commodores and L.T.D. jammed 18,800 fans into Philadelphia's Spectrum on October 9, and Styx and Thin Lizzy drew nearly 30,000 fans to the Coliseum in Seattle on October 10 and 11.

Executives of MCA Records were treated to a surprise appearance by Elton John, his first U.S. performance in two years. The astounding Elton pounded out two hours worth of old and new songs at their convention on October 13 and 14. On October 14 and 15, nearly 100,000 crowded the six blocks surrounding city hall for Los Angeles's first L.A. Street Scene Festival. The outdoor event featured free performances by such stars as Chicago,® Nancy Wilson, Freddy Fender, David "Fathead" Newman, the L.A. Philharmonic, the Clara Ward Singers, the Frankie Valli Revue, the Sylvester Revue, and many other acts.

November 1978

The Commodores with the Brothers Johnson drove 18,360 fans to a frenzy on November 5 in Denver's Sports Arena, while New York City's Madison Square Garden barely contained the 18,300 bouncing fans who packed it on November 9 for the Marshall Tucker Band and Firefall.

Other bands Americans gave thanks for in November 1978 were the Moody Blues and Jimmy Sheres, who drew 18,600 fans to Philadelphia's Spectrum on November 22; Aerosmith and Golden Earrings, who blasted 19,500 at the Spectrum on November 25; and Bob Seger, who, with Le Roux, drew 17,300 boogiers to Lexington, Kentucky's Rupp Arena on the 25th.

December 1978

December was a month for hard rockers, beginning with Kiss's Paul Stanley, who delighted a crush of 4,000 Cincinnati fans when he appeared at the Record Theatre record store on December 1. Stanley stayed for nearly three hours, greeting his fans with the same enthusiasm they showed for him. Foreigner and the Cars packed 19,600 rockers into Philadelphia's Spectrum on December 1; the J. Geils Band, Southside Johnny and the Asbury Jukes, and Richard T. Bear were the attractions for 16,000 fans at the Cleveland Coliseum on December 3; and Black Sabbath with Van Halen drew nearly 15,000 heavy metal screamers to Oakland's Coliseum on December 12.

On December 31, in an emotion-filled evening, a legendary hall closed its doors when Bill Graham mounted the final concert in Winterland, San Francisco's rock palace. The beloved venue hosted 556 concerts in its twelve-year history, beginning on September 23, 1966, with a concert by the Jefferson Airplane, the Butterfield Blues Band, and Muddy Waters; through the years it showcased such top names as the Who, the Rolling Stones, Jimi Hendrix, Traffic, Cream, Fleetwood Mac, the Band, and hundreds of others, particularly the bands that made up San Francisco's teeming late-1960's rock scene. Appropriately, the Grateful Dead, the band that symbolized that period, headlined the final show, which also included the New Riders of the Purple Sage® and the Blues Brothers. Graham received more than 25,000 requests for the thirty-dollar tickets from rock lovers from across the country. Some 5,400 of them, chosen by lottery, filled the hall for a bountiful evening of superb music, ending after 6 A.M. with a bacon and eggs breakfast.

January 1979

The Grateful Dead, who closed San Francisco's year so successfully, opened 1979 with a bang, selling out every venue they played throughout the month of January, from New York's Madison Square Garden to the Providence, Rhode Island, Civic Center to New Haven's Coliseum.

On January 26, top promoters Chuck Morris and Barry Fey opened the Rainbow Music Hall in Denver with a sold-out concert featuring Jerry Jeff Walker and Gail Davies.

February

February's biggest musical draws were performers with vastly different musical styles and audiences. The inimitable Parliament/Funkadelic along with the Brides of Funkenstein drew 41,000 fans of funk to Landover, Maryland's Capital Centre on February 1 and 2. On February 24 and 25 nearly 44,000 members of Neil Diamond's huge adoring army flocked to Seattle's Coliseum to watch him perform.

Preceding page: *Grammy-winner Kenny Rogers achieved crossover success in 1979 with "She Believes in Me."* Above: *Cher at a Brooklyn, New York roller disco.* Opposite, top: *The Doobie Brothers at an early 1979 concert, before new members McCracken, McFee, and Bumpus joined.* Opposite, bottom: *Mick Jagger never fails to provide the unexpected.*

Robin Platzer

Far Left: *Glowing Olivia Newton-John won new fans in 1979 with her hard rocking album* Totally Hot. *Opposite:* Engelbert's compelling stage presence and warm voice have made him a long-time favorite of women around the world. *Above: The unbeatable Bee Gees swept through 1979 in high style, beginning the year with their televised "A Gift of Song" UNICEF benefit, and racking up three top songs by June.*

In late 1978 and throughout 1979 top comics combined lunacy with music.
Below left: *Steve Martin's wacky King Tut routine was the perfect
antidote to the King Tut exhibition's high seriousness. Below right:
With the song "Dancing Fool" Frank Zappa poked gentle fun at discos.
Right: Dan Aykroyd and John Belushi made best-selling music as the Blues
Brothers. Following page: Gilda Radner, whose one-woman show scored
on Broadway, does an inspired Patti Smith take-off.*

Charlyn Zlotnik

Chuck Pulin

Lynn Goldsmith

March

March's biggest, noisiest, and most colorful musical event was Mardi Gras in the Superdome—the World's Biggest Disco. In addition to enjoying supercharged performances by the Trammps, Gloria Gaynor, K.C. and the Sunshine Band, Vince Vance and the Valiants, Doug Kershaw, and Le Roux, the audience was treated to a closing parade of twenty-two carnival floats that circled the arena.

Other big concerts included Alice Cooper and the Babys, who captured 16,500 fans in a hard-driving show at Louisville's Freedom Hall on March 3. The Beach Boys easily sold out Radio City Music Hall for the first three evenings in March, delighting New York fans with their California sunshine. Boston and Sammy Hagar raised a ruckus in the St. Louis Checker Dome on March 9 with their hard rocking; Santana and Eddie Money squeezed 19,600 fans into Madison Square Garden on March 15. Kenny Rogers' March 22 appearance at Carnegie Hall filled that prestigious venue, while Rogers, Dottie West, and the Oak Ridge Boys jammed more than 15,500 fans into Landover, Maryland's Capital Centre on March 23. The Statler Brothers and Barbara Mandrell drew 15,000 to Louisville's Freedom Hall on March 17.

April

The year's first mammoth musical event, the first annual California World Music Festival, drew 106,000 rock fans to the Los Angeles Coliseum on April 7 and 8 to see Aerosmith, Ted Nugent, Cheap Trick, Van Halen, Toto, Eddie Money, REO Speedwagon, the Boomtown Rats, April Wine, Cheech & Chong, and the Fabulous Poodles, among others. Cheap Trick's Rick Nielsen gave away a $700 guitar to the crowd, and Ted Nugent wrote his name in fireworks across the sky. Although promoter Jim Rissmiller reported that he lost money on the festival, he was delighted with the results, seeing the peaceful event as the springboard to more massive outdoor festivals.

April's other big attractions were then-expectant father Rod Stewart, who began his sold-out tour at Vancouver, British Columbia's Pacific Coliseum on April 14 and 15, drawing 35,000 lucky fans. Yes delighted 17,500 rockers at their April 11 concert in Pittsburgh's Civic Arena. Eric Clapton with Muddy Waters' Blues Band filled houses wherever they went, and Clapton joined B.B. King onstage at Atlanta's Great Southeast Music Hall on April 19 for a thirty-minute jam. On April 19 and 20 the music master Ray Charles appeared with the Raeletts and the Ray Charles Orchestra at the Marin County Veterans Auditorium in San Rafael, California, while Chet Atkins, Mr. Guitar, appeared on April 20 at San Francisco's Masonic Auditorium. On April 8, Harry Chapin organized a benefit for a Long Island ballet group and two Long Island symphony orchestras, appearing at the Nassau Coliseum along with Dave Mason, Gordon Lightfoot, and Waylon Jennings in a four-hour concert that highlighted each man's different style.

May

The big summer festival season began in May, Bill Graham's Day-on-the-Green #1, with Boston, Sammy Hagar, Eddie Money, and U.K., leading the way at the Oakland Stadium on

Sunday May 6. On May 13, Colorado University's Folsom Field in Boulder rang with the music of the Doobie Brothers, Boston, Bob Welch, Poco, and Country Joe and the Fish, all entertaining a massive crowd of 50,400.

Some 70,000 funk fans were treated to the World's Greatest Funk Festival in the Los Angeles Coliseum on May 26. There they boogied with such favorites as Parliament/Funkadelic, Bootsy's Rubber Band, Rick James, the Bar-Kays, the Brides of Funkenstein, Con Funk Shun, and Parlet.

Bad Company and Carillo were on the road in May, selling out Cincinnati's Coliseum on May 13, Knoxville's Civic Auditorium on May 12, Cleveland's Coliseum on May 15, Detroit's Cobo Arena on May 16, and Indianapolis's Market Square Arena on May 18.

Between May 25 and June 10, Charleston, South Carolina, was transformed for the third year into Spoleto, U.S.A., home of America's counterpart of Italy's traditional festival of the arts. The 1979 extravaganza drew more than 100,000 people to see and hear *The Desperate Husband,* an eighteenth-century opera; a thirteenth-century liturgical music play, *The Play of the Three Maries;* and contemporary jazz by such bands as Buddy Rich, Woody Herman, and the New Orleans Heritage Hall Jazz Band.

On May 27, Kool Jazz Festivals sponsored Soul on the Green at the Oakland Stadium, featuring the Emotions, the Bar-Kays, Chic, Peabo Bryson, Rose Royce, and B.B. King in a sparkling day of fine soul and disco.

On May 21, Elton John detonated a cultural explosion in Leningrad when he appeared in the elegant Bolshoi Oktyabrsky Concert Hall. His Russian fans burst into a frenzy when he closed the first of eight Russian concerts (four in Leningrad and four in Moscow) with a spontaneous performance of the Beatles' "Back in the USSR."

After a year of panic during which the owners were planning to tear down the money-losing theater, lovers of New York's famed Radio City Music Hall managed to have the building's interior declared a national landmark. The grand lobbies were unstintingly restored to their original art deco grandeur, and on May 31 the hall reopened as a musical theater. During the summer of 1979 out-of-towners cheered *A New York Summer,* a spectacle rising and falling on the great stage's many platforms, featuring the great Wurlitzer organ, and, of course, the inimitable Rockettes.

June

June came alive with several massive festivals, the biggest being the 81,000 people drawn by Boston, Heart, Van Halen, Blue Öyster Cult, Nazareth, Sammy Hagar, and TKO to the Louis Messina Cotton Bowl in Dallas, Texas, on June 9. On June 10 a crowd of 62,000 jammed the New Orleans Superdome to see the same lineup with the Granati Brothers substituting for TKO. Some 55,000 fans braved gasoline shortages and cheerfully sat through a downpour to see Boston, the Outlaws, Poco, and Todd Rundgren and Utopia at New Jersey's Giants Stadium on June 17. Ted Nugent, Heart, the Cars, UFO and the Rockets drew 51,500 to Denver's Mile High Stadium on June 16, and 42,000 fans thronged Arrowhead Stadium in Kansas City, Missouri, on June 17 to see Nugent, Heart, the Cars, Sammy Hagar, and Missouri. The Bee Gees and Sweet Inspiration were on the road in June; their most spectacular concert was the June 30 evening at Houston's Summit when they were joined by John Travolta. On

Above: *One of rock's finest leapers, David Lee Roth's raw physicality helped jet the band Van Halen to its sizzling success.*

the road also were Supertramp, Yes, and the Village People.

On June 17, Rita Coolidge beat out ten other international music stars to snatch the grand prize at the eighth Tokyo Festival International Contest for her performance of "Don't Cry Out Loud." Other American prizewinners were A Taste of Honey, who won a gold prize for "Do It," and Al Jarreau, who won a silver prize for "All." Donna Summer appeared as a special guest star.

July

Fourth of July musical fireworks popped in Staunton, Virginia, where the Statler Brothers held their tenth annual Happy Birthday U.S.A. Celebration, near Austin, Texas, where Willie Nelson held his seventh, and at Oakland Stadium, where Bill Graham presented an All-American Rock and Roll Show featuring Journey, Van Halen, the J. Geils Band, and Nazareth.

On July 15 competitions began in the Slingerland/Louis Bellson National Drum Contest, with winners eligible for part of $30,000 in prizes and scholarships and an appearance in Las Vegas with Louis Bellson and his band, Explosion.

On July 17, as part of a seven-and-a-half-month world tour, Harry Belafonte appeared at Los Angeles's Greek Theatre, treating his audience to his electric personality and eclectic blend of songs, with, as always, the spirited emphasis on West Indian and African music.

Other July festivals included a July 7 performance by four jazz piano greats: Eubie Blake, Teddy Wilson, Marian McPartland, and George Shearing. Called Great Jazz Pianos, the concert was held at Wolf Trap Farm Park in Vienna, Virginia.

On July 30 the Sheep Meadow in New York's Central Park was packed with an estimated quarter of a million rock fans who came to hear James Taylor. Determined listeners began arriving at dawn for the 5:30 P.M. concert. Sponsored by Gloria Vanderbilt and New York's radio station WNEW-FM, the free concert raised some $20,000 through the sale of T-shirts and buttons to help restore the much-used Sheep Meadow. Taylor's performance was as mellow and relaxed as if he had been playing for a small crowd of his most devoted fans; the audience was well-behaved, and, best of all, helped clean up after the show.

August

The biggest August musical event took place in the windy city, as the ten-day ChicagoFest, at first opposed by Chicago Mayor Jane Byrne, drew nearly 700,000 people to the Navy Pier on the shores of Lake Michigan. The star acts that appeared included Chicago® for whom a crowd of 120,000 turned out, Helen Reddy, Bobby Vinton, and Pablo Cruise, as well as dozens of midwestern performers. The event was so successful that there are plans for a winter ChicagoFest.

In August, Kiss stomped the country in their explosive seven-league boots; Supertramp drew 40,000 to Empire Stadium in Vancouver, Canada, on August 11; REO Speedwagon and Missouri drew more than 17,000 fans of their hard-trucking sound to the St. Louis Checkerdome on August 10. On August 17, St. Paul's Midway Stadium was filled with nearly 33,000 fans of the Doobie Brothers, the Cars, and Night; 22,500 fans of Blue Öyster Cult, Cheap Trick, Pat Travers, and Shakin' Street were treated to high-energy performances at the Sacramento State Fair on August 18, while on August 19, some 22,000 of those bands' fans showed up to see them at San Jose's Spartan Stadium.

Other top concert draws in August were the Grateful Dead, Joni Mitchell with the Persuasions, Teddy Pendergrass, and Heart with the Dixon House Band.

September

From September 4 through September 14, New Yorkers were treated to the dynamite voice and presence of Liza Minnelli at Carnegie Hall. On September 19, 20, and 21, three sold-out concerts featured such artists as Jackson Browne, the Doobie Brothers, John Hall, Graham Nash, Bonnie Raitt, James Taylor, Bruce Springsteen, Chaka Khan, Ry Cooder, Jesse Colin Young, and Sweet Honey in the Rock at Madison Square Garden. Organized by Musicians United for Safe Energy (MUSE), the concerts were benefits to raise money for campaigns opposing the use of nuclear energy.

Across the country in Monterey, California, the first rock festival since 1967 was held at the Monterey Fairgrounds on September 8 and 9. Called the Second Annual Tribal Stomp, the event featured the Clash, Peter Tosh, and such 1960s names as the Blues Project, Country Joe and the Fish, and the Chambers Brothers.

Although the much-rumored Woodstock II never materialized, at Parr Meadows in Brookhaven, Long Island, a ten-hour festival called the Reunion Concert was held on September 8, featuring such Woodstock survivors as Stephen Stills, Canned Heat, Paul Butterfield, Rick Danko and Friends, Jorma Kaukonen, Country Joe McDonald, Johnny Winter, and John Sebastian. During the first week in September, the Who, also Woodstock performers, treated New York audiences to a week of sold-out Madison Square Garden shows plus several other concerts in smaller halls.

Halfway around the world, in the shadow of the pyramids, Frank Sinatra accepted the invitation of Madame Anwar Sadat and performed a benefit to aid an Egyptian medical center, drawing a chic, jet-set crowd.

October

On October 2, Earth, Wind & Fire displayed their elemental talents at Philadelphia's Spectrum. On the seventh the Doobie Brothers filled that venue. Madison Square Garden rang with the sound of Ian Anderson's flute as Jethro Tull drew SRO crowds on the ninth and tenth. In the Oakland Coliseum on October 12 Waylon Jennings charmed with his fast-moving show. The Grateful Dead took command of the New Haven Coliseum on October 25.

TOURS

Tour information courtesy *Performance* Magazine. Unless otherwise indicated, all dates are 1979.

Allman Brothers: Began April 8 in Jacksonville, Florida, played through the summer.

Bad Company: Began April 30 in Houston, Texas; ended July 22 in Philadelphia, Pennsylvania.

Bee Gees: Began June 18 in Fort Worth, Texas; ended October 6 in Miami, Florida.

George Benson: Began April 13 in Portland, Oregon; ended May 26 in Maui, Hawaii.

Blondie: Began October 20, 1978, in Willimantic, Connecticut; ended December 29, 1978, in Wharton, Texas. Began June 27 in Shelton, Connecticut; ended August 16 in Los Angeles, California.

Peabo Bryson: Began March 2 in Fresno, California; ended August 11 in the Meadowlands, New Jersey.

Cars: Began June 12 in Hamilton, Canada; ended August 24 in New York City.

Cheap Trick: Ended lengthy fall tour December 31, 1978, in Long Beach, California. Toured England, Europe, and Japan from January through March. Began U.S. tour May 4 in Rochester, New York, ended September 3 in Salem, Wisconsin.

Chicago: Began July 21 in Eugene, Oregon; ended September 20 in Bloomington, Indiana.

Clash: Toured the United States in spring and fall.

Natalie Cole: Began October 27, 1978, in St. Louis, Missouri; ended November 19, 1978, in Cincinnati, Ohio.

Judy Collins: Began March 19 in Schenectady, New York; ended July 27 in Highland Park, Illinois.

Rita Coolidge: Began July 16 in Vienna, Virginia (Wolftrap); ended September 6 in Los Angeles, California.

Elvis Costello: Began February 6 in Seattle, Washington; ended April 14 in Providence, Rhode Island.

Dire Straits: Toured the United States in March and September.

Doobie Brothers: Began April 20 at University of Montana; played through the summer.

Bob Dylan: Ended extensive fall and early winter tour December 16, 1978, in Miami, Florida.

Fabulous Poodles: Played first U.S. dates in spring.

Firefall: Began October 2, 1978, in Aspen, Colorado; ended December 16, 1978, in Anaheim, California. Began March 31 in Flagstaff, Arizona; ended May 1 in Boston, Massachusetts.

Foreigner: Ended world tour December 3, 1978, in Boston, Massachusetts. Began August 24 in East Troy, Michigan.

Peter Frampton: Began June 21 in St. Louis, Missouri.

Nick Gilder: Began October 6, 1978, in Chicago, Illinois; ended October 26, 1978, in Hartford, Connecticut.

GQ: Began April 20 in Greensboro, North Carolina; ended June 15 in Anaheim, California.

Leif Garrett: Began June 25 in Del Mar, California; ended September 22 in Seattle, Washington.

Marvin Gaye: Began February 2 in Atlanta, Georgia; ended March 4 in New York City.

Gloria Gaynor: Began April 18 in Cleveland, Ohio; ended June 25 in Philadelphia, Pennsylvania.

Heart: Began late summer, 1978; ended December 8, 1978, in Phoenix, Arizona.

Instant Funk: Began March 31 in Buffalo, New York; ended June 11 in New York City.

Jacksons: Toured Britain in February. Began April 12 in Cincinnati, Ohio; ended June 10 in Greensboro, North Carolina.

Al Jarreau: Began November 17, 1978, in Nashville, Tennessee; ended December 31, 1978, in New York City.

Billy Joel: Ended fall tour December 16, 1978, in New York City. Toured Europe in February. Began March 24 in Starksville, Mississippi; ended May 17 in Honolulu, Hawaii.

Elton John: Began September 19 in Phoenix, Arizona; ended November 11, in Houston, Texas.

Kansas: Began June 28 in Huntsville, Alabama; ended September 2 in Providence, Rhode Island.

Kiss: Began June 14 in Lakeland, Florida; ended September 19 in Evansville, Indiana.

Knack: Toured Far East in August. Began U.S. tour in late September.

Little River Band: Began August 16 in Las Vegas, Nevada; ended November 4 in Los Angeles, California.

Kenny Loggins: Began October 11, 1978, in Norfolk, Virginia; ended October 29, 1978, in Miami, Florida.

Chuck Mangione: Began June 30 in Kansas City, Kansas; ended August 25 in Westbury, New York.

Steve Martin: Began June 7 in Las Vegas; ended October 1 in Lake Tahoe, Nevada.

Eddie Money: Followed European tour with late February–early March U.S. dates. Began second string of U.S. dates in mid-July in Los Angeles.

Joni Mitchell: Began August in Oklahoma City, Oklahoma; ended September 16 in Los Angeles, California.

Nazareth: Toured Japan in May. Began U.S. tour May in La Crosse, Wisconsin; ended July 8 in Portland, Oregon.

Olivia Newton-John: Toured Australia and Europe, November 1978.

Ted Nugent: Began November 27, 1978, in Chicago, Illinois; ended February 19 in San Diego, California. Toured Europe end April–mid May. Began spring and summer tour May 25 in Louisville, Kentucky.

Teddy Pendergrass: Began June 1 in Sacramento, California; ended September 9 in Los Angeles, California.

Pointer Sisters: Began April 20 in Seattle, Washington; ended May 17 in Washington, D.C.

Suzi Quatro: Began July 12 in San Diego, California; ended August 22 in Atlanta, Georgia.

Queen: Began October 28, 1978, in Dallas, Texas; ended December 18, 1978, in Los Angeles, California.

Linda Ronstadt: Toured South and West Coast between December 15, 1978, and December 24, 1978.

Santana: Began January 19 in Chicago, Illinois; ended March 17 in Detroit, Michigan.

Al Stewart: Began October 8, 1978, in Berkeley, California; ended November 19, 1978, in Washington, D.C.

Rod Stewart: Began April 12 in Edmonton, Canada; ended June 25 in Los Angeles, California.

Styx: Began March 12 in Jacksonville, Florida; ended April 4 in Portland, Oregon.

Donna Summer: Began April 5 in Las Vegas, Nevada; ended August 14 in the Universal Amphitheatre, Los Angeles, California.

Supertramp: Began April 3 at the Forum, Los Angeles, California; ended June 17 in Alpine Music Theatre, East Troy, Wisconsin.

James Taylor: Began July 3 in Memphis, Tennessee; ended August 4 in Columbia, Maryland.

Toto: Began February 2 in Chicago, Illinois; ended April 30 in Toronto, Canada.

Gino Vannelli: Began March 9 in Charlotte, North Carolina; ended May 6 in Vancouver, Canada.

Village People: Began June 1 in Salt Lake City, Utah; ended June 25 in New York City.

Grover Washington Jr.: Began June 1 in Louisville, Kentucky; ended July 2 in Hampton, Virginia.

Weather Report: Began November 3, 1978, in New York City; ended November 26, 1978, in Berkeley, California.

Who: Played only U.S. dates September 13–18 at Madison Square Garden, New York City.

Charlyn Zlotnik

Clockwise from below: *Gordon Lightfoot, Waylon Jennings, and Harry Chapin blended their talents in an April benefit for the André Eglevsky ballet. Nancy Wilson's guitar may be acoustic, but the authority with which she plays lights up the stage. Willie Nelson reigns as the red-haired king of country.*

Charlyn Zlotnik

STARS OF
YEAR IN M

A

ALLMAN BROTHERS BAND

Gregg Allman—Vocals, organ

Dickey Betts—Guitar

Dan Toler—Guitar

David Goldflies—Bass

Jaimoe—Drums, congas

Butch Trucks—Drums, percussion

The late Duane Allman, whose breathtaking bottleneck slide guitar was the beating heart of the original, legendary Allman Brothers Band, often referred to the group as enlightened rogues. So *Enlightened Rogues* was a natural choice for the title of an invigorating reunion album that's sparked by sizzling hot performances from Gregg, Dickey, Jaimoe, and Butch and newcomers Dan Toler and David Goldflies. The original Allman ensemble, formed in the spring of 1969, was immediately successful with its first album, *The Allman Brothers Band*, a disk supercharged by the scintillating interplay of Duane Allman's and Dickey Betts's guitars. Two more albums, *Idlewild South* and *At Fillmore East*, came out in 1970 and 1971, nailing down their reputation as the most original and dynamic blues and rock band to emerge from a high-powered pack. On October 29, 1971, Duane Allman was killed in a motorcycle accident, and the music world reeled with shock. The band pulled itself together and completed *Eat a Peach*, which many regard as their finest album. They were rehearsing their next album, *Brothers and Sisters*, when they were deeply shaken by another blow: Bass player Berry Oakley was killed in another motorcycle crash, uncannily close to the spot where Duane had his accident.

Stunned once again, the band nevertheless went on to record *Brothers and Sisters*, replacing Berry Oakley with Lamar Williams, who had worked with Jaimoe. But the two tragedies had put a strain on the band members; some spark had gone out of the music, and their next album, *Win, Lose or Draw*, lacked the fire and conviction of earlier albums. By the mid-seventies the band was faltering; they finally split up, Gregg Allman touring with his own band and Dickey Betts forming Great Southern.

But the original chemistry that had cooked between Gregg, Dickey, Butch, and Jaimoe is now again evident, and the Allman Brothers have returned with some aggressively hard rock, delighting their fans in 1979 with both a gold album and a wildly successful American tour.

1978/79 Discography: *Enlightened Rogues*

ASHFORD AND SIMPSON

Nicholas Ashford—Vocals

Valerie Simpson—Vocals

They were songwriters to begin with, Valerie a slick seventeen, Nick a street-sharp twenty-one, when they first saw each other on a Harlem street. Their eyes met, locked, and before too long their conversation became melodic, as they discovered each other's musical gifts. Since then they've penned such pop powerhouses as the Ray Charles monster "Let's Go Get Stoned" and such rousers as "Ain't No Mountain High Enough," "Ain't Nothing Like the Real Thing," "Reach Out and Touch (Somebody's Hand)," and "Remember Me." Today, their careers have a new glow as their own warm vocal style shines out.

In the late 1960s, while they were working as writers, arrangers, and producers for Motown, Valerie took the first tentative steps into performing, beginning by singing on several Quincy Jones albums. Emboldened, she recorded two solo LPs, *Exposed!* and *Valerie Simpson*; along the way, she had an R & B hit single with "Silly, Wasn't I?" After some touring, she locked her eyes with Nick's once more, and in September 1973 the two of them set out to record their first album as a team, *Gimme Something Real*. They barrelled into their second joint effort, *I Wanna Be Selfish*, in May of 1974. Much of 1975 was devoted to personal life—decorating a new home, celebrating the birth of a child. Then came two chart-climbers, *Come As You Are* and *So, So Satisfied*; from the latter came the hit singles "Over and Over," "Tried, Tested and Found True," and the title song. Audiences were beginning to listen for the Ashford and Simpson touch, and in September 1977 they released the album that was to win them their first gold disk, the animated *Send It*. The continued success of this versatile duo seems assured as their latest album, *Is It Still Good to Ya*, also zoomed to gold.

1978/79 Discography: *Stay Free*

B

BAD COMPANY

Paul Rodgers—Vocals

Mick Ralphs—Guitar

Boz Burrell—Bass

Simon Kirke—Drums

The dynamite charge that calls itself Bad Company exploded once more in 1979 with a million-selling album called *Desolation Angels*, a commanding single called "Rock 'n' Roll Fantasy," and a thundering tour of the United States, their first since 1977. American rock fans were starved for their sound. In California, tickets for a June performance at Inglewood's 18,000-seat Forum were sold out in six hours, and demand for Bad Company was so great that a second sold-out show was added.

American fans aren't the only ones who love Bad Company, however. Led Zeppelin, who signed them to Led Zep's own record label, Swan Song, is increasingly enthusiastic about the band it discovered. When Bad Company performed in Birmingham, England, this year, Jimmy Page, Robert Plant, and John Bonham joined them onstage for their encore.

Coming out of the British bands Free, Mott The Hoople, and King Crimson, the four joined forces in 1973. Once they signed with Swan Song, their career moved fast. Their first single, "Can't Get Enough," was an international number one; in 1974 pop polls voted them the best new group of the year. A 1975 tour of America was almost instantly sold out, and they scored in 1975 with both their second single, "Feel Like Makin' Love," a top-ten winner, and their second album, *Straight Shooter*, which was in the top five on the pop charts for more than a month. *Run With the Pack*, their third album, sold half a million copies within two weeks after its release and stayed on the charts for nine months. In 1977 their fourth album, *Burnin' Sky*, became a top-twenty charter, and their 1977 tour of the United States was a rousing critical and financial winner.

1978/79 Discography: *Desolation Angels*

The Allman Brothers Band

Ashford and Simpson

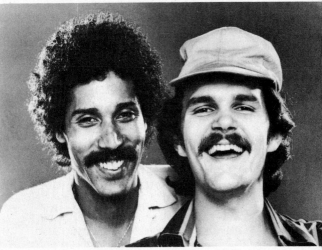

Bad Company

Bell and James

The Bee Gees

George Benson

BEE GEES

Barry Gibb	Vocals, guitar
Maurice Gibb	Vocals, bass
Robin Gibb	Vocals
Alan Kendall	Guitar
Dennis Byron	Drums
Blue Weaver	Keyboards

What could they do to follow up 1978's *Saturday Night Fever*, the multimillion-selling sound track that won them three Grammies: album of the year, producer of the year, and vocal performance by a duo, group or chorus, and contained the Grammy-winning song "Stayin' Alive" as well as "Night Fever," the most frequently performed song of 1978. Even *Sesame Street Fever*, featuring Robin Gibb and Big Bird, went gold. In 1979 the brothers Gibb effortlessly maintained their positions in the stratosphere of pop with the album *Spirits Having Flown*, a hot/sweet continuation of the quavery disco sound that has become their trademark. The album itself shipped platinum and has since gone on to sell more than four million copies. By June of 1979 it had spawned three ubiquitous, hummable singles— "Too Much Heaven," "Tragedy," and "Love You Inside Out." The last was their sixth number-one single in a row, their ninth in the 1970s, placing them far ahead of their competition, Wings and Elton John, with six each. Their special performance in January at the United Nations was a gala event, sparkling with such guest stars as Rod Stewart and Olivia Newton-John. With all profits going to UNICEF, the benefit was a huge success; keynote to a full year that included an instantly sold-out three-month, fifty-eight-concert tour (featuring a surprise appearance by John Travolta at Houston's Summit Sports Arena that brought an already howling audience to even louder shrieks), a new movie, a new album, a David Frost television special, and an almost 100 percent certainty that Barry Gibb would be chosen to play Che Guevara in Robert Stigwood's movie version of *Evita*.

The personal and professional lives of the brothers Gibb have not been all beer and skittles, however. Their childhood was fragmented by a series of moves from Australia to England, the family following their bandleader father as he moved from job to job. Often outsiders in the schools they attended, the brothers stuck together closely for self-defense. This closeness is evident today, with twins Maurice and Robin often displaying an eerie extrasensory communication.

Music was always part of their lives. In 1958 the brothers, not yet in their teens, began singing together professionally in Australian speedway ovals. They worked for years in Australia, trying to hit the top. Despite gaining a large local following and their own television show, a dozen attempts at a winning single were all failures.

Disgusted, the brothers were delighted to leave Australia with their parents and head for England once again in 1967, just as their single "Spicks and Specks" was on its way to the number-one spot Down Under. The move to England was fortuitous, however, as entrepreneurial genius Robert Stigwood saw their potential and eagerly signed them on. Their first song under his aegis, the mournful "New York Mining Disaster, 1941," became a smash in Britain and the United States in the spring of 1967 and was followed by a string of hits— "To Love Somebody," "Holiday," "Massachusetts," "I've Gotta Get a Message to You," and "I Started a Joke."

The brothers were on their way, but success went to their heads in the form of overindulgence in drugs and sibling rivalry. In 1969, tensions, largely between Barry and Robin, the two songwriters of the trio, forced them apart. Barry and Maurice made a record called *Cucumber Castle* as the Bee Gees, and Robin cut a record called *Robin's Reign*. Neither was successful, and by 1971 the brothers came together again. Such new songs as "Lonely Days" and "How Can You Mend a Broken Heart" continued the plaintive-ballad mold with which they had become identified. Their careers faltered until 1973 when they teamed up with Atlantic Records R & B producer Arif

Mardin. Their first album with him, *Mr. Natural*, was still full of sugar and sweet ballads, but their second, *Main Course*, was a disco-flavored popper with such songs as "Jive Talking." It pulled them out of their honeyed rut and up into a new orbit of success.

Although the Bee Gees and Mardin were a natural smash combination, they were forced to part company when the Robert Stigwood Organization switched distribution to Polygram. Luckily, they found a similar rapport with producers Albhy Galuten and Karl Richardson and the hits started to come—the singles "Nights on Broadway" and "You Should Be Dancing," and the explosive, *Here At Last ... Bee Gees ... Live*, a two-record collection of twenty-two of their greatest hits, recorded on their crackling 1976 tour of the United States. 1978/79 Discography: *Spirits Having Flown*

BELL AND JAMES

Casey James	Drums, vocals
Leroy Bell	Guitar, vocals

With the solid-gold success of their exuberant "Livin' It Up (Friday Night)," Leroy Bell and Casey James, better known as Bell and James, have come out of the secluded background they had known as songwriters and entered the performers' arena.

Sharp-as-a-tack Casey James masks his penetrating mind with an easygoing wit. "I started out as a genius and it's been downhill from there," he grins, pulling his baseball cap down over his face. Born in Portland, Oregon, he played the drums, piano, and guitar when he was a young boy. Before long he was performing with Pacific Northwest bands, moonlighting as a percussionist with the Portland Symphony and the Portland Opera Company. He won a B.S. degree in biology from the University of Washington, but he spent most of his free college hours working with a drum teacher and surreptitiously writing songs. "I was definitely a closet writer; I never played my songs for anyone."

Leroy Bell was born in Florida but spent most of his childhood in Germany with his army father, learning the guitar when he was thirteen. "I went *wild* with the music," he recalls. "I found out pretty young that music was the only thing I wanted to do." He too had been writing songs. With the help and guidance of uncle Thom Bell, producer/arranger/songwriter for the team of Gamble and Huff, Leroy began to develop as a songwriter. His first recorded song, "You're All I Need In Life," written with Linda Creed, was sung by the Spinners. He met James when the two played in a band called Special Blend, and they began to write together. With further guidance by Thom Bell, the two began to hone their craft. They made demo records for Bell's Mighty Three Music, playing all the instruments themselves. They shot out tons of material to producers and artists, and their songs were snapped up by the Spinners, the O'Jays, Elton John, Maxine Nightingale, the Pips, Freda Payne, Pockets, and L.T.D. Someone—they claim they can't remember who—sent a demo to A & M Records, and, before they knew what was happening, A & M offered them a recording contract. They completed scoring the movie *The Fish That Saved Pittsburgh* and zipped into *Bell and James*, their first album. 1978/79 Discography: *Bell and James*

GEORGE BENSON

His string of platinum albums began in 1976 with *Breezin'*, the first jazz disk ever to sell a million copies; with almost three million copies sold, it's still the best-selling jazz album of all time. The consummate musician with the smooth style also picked up three Grammy awards in 1976 for his scintillating guitar work. His fabulous success continued with 1977's *In Flight* and 1978's *Weekend in L.A.*, from which came his Grammy-winning full-steam-ahead treatment of the Drifters' classic "On Broadway." This year's electronic *Livin' Inside Your Love* is

Courtesy Chrysalis Records

Blondie

The Blues Brothers Courtesy Atlantic Records

Claude Bolling Courtesy Columbia Records

Boston Ron Pownall/Courtesy Epic Records

The Brothers Johnson Courtesy A&M Records

Chuck Brown and the Soul Searchers Courtesy MCA Records

a gold-winner on its way to platinum, perching in the number-one jazz album spot for more than three months and rising high in the soul and pop charts as well. But for George Benson perhaps 1979's greatest thrill was the opportunity to design his own personalized guitar, hand-made and distributed by Ibanez.

Benson's music has universal appeal, but his roots are firmly in the jazz idiom he learned as a child. The precocious musician won his first contract with RCA records when he was ten years old, but it took ten more years until his talents were fully appreciated. He played with Jack McDuff's funky R & B band, but Benson eventually felt limited by that genre and left the group in 1965, bringing together Lonnie Smith on organ, Ronnie Cuber on baritone, and Phil Turner on drums for his own ensemble.

With this group, he recorded for Creed Taylor and CTI records through the mid-sixties to the early seventies, during which time, because his guitar work was so much in demand, he never got a chance to sing. All that changed with *Breezin'*, when his velvety voice rang out on "This Masquerade," the top single from that album. After the fabulous success of *Breezin'* in America, Benson went on to conquer the world, exalting fans in Europe, Japan, and Australia. He continued to sail ahead with *In Flight*, his second platinum-winner, and the soundtrack for the Muhammed Ali film *The Greatest*, which featured the top hit "The Greatest Love of All."

During one long weekend in the summer of 1977 Benson's guitar dominated New York City, as loving New Yorkers followed their idol from the Metropolitan Museum of Art to the Palladium Theatre, from Avery Fisher Hall to the Dance Theater of Harlem. By the end of 1977 *Billboard* rated Benson the top box-office attraction in small concert halls. Throughout 1978 Benson toured the world, was featured at the historic White House tribute to the Newport Jazz Festival's 25th Anniversary, starred at New York's Belasco Theater in "On Broadway," and appeared for five sold-out nights at Los Angeles's Universal Amphitheatre.
1978/79 Discography: *Livin' Inside Your Love*

BLONDIE

Debbie Harry—Lead vocals

Chris Stein—12-string guitar, E-bow

Jimmy Destri—Keyboards

Frank Infante—Guitars

Nigel Harrison—Bass

Clem Burke—Drums

The year 1979 was the year of Blondie, the first new wave group to break through commercially with a number-one single and a top-ten gold album. With its irresistible melodic swoops, "Heart of Glass" was an emphatic pop charger and a disco hit as well. It was followed by the insinuating pulse of "One Way or Another," both singles driving the album *Parallel Lines* to gold sales. Blondie has always enjoyed international fame, but their first two albums, 1976's *Blondie* and 1977's *Plastic Letters*, sank without a trace in America. They broke big in the United States in 1979 with the help of television exposure, particularly their January 19 appearance as hosts of "Midnight Special."

When people think of Blondie, they think of Debbie Harry, whose clear, dead-ahead voice and full throttle stage act is the obvious visual center of the band. In miniskirts and spike heels, she was also a campy fashion trend setter, although she says that her thrift shop days are over now that she can afford to buy good clothes. Born in Miami and raised in New Jersey, Debbie left home for New York's St. Marks Place in the psychedelic cauldron of the 1960's East Village. She began her musical career singing with a soft rock group called Wind

in the Willows, and when they broke up she supported herself with a string of odd jobs until she got her next singing stint with a band called the Stilettoes. Guitarist/songwriter Chris Stein joined the band, and he and Debbie linked romantically and musically. The Stilettoes soon evaporated, but Debbie and Chris remained together and formed Blondie by gathering drummer Clem Burke, bass player Gary Valentine, and keyboard master Jimmy Destri.

Performing in the famed CBGB, New York's gritty punk palace, they were spotted by Richie Gottehrer. He became their manager and producer and got them heard and signed by Private Stock Records. After a smash debut at Los Angeles's Whiskey in February of 1977, they were chosen to tour with Iggy Pop and David Bowie that spring. In July of 1977 Gary Valentine split; Frank Infante joined as bass player for the album *Plastic Letters*. He moved to guitars when Nigel Harrison came in on bass.

Together with their second manager, Peter Leeds, they decided they weren't being supported enough by Private Stock. Leeds raised $500,000, bought out their contract and took Blondie to Chrysalis. Although Leeds and the band are now engaged in acrimonious disputes, his choice of Chrysalis was inspired as the small, aggressive label threw its entire weight behind the group. Also inspired was their choice of Mike Chapman, 1979's hot producer, to produce *Parallel Lines*.

In the summer of 1979 they became heroes in their own country at last, capping their recording success with a glorious American tour.
1978/79 Discography: *Eat to the Beat*

BLUES BROTHERS

Dan Aykroyd—Elwood Blues, Harmonica

John Belushi—Jake Blues, Vocals

Their first appearance at Los Angeles's Universal Amphitheatre was preceded by their own intense nervousness and the audience's equally intense curiosity. Steve Martin headlined that show in the fall of 1978, but the audience had come to see just what Dan Aykroyd and John Belushi were up to. What was this Blues Brothers? Was their performance going to be another "Saturday Night Live" satire? Could these two men, who inspire gales of laughter just by looking at them, be serious about music?

In their slightly undersized porkpies, their discreetly dark Ray-Bans, and their identical black suits, the duo certainly looked a mite daffy. But within seconds, as guitarist Steve Cropper, bassman Donald "Duck" Dunn, drummer Steve Jourdan, and horn players Tom Scott, Al Rubin, and Lou Marini hit their first feverish blast, the crowd knew this was no laughing matter. And Aykroyd and Belushi, firmly in character as Jake and Elwood, did not disappoint but played and sang with geniune involvement.

The promise of that first night was fulfilled during the next eight nights of the Universal engagement and during a slamming tour of the country. The album *Briefcase Full of Blues* bulldozed its way to platinum sales and spawned two hit singles, a slam-bang version of Sam and Dave's "Soul Man" and the infectious, lunatic "Rubber Biscuit."
1978/79 Discography: *Briefcase Full of Blues*

CLAUDE BOLLING

Although Claude Bolling has won the Grand Prix du Disque six times, the former child jazz piano prodigy is best known in America for two albums: his best-selling jazz/classical melds, *Suite for Flute and Jazz Piano*, recorded with Jean-Pierre Rampal, and 1979's *Suite for Violin and Jazz Piano*, with Pinchas Zuckerman.

Born in Cannes, France, Bolling was formally trained in harmony and counterpoint, but his real love was jazz and his greatest musical hero, the legendary Duke Ellington. Ellington and Bolling later met and became friends, and Duke was among Bolling's greatest fans.

In the course of his sparkling career, Bolling has performed and recorded with such jazz greats as Roy Eldridge, Sidney Bechet, Kenny Clarke, Paul Gonsalves, Sam Woodyard, and Lionel Hampton. He has arranged songs for such vocalists as Liza Minnelli, Sacha Distel, and Juliette Greco, and he has composed scores for movies and television, the most famous of which was his music for the film *Borsalino*.

1978/79 Discography: *Suite for Violin and Jazz Piano*

BOSTON

Tom Scholz—Guitar, keyboards

Bradley Delp—Vocals

Barry Goudreau—Guitar

Fran Sheehan—Bass

Sib Hashian—Drums

At last count, Boston's first album, 1976's *Boston*, had racked up more than four million American sales. It was followed smartly by 1978's *Don't Look Back*, which sold four million copies in America and another two million internationally. In 1979, wherever the band appeared, fans packed in to see them and roared approval of such favorite songs as "Don't Look Back," "More Than a Feeling," and "Peace of Mind." Not a bad three years for a band that had never even played together when its first album was released.

At the core of Boston's sensational success is the genius and persistence of mechanical engineer Tom Scholz, an MIT graduate whose head was in his daytime job at Polaroid but whose heart was in the stinging guitar riffs he played in Boston clubs at night. Working in a handcrafted twelve-track home studio, Scholz and singer Bradley Delp put together a handful of tapes augmented by the separately recorded tracks of Barry Goudreau, Fran Sheehan, and Sib Hashian. Delp and Scholz eagerly mailed these tapes out to record companies, only to meet with one rejection after another. Independent record producers Paul Ahearn and Charlie McKenzie, however, were enthusiastic about the sound. They kept banging on doors until they got the band airplay and a contract with Epic Records.

The first album exploded with such force that the band had to begin touring. The five musicians got together for the first time, rehearsed intensely for weeks, and sallied out on a four-month blitzkrieg of a tour. Their astonishing success in person and on record is as strong as ever in 1979.

BROTHERS JOHNSON

With three out of three albums platinum, the Brothers Johnson have lived up to the expectations of Quincy Jones, who was bowled over by their buoyant sound when he invited them to play on *Mellow Madness* in 1975. Quincy's call for the two young jazzmen came not a moment too soon for the brothers. Eight months earlier guitarist George and bass player Louis had left the security of steady work with Billy Preston's band to create their own music. During those eight months they wrote and recorded for ten hours a day, but the tapes they hopefully sent out to record companies invariably came back. To keep a roof over their heads, the brothers finally decided they needed nine-to-five jobs, a dismal prospect for the veteran musicians, who,

when they were twelve and thirteen, had opened shows for the Supremes. Chuckling, Louis remembers, "The day that Q called, I had just gotten a gig working at a pizza place. I had to ask the boss for time off on the first day to go do the session with Quincy. I don't know how I pulled that one off!"

The two impressed Jones so much that he hired them to tour Japan with him and used four of their songs on *Mellow Madness*. Their own first album, *Look Out for #1*, was a gold-seller within three months of its release and platinum soon after; it also included two million-selling singles, "I'll Be Good to You" and "Get the Funk Out Ma Face." It won them a Grammy nomination as the best new artist of 1976 and a slew of similar awards from the music trade papers. The brothers felt intense pressure to outdo themselves on the second album. They did. *Right on Time*, released in the spring of 1977, was another monster, a million-seller in less than a month, and contained both the million-selling single "Strawberry Letter 23" and "Q," their tribute to Quincy Jones that won them a Grammy for best instrumental performance of the year. Their tours of Europe and Japan created near-riots.

On *Blam!*, another platinum, the brothers continue their musical growth, using their touring band rather than studio musicians to give the album a taste of their live energy. Their 1978 eight-city headline tour of the United States was another wild rocket-ship ride for the brothers and their fans. That they'll keep striving for even greater heights is obvious. As they say, "Why reach for the ceiling when there's a moon up there?"

1978/79 Discography: *Blam!*

CHUCK BROWN AND THE SOUL SEARCHERS

Chuck Brown—Guitars, lead vocals

Donald Tillery—Trumpet, percussion, vocals

John Buchanan—Keyboard, synthesizer, trombone, vocals

LeRoy Fleming—Saxophone, percussion, vocals

Ricardo Wellman—Drums

Jerry Wilder—Electric bass, vocals

Gregory Gerran—Congas, percussion

Curtis Johnson—Organ

In early 1979, with "Bustin' Loose," a solid-gold single, socked into the number-one spot on the soul charts for a month and the self-titled album a top soul LP, Chuck Brown and the Soul Searchers returned triumphantly from a four-year recording break. For the past eight years, Brown and his funky band have been one of the hottest groups in the Washington-Baltimore-Richmond area, performing an average of five shows a week in clubs and concert halls to fill the demand for their rousing music. In 1972 they were signed to Sussex Records; their first album contained two hits, "We the People" and "All in Your Mind." Their next album, 1974's *Salt of the Earth*, contained the smash single "Blow Your Whistle."

But Sussex Records folded, and Brown and the Soul Searchers were left without a label. They decided to channel their energies into live performances, and between 1974 and 1978 they appeared with such top artists as the O'Jays, Parliament-Funkadelic, Earth, Wind & Fire, and the Commodores. In 1978 producers James Purdie and David Carpin signed the band to Source Records and succeeded in capturing their energetic live sound.

1978/79 Discography: *Chuck Brown and the Soul Searchers*

PEABO BRYSON

His silken voice reveals strong traces of his Greenville, South Carolina, boyhood; but his soulful love songs are worlds away from the sly, pounding rock and roll of Chuck Berry and Little Richard, his favorite boyhood artists. Today, Peabo Bryson has parlayed his natural romanticism into two gold albums, 1978's *Reaching for the Sky* and *Crosswinds*, released in November of 1978 and gold by February of 1979.

"As far back as I can remember, I've always been into music," the gentle producer/singer/songwriter says; at the age of fourteen he was already a veteran of local bands. Although he tried college for a couple of years, he soon decided that he wanted to pursue music full time. He left school and joined the group the Textile Display. With them he put in his hard years on the road, between 1968 and 1973 touring the country and performing overseas in such diverse places as the Caribbean and Vietnam.

After working for several years as a producer for Bang Records, he scored his first soul hit in 1976 with "Underground Music." His first album, *Peabo*, made the charts and gave him two more top-thirty hits, "Just Another Day" and "I Can Make it Better." From his *Crosswinds* album comes the top-five soul single "I'm So Into You."
1978/79 Discography: *Crosswinds*.

B.T.O.

Fred Turner—Guitars, vocals

Blair Thornton—Guitars

Jim Clench—Bass

Robbie Bachman—Drums

Bachman-Turner Overdrive was a 1970s band of hard-as-nails rockers. Led by Randy Bachman, former writer and guitarist for the Guess Who, Bachman Turner Overdrive scored six gold albums in the space of three years, with their third album, *Not Fragile*, a platinum gorilla. They delivered such pounding singles as "Let it Ride," "Taking Care of Business," and the million-selling "You Ain't Seen Nothing Yet."

Their seventh album, *Freeways*, however, moved in a softer direction. The music was light and disco influenced, and critics accused Randy Bachman of being self-indulgent. In addition, his strict Mormon life-style had always been a source of conflict and friction within the band. In 1977, as tension within the band was about to reach the breaking point, he left, taking the name Bachman-Turner Overdrive and its logo. The new band, under brother Robbie Bachman, was eager to rock on. They officially changed their name to B.T.O. and in 1978 released *Street Action*, a return to muscular music. *Rock 'n' Roll Nights* followed in 1979, supported by a sold out eighty-date tour in the spring.
1978/79 Discography: *Rock 'n' Roll Nights*

CARS

Ric Ocasek—Rhythm guitar, vocals

Ben Orr—Lead vocals, bass

Greg Hawkes—Keyboards, saxophone, guitar, back-up vocals

Elliot Easton—Lead guitar, back-up vocals

David Robinson—Drums, percussion, electronic drums

Tall, gaunt, black-haired guitarist Ric Ocasek and short, blond, stocky singer/bass player Ben Orr first met in Cleveland, where Ocasek had been writing songs. Orr, who had already made a couple of local hits with his group the Grasshoppers, had been singing since he was a child, entertaining his parents and their friends with his Elvis Presley imitations. The two of them teamed up, toured, and stayed a step ahead of starvation. They moved to the East Coast, settling into Cambridge where they performed as a duo and recorded with a folk trio called Milkwood. Through that group they met Greg Hawkes, an expert music arranger who played keyboards and saxophone. After a couple of years, during which time Ocasek formed and disbanded a number of less-than-satisfactory groups, they were ready to roll, in early 1976, with a band called Cap'n Swing that included crack guitarist Elliot Easton. Knocked out by their live sound, Boston WBCN-FM deejay Maxanne Sartori began airing their demos; on the strength of those demos the band scooted to New York to expose their talents to some major managers. The trip was a failure, but it gave Ric determination to rearrange the band into the current lineup, complete when drummer David Robinson was brought in from DMZ. The fledgling band descended into Ocasek's basement to put their first album together during the fall and winter of 1976. The album was eagerly snatched by Elektra, and *The Cars* accelerated quickly, winning critical cheers and burning rubber all the way to platinum; from the album came two rollicking, hard-edged new wave singles, "Just What I Needed" and "My Best Friend's Girl."
1978/79 Discography: *Candy-O*

CHEAP TRICK

Robin Zander—Vocals

Rick Nielsen—Guitars

Tom Petersson—Bass

Bun E. Carlos—Drums

Beneath the surface of the boisterous cartoon characters who make up Cheap Trick are four midwestern boys who have been transmuted by the love of rock and roll into one of 1979's most dynamic, aggressive bands. They've made music together since 1974, cutting their performing teeth in small clubs and as openers for such groups as Kiss, the Kinks, Santana, and Boston. The powerhouse quartet maintains a gruelling 250-performance-a-year schedule, thanks in part to manager Ken Adamany. Since Adamany, a midwestern booking agent, controls much of the club and concert activity in the northern

Peabo Bryson   Courtesy Capitol Records

B.T.O.   Courtesy Mercury Records

heap Trick   Courtesy Epic Records

The Cars   Elliot Gilbert/Courtesy Elektra Records

Courtesy Atlantic Records

Chic

Cher   Courtesy Casablanca Records and Filmworks

91

Illinois area, he saw to it that his band was almost constantly onstage right from the beginning.

The band signed with Epic Records in August 1976 and cut *Cheap Trick*, a critically appreciated but underbought first album, with heavy metal instrumentals wed to clever lyrics. Six months later, they released the lighter and more melodic *In Color*; despite the album's neatly turned tunes and an increasingly colorful road show, they didn't get the reaction they wanted. However, two singles from *In Color*, "Clock Strikes Ten" and "I Want You to Want Me," reached number one on the Japanese charts. The major Japanese music magazines began to pursue Cheap Trick for interviews, and in 1978, when *Heaven Tonight* was released, the band toured Japan. Although that tour was wildly successful, *Heaven Tonight* still did not penetrate the American market, rising only to the forties on the pop charts before dropping off.

The American breakthrough came, unexpectedly, from an album recorded on the 1978 Japan tour and initially released only for the Japanese market. Called *Cheap Trick Live at Budokan*, it contained the best songs from the first three albums. Japan loved it, and even more thrilling for the band, Americans loved it too. American fans snapped up rare imported copies at twenty dollars a disk, and Epic rushed out an American pressing. New Cheap Trick fans bought over a million of them. By this time *Heaven Tonight* had gone gold and the single "Surrender," with its irresistibly ebullient hooks, had become a pop hit. "I Want You to Want Me" was the next smash single from the album; a studio album, *Dream Police*, was ready by early summer. At the beginning of 1979 the group toured Europe and throughout the spring and summer headlined in the United States.

1978/79 Discography: *Cheap Trick Live at Budokan*
Dream Police

CHER

Cher is back and Bogart's got her! Delighted with the acquisition of the glamorous singer, Casablanca Records and Filmworks' president Neil Bogart says of his new star: "Her gifts are unique, and I think, in the past, she only scratched the surface of the talent she has."

He saw to it that Cher got to play out one of her erotically underdressed fantasies in Ron Frasetta's look-again artwork for the jacket of her first Casablanca album. That LP, *Take Me Home*, Cher's first venture into disco, has already repaid Bogart's faith; both it and its title single have won gold.

At seventeen, already self-possessed and maturing into a woman of regal stature, Cher began her career when she was asked to fill in for a missing back-up singer during a Phil Spector recording session. Spector, impressed, asked her back to sing on two of his greatest hits, "Be My Baby," and "You've Lost That Lovin' Feeling."

She soon married Sonny Bono, and their duet of "I Got You, Babe," in 1965 became a dizzying smash. The duo made more hit records, made the films *Goodtimes* and *Chastity*, and beginning in 1971, starred in *The Sonny and Cher Comedy Hour*. Cher's solo recording of "Gypsies, Tramps and Thieves" was another blockbuster. Her divorce from Sonny in the mid-seventies made headlines, as did her brief marriage to Gregg Allman and her whirlwind romance with Kiss star Gene Simmons. In 1978 her television extravaganza, "Cher...Special," was a smash success, and she, almost singlehandedly, has made roller disco a chic pastime.

1978/79 Discography: *Take Me Home*

CHIC

Bernard Edwards	Bass
Nile Rodgers	Guitar
Tony Thompson	Drums
Alfa Anderson	Vocals
Luci Martin	Vocals

Light, zippy, quintessentially disco, Chic's first single, 1977's "Dance, Dance, Dance," skyrocketed the then-unknown group to the top of the charts. One smash followed another, and they closed 1978 with the chart-topping platinum "Le Freak" and the stirring "I Want Your Love."

The core of the group is Bernard Edwards and Nile Rodgers, two New York city boys who met in 1972 in a group called the Big Apple Band. Bernard was a soul man and Nile was a rocker who had moved through classical and was dabbling with a bit of jazz, but the two of them hit it off and cut a demo record that included a song called "Everybody Dance" early in 1977. Rob Drake, deejay at New York's Night Owl disco, played the record and attracted a large group of fans. Another cut, "Dance, Dance, Dance," set record companies bidding. Drummer Tony Thompson and singer Norma Jean Wright joined the group, "Dance, Dance, Dance" caught on, and by early 1978 Chic was ready to make their first live appearances, touring coast-to-coast with such top groups as the O'Jays, Rufus, Heatwave, the Isley Brothers, and Peter Brown. Chic crisscrossed the country throughout the summer and fall of 1978, finishing September in Rio and São Paulo. When Norma Jean went out on her own, she was replaced by lead singer Alfa Anderson, who comes to Chic with credentials including the soundtrack of *The Wiz* and vocals on Ray Baretto's song "What Part of Heaven Do You Come From?" Luci Martin, the other new female singer, has studied dance with Alvin Ailey and appeared in the road companies of *Hair* and *Jesus Christ Superstar*. In the summer of 1979 the band climbed the pop, soul, and disco charts with the bouncy "Good Times."

1978/79 Discography: *C'est Chic*
Risqué

CHICAGO

Peter Cetera	Bass
Donnie Dacus	Guitar
Laudir De Oliveira	Percussion
Robert Lamm	Keyboards
Lee Loughnane	Trumpet
Walt Parazaider	Woodwinds
James Pankow	Trombone
Daniel Seraphine	Drums

A little more than ten years ago a monolithic band with the unlikely name of Chicago Transit Authority lumbered onto the rock scene. Complete with trumpet, trombone, and woodwinds, their stage-crowding eight-man presence startled audiences who, in those days, expected to see a rock stage filled with towering amplifiers, not live musicians. Even their first album, *Chicago Transit Authority*, was larger than usual—a two-record set in an era when double albums were a rare breed. The bigger-than-life aura that surrounds the group extends to their sales figures as well: Every one of their thirteen albums—including the 1979-winner *Hot Streets*—has hit the million mark. Such songs as "Does Anyone Know What Time It Is," "Beginnings," "25 or 6 to 4," "Color My World," "Saturday in the Park," "Just You'n Me," "Feelin' Stronger Every Day," "Wishing You Were Here," "Call on Me," "If You Leave Me Now," "Baby What a Big Surprise," "Hot Streets," and "Alive Again," are all tuneful modern classics.

They didn't fall into their success accidentally. Transported from their namesake native city to Los Angeles by crack producer James Guercio, they trained intensively before recording that first album. Guercio, as tough as the crustiest athletic coach, drove them eight hours a day, seven days a week, until they had hammered their disparate elements into a smooth, dynamic sound.

With the release of the first album came national tours—first with Janis Joplin and then with Jimi Hendrix. If audiences were startled by the size of the band, they were also entranced by its power. The group toured year after year to sold-out houses, here and in Europe, where audiences immediately became ecstatic fans.

In 1978 they were shaken by the death of guitarist Terry Kath, who will always have a place in their hearts. New guitarist Donnie Dacus, however, provides his own sizzling style. Musically, the band members have always found their greatest pressure comes from their own desire to improve. "We always must try to be better than we were the last time," says drummer Danny Seraphine.

1978/79 Discography: *Hot Streets*
          Chicago 13

CLASH

Joe Strummer—Lead vocals

Mick Jones—Guitars

Paul Simonon—Bass

Topper Headon—Drums

William Morris booking agent Wayne Forte was not surprised that the Clash, Britain's new kings of punk, sold out their first American tour without a hit record; indeed, without much airplay. "There is a buzz coming from the streets about the band," he explains. Not the overblown, prepackaged hype that had accompanied the ill-fated Sex Pistols' tour, but a genuine reaction to fierce personal songs, played and sung with a stunning passion. The Clash brings to America a music combining all the rawness of early rock and roll with the sophistication of four accomplished musicians whose influences include the early Rolling Stones and the Who; the aggressive atonality of the New York Dolls, the Stooges, and Captain Beefheart; and strong flashes of reggae. Resisting all attempts at polish, the rough-hewn band comes to the States in combat boots, ready to battle the overproduced, overpromoted, overpriced dinosaur that once was rock and roll.

They refuse to be manipulated or pushed around, not even by Epic Records. When Epic's publicity people tried to herd them all into a group photograph after they had driven all night on a tour bus, they refused violently. As Joe Strummer explained to *Billboard* reporter Roman Kozak, "If you let them do this to you, you'll have no soul left, and if you have no soul left you cannot make records. And we'd rather make our records, even if they don't make the top one hundred."

Although their first album, *Give 'Em Enough Rope*, barely skimmed the charts, the Clash has the potential to be to the music of the eighties what Elvis Presley was to music of the fifties.

1978/79 Discography: *Give 'Em Enough Rope*

LINDA CLIFFORD

At the age of four, Linda Clifford was already taking tap, jazz, and ballet lessons. Unlike most toddlers, Linda was blessed with an impressive attention span; she stuck to her dancing, and by the time she was seven she was appearing on such television programs as "Startime" and "The Merry Mailman." When she was ten years old she appeared on a television special for the NAACP with Harry Belafonte and Sidney Poitier; at seventeen, already a seasoned veteran, she was touring nationally.

Her first hit record was "Long, Long Winter" for a small record company called Gemigo Records. Marv Stuart, co-president of Curtom Records, heard the song and brought Linda into Curtom, which released her debut album, *Linda Clifford*. That LP won her some fans, but it was 1978's wickedly boisterous "If My Friends Could See Me Now," the title cut from her second album, that established her as a top disco contender. Her second 1978 single, "Runaway Love" and 1979's "Don't Give It Up" were also exciting successes, establishing her as a solid disco star.

NATALIE COLE

A riveting powerhouse onstage, dynamic Natalie Cole never completely plans a performance. "I'm very emotional onstage. Every move is spontaneous. If I tried to put everything into a structured format, it just wouldn't work for me." Perhaps that attitude is a result of her college training in psychology and sociology. Or perhaps her openness grows out of the confidence she naturally developed growing up as the daughter of the great Nat King Cole. In a house full of love, she was surrounded by such music-business titans as Pearl Bailey, Nancy Wilson, Count Basie, Ella Fitzgerald, and Sarah Vaughan.

Whatever the mood of her music, funky or romantic, upbeat or blue, sophisticated or simple, her fans get the message. And as long as the word comes from Natalie, they adore it, turning every one of her albums to gold or platinum. Her explosive first album, 1975's *Inseparable*, not only flew to the top of the soul charts, it also rose high on the pop charts, reaching gold certification in a flash and remaining a charted album for more than a year. The single "This Will Be" won her two Grammies as new artist of the year and best female R & B vocal performance in 1976. From her second album, *Natalie*, came "Sophisticated Lady" and "Mr. Melody." This album also went gold, and 1976 was capped by two prestigious awards—a third Grammy for best female R & B vocal performance and the grand prize in the Fifth Tokyo Music Festival.

Unpredictable in 1977 was Natalie's first million-selling album, containing the gold single "I've Got Love on My Mind" and "Party Lights," another big hit. Her fourth album, *Thankful*, released in November 1977 was another platinum-winner and contained her second gold single, "Our Love." In June 1978 she released *Natalie . . . Live!*, which captured her in-person authority and power and was another gold-winner for Natalie.

Her latest gold disk, *I Love You So*, contains a variety of music and moves Natalie into new areas. It offers songs with touches of country, gospel, soul, jazz, and Broadway.

1978/79 Discography: *I Love You So*

JUDY COLLINS

As durable and as fresh as the first day of spring, Judy Collins has always followed her own star. Her impeccable taste and artist's intuition have guided her from one style to another, her music always changing and growing, but always illuminated by a gentle and compassionate consistency of tone.

From 1961, when critics and fans first thrilled to her voice in *Maid of Constant Sorrow* and *Golden Apples of the Sun*, she always stood out from the crowd. In the days when folk singers were all protest or resignation, Judy Collins included on her second album the totally lovely and otherworldly musical setting of the W. B. Yeats poem "The Song of the Wandering Angus." Throughout her seventeen albums she explored not only folk and protest, but such contemporary composers as Joni Mitchell and Leonard Cohen; she sang the theatrical music of Bertolt Brecht, Kurt Weill, and Jacques Brel long before it became fashionable to do so.

In the mid-1960s she became politically active and, as a result of her involvement in the Woman's Strike for Peace, coproduced an album called *Save the Children*, which contained songs and recitations by herself, Joan Baez, Mimi Fariña, Janis Ian, Odetta, Viveca Lindfors, and the Pennywhistlers. Her seventh album, *Wildflowers*, became her first gold disk; it was the first to feature her own compositions. Since that winner five more of her albums have sold half a million copies each: *In My Life, Who Knows Where the Time Goes, Whales and Nightingales, Colors of the Day (The Best of Judy Collins)*, and *Judith*.

In 1969 she wrote *The Judy Collins Songbook*, which, in addition to her songs, contained stories of her life and career. That book led her to write several magazine articles, and when she planned an interview for *Ms.* magazine with conductor Dr. Antonia Brico, a friend suggested that she film it. She and filmmaker Jill Godmilow were so delighted with the results that they decided to turn the brief interview into a full-scale documentary on Dr. Brico's life, and in 1974 Judy's first film, *Antonia: A Portrait of the Woman*, opened to rave reviews. It has since received a handful of awards.

1978/79 Discography: *Hard Times for Lovers*

JOHN CONLEE

John Conlee didn't start out to be a musician. His first job was a funeral director; luckily for country music fans, his interest in music lured him from that profession to become a disk jockey on pop radio stations near his hometown of Versailles, Kentucky. He soon moved to Nashville, where he worked for station WLAC-AM, and began to crave a recording career for himself.

In 1976 he released a song called "Backside of Thirty," which didn't make much of a splash. He worked away for the next two years, polishing his style and refining his craft. In late 1978 a song called "Rose Colored Glasses," from the album of the same name, shot to number one on the country singles charts, was named one of the top fifteen songs of the year by the Nashville Songwriters' Association, and won him *Billboard*'s award as new country singles artist of 1978. He began 1979 with his second hit single, a song called "Lady Lay Down," and, in the middle of 1979, MCA, his record company, pulled out "Backside of Thirty," 1976's flop, and watched it zip to number one on the country singles charts. Conlee made his television debut in the ABC made-for-television movie "The Girls in the Office."

1978/79 Discography: *Rose Colored Glasses*

RITA COOLIDGE

For singer Rita Coolidge 1979 was a year of international acclaim. She opened the year with an appearance on the Bee Gees' UNICEF benefit, "A Gift of Song." In the spring she appeared with husband Kris Kristofferson at Columbia Records' Havana Jam in Havana, Cuba. In June she won grand prize in the eighth Tokyo Music Festival. Her worldwide success has been growing since 1976, when *Anytime . . . Anywhere*, with its honey-dipped version of Jackie Wilson's "Higher and Higher," became a two-million-seller. Other hit singles that spun off that album were "We're All Alone" and "The Way You Do the Things You Do." Her 1978 album, *Love Me Again*, quickly sold half a million copies, and "You," a song from that album, was an easy-listening success.

Although Rita was drawn to music early in her life, performing in her minister-father's church choir and then touring with sisters Priscilla and Linda as the Coolidge Sisters, she went to Florida State University to study art. In her college days she took singing jobs only to help her pay for art supplies. One of her jobs was working for a Memphis company that created jingles. "Turn Around and Love You," a song she made for them, was released as a single and became a top-ten hit in Los Angeles. When rockers Delaney and Bonnie visited Memphis they were so excited by Rita's voice that they asked her to come back to Los Angeles with them and record on their *Accept No Substitutes* album. Rita agreed and left school for the West Coast; when she arrived she was amazed to find that her single had made her famous in L.A. She loved it. "I never even went back to Memphis," she says, "I just left everything behind and started again."

The beginning was an explosive tour with Joe Cocker's Mad Dogs and Englishmen in 1969, a celebrated cross-country extravaganza that symbolized the madness of the decade. In 1970 she met Kris Kristofferson on a flight to Memphis. He was so entranced by Rita that he never made it to Nashville, his own destination. The two were soon married. Back in L.A., Rita found her talents were much in demand; she sang on albums by Stephen Stills, Eric Clapton, and Dave Mason, all of whom, in turn, provided sparkling studio work on her first album, *Rita Coolidge*.

When they're not touring together in their sensational stage show, Rita and Kris live quietly at home with daughter Casey. In 1979 they released an album called *Natural Act*.

1978/79 Discography: *Natural Act* (with Kris Kristofferson)
Satisfied

ELVIS COSTELLO

The viperish, owl-eyed Elvis Costello was a terror on his 1979 American tour. Although a frenzied Boston audience gave him the adulation he desires, much of the tour was marred by his rage, his sometimes insultingly short sets performed at hell-for-leather speeds, his barbed words for radio stations that didn't play his songs enough, his refusal to do interviews, his manager's loud threats, and his tour manager's rage against photographers and tapers. The climax was his verbal blasts at Ray Charles and James Brown, made in a Columbus, Ohio, bar during an argument with Bonnie Bramlett and Stephen Stills and their entourage. At a later press conference, Costello attempted to explain away his harshness, but only the high quality of his music could make people forget his words.

Considered by many to be the new wave fountainhead and major talent, Costello came to America with the backing of his three whistle-clean, demonically driving albums: 1977's *My Aim Is True*, 1978's *This Year's Model*, and 1979's *Armed Forces*, his first gold-winner. He also arrived with unplumbed depths of bitterness, perhaps dating back to his years of trudging from record company to record company in London, carrying a homemade cassette and a guitar.

Thanks to the help of singer/songwriter/producer Nick Lowe, Elvis was finally signed by Stiff Records, Britain's new wave label. He was a smash in England; his provocative, irresistible rhythms and his unflinchingly harsh lyrics softened by seductively catchy melodies have won him fame in America as well.

Despite all the furor, his legion of fans continues to grow. The reason was succinctly stated by the *Cleveland Plain Dealer*'s rock writer, Jane Marie Scott. After one brief run-in with the famed Costello scorn she told *Rolling Stone* reporter Lee Abbott, "He's scum. But he sure can write."

1978/79 Discography: *Armed Forces*

The Clash

Chicago   Courtesy Columbia Records

Judy Collins

Natalie Cole

John Conlee   Courtesy MCA Records

Rita Coolidge

CRUSADERS

Nesbert "Stix" Hooper—Drums

Joe Sample—Keyboards

Wilton Felder—Tenor saxophone

The three men that make up the Crusaders are often referred to as musicians' musicians. As session men or in guest appearances, they can be heard on more than two hundred gold-winning records. Their own disks consistently win a huge audience, often selling more than half a million copies.

The group began in Houston, Texas, where Nesbert Hooper, Joe Sample, Wilton Felder, and several other musicians formed the Swingsters, a group that played the blues of B.B. King and Lightnin' Hopkins along with the jazz of Dizzy Gillespie, Max Roach, Charlie Parker, Chico Hamilton, and Stan Kenton. Blues and jazz blended into the distinctive Gulf Coast sound.

Texas fans loved them, and Hooper urged the band, which then included trombone player Wayne Henderson, to brave Los Angeles in the hopes of winning a long-term record contract. Their first months in Los Angeles were not easy, and band members kept body and soul together by doing studio work. Before long they were being called on to record more sessions than they could handle, and they were eventually signed to a record contract as the Jazz Crusaders.

The word *jazz* in their name was a mistake. It kept away fans who didn't like jazz, and those that did were taken aback because these Jazz Crusaders weren't playing traditional cool jazz, but music with a beat. So the band became simply the Crusaders and began enjoying heavy AM airplay, pop sales, and critical acclaim. In 1975 the band was chosen by the Rolling Stones to tour England with them, and the group completed its first solo tour of Europe in September of 1976. European audiences loved them. In 1978 they toured the capital cities of Europe in an SRO tour; a mini-tour of Japan was also sold out immediately.

Back home in the United States, they played large auditoriums and amphitheaters and were greeted by the same enthusiastic reaction. In 1978 their album *Images* was at the top of the national jazz charts for more than three months and won them a gold disk. Their 1979 album, *Street Life*, with talented singer Randy Crawford on the title track, also soared to the top of the jazz charts. In addition, individual band members have scored with new albums; Joe Sample's solo album debut, *Rainbow Seeker*, was high on the jazz charts for more than forty weeks, and in 1979 his *Carmel* was a top jazz LP as well. Wilton Felder's solo album, *We All Have a Star*, was also a critical and commercial success.

1978/79 Discography: *Street Life*

D

DAVE AND SUGAR

Dave Rowland—Vocals

Vicki Hackeman—Vocals

Sue Powell—Vocals

Although the name sounds like a duo, Dave and Sugar is a country trio: three fresh voices whose stinging sweet harmonies made Minnie Pearl exclaim, "I haven't heard such a sound since the Carter Sisters!"

They've been together for only a few years, but from the begin-

ning every one of their songs has zipped up the country charts. Their powerful hits include the top twenty "Queen of the Silver Dollar" and the number-one country singles "The Door Is Always Open," "I'm Gonna Love You," "Tear Time," and "Golden Tears."

Before coming together as Dave and Sugar, each member of the group was a recognized country talent. Dave, who plays piano, drums, guitar, bass guitar, and trumpet, was the vocalist for a seventeen-piece band and played the trumpet for the 75th Army band. He toured with Elvis Presley, was a regular on the Grand Ole Opry, and has appeared on "The Merv Griffin Show," "Dinah Shore Show," "Phil Donahue Show," "Mike Douglas Show," and "Midnight Special." Vicki Hackeman sang in church choirs, the school chorus, and with a pop group during high school. Afterwards, she moved to local radio and television shows and toured with a group called the Dallas Star, which appeared with such headliners as Bob Seger, Buddy Miles, Cactus, the Association, and Crazy Horse. Sue Powell, the other half of Sugar, was born to a musical family. Her mother, Patty Powell, was a singer, and her father had built his own recording studio. Sue started singing in country shows in the Louisville area at the age of seven, and her father recorded Sue's first record when she was eight. When Sue was thirteen, she had her first hit, "Little People," which reached number two on the local country charts.

The three are in great demand on the country circuit, whether on their own or as back-up singers for Charley Pride.

JOHN DENVER

His latest gold album is called simply *John Denver* and is the fourteenth of his disks to reach gold or platinum certification. His total record sales are now well beyond the 100 million mark. John Denver, with his sparkling songs and warm presence, is a maximal star.

Since his first "John Denver Show" in March 1974, he has hosted a number of television specials, including several stints on "The Tonight Show" and a series of specials for the BBC in London. In 1979 he appeared on The Bee Gees' televised UNICEF benefit, "A Gift of Song," hosted the Grammy awards presentation, appeared in "Denver and the Ladies," and "The Third Barry Manilow Special." His concerts are always sold out, and in 1978 Madison Square Garden honored him with their Golden Ticket Award for ticket sales of more than 100,000; when he appeared with Frank Sinatra at Harrah's in Lake Tahoe, Nevada, in 1976, announcement of their show jammed the switchboards with 600,000 phone calls for reservations. Such varied stars as Frank Sinatra, Peggy Lee, Arthur Fiedler, Andre Kostelanetz, Julie Andrews, Lawrence Welk, Carol Burnett, the Osmond Brothers, Engelbert Humperdinck, and Olivia Newton-John have recorded his songs. In addition to an Emmy award, Denver has won the Country Music Association's awards for entertainer of the year and song of the year (for "Back Home Again"). John Denver's stunning success grows directly out of the buoyant joyfulness of his music, its celebration of nature, the flow of life, and the power of love.

Born Henry John Deutchendorf, Jr., on New Year's Eve, 1943, in Roswell, New Mexico, he spent his youth traveling from one military base to another with his father, an air force pilot. He got his first guitar when he was eight years old, a present from his grandmother, and music quickly became his passion. Although he studied architecture at Texas Tech, his mind and heart were with his guitar rather than his T-square, and in his junior year he packed up his 1955 Chevy and tooled out to Los Angeles, where he felt his folk-influenced music would have a better chance of being heard.

Once in L.A., he worked as a draftsman during the day and sang in coffeehouses at night. He changed his name to John Denver, after his favorite city, and cut some demo records. One of those demos led to an invitation to audition for the Chad Mitchell Trio as Chad Mitchell's replacement. John flew to New York where he beat out 250 applicants for the job, which he kept for two-and-a-half years. At the end of that time he decided he was ready for a solo career and recorded his first album, *Rhymes and Reasons*. The album didn't win much recognition until Peter, Paul and Mary picked up his song "Leaving On a Jet Plane," which swept the country.

Denver became the darling of the college circuit; "Take Me Home, Country Roads" became his first smash single, and from then on his career has been lit by one success after another.

1978/79 Discography: *John Denver*

NEIL DIAMOND

From a thirty-five-dollar a month attic office on Broadway to a lavish American Dream life-style was not a swift and easy journey for singer/songwriter Neil Diamond. For seven years he poured his heart out into songs that nobody else wanted to hear, struggling constantly to keep going, writing day and night, buoyed only by the knowledge that he was a good songwriter and the faith that someday he would succeed. At the end of those seven years, desperate to present his music to the public, he began singing in Greenwich Village coffeehouses. Record producers Jeff Barry and Ellie Greenwich heard him and eagerly signed him to their small label, Bang Records. His first three records for them, "Solitary Man," "Cherry," and "I Got a Feeling," were smashes, introducing a sizzling talent. At the same time, two songs he had written, "I'm a Believer" and "A Little Bit Me, A Little Bit You" became hits for the Monkees.

Diamond then moved to the Uni label. Over the next five years, he recorded eight albums for them, each of which was a gold-winner.

In addition to recording, throughout these years Diamond toured and traveled, driving himself continually. At first he enjoyed the adulation he had dreamed of during his years of struggle. But after six years he began to feel the strain. He wanted time to look at his life, to spend with his family, to plan his future. So, at the end of 1972, he announced he was going to retire from performing.

He had no intention of stopping his flow of music, however, and when Columbia Records offered him a multimillion-dollar, five-year, five-album contract, he accepted. *Jonathan Livingston Seagull,* the first album he created for them, instantly became a monster best-seller in the United States and abroad.

By 1976 Diamond was rested and ready to go back onstage. He gave his first concert in Auckland, New Zealand, where he set an all-time attendance record of 37,500. He appeared for eight thrilling, sold-out nights in Los Angeles's Greek Theater; from that power-packed week came *Hot August Night,* an album that sold more than eight million copies. In 1978 his album *I'm Glad You're Here with Me Tonight,* from his late 1977 television special, became his third platinum LP. In 1978 he became father to a son, Michael Joseph.

In late 1978 Diamond's music continued to delight fans. *You Don't Bring Me Flowers* became his fourth platinum album; the title cut, recorded with Barbra Streisand, was a top single. "Forever in Blue Jeans" and "Say Maybe" were two 1979 hit singles, and in June of the same year Diamond announced, after some months of indecision, that he would play the lead in the upcoming remake of *The Jazz Singer.*

1978/79 Discography: *You Don't Bring Me Flowers*

DOOBIE BROTHERS

Chet McCracken—Drums, vibes

John McFee—Guitar, violin

Patrick Simmons—Guitar, vocals

Michael McDonald—Keyboards

Tiran Porter—Bass, vocals

Keith Knudsen—Drums, vocals

Cornelius Bumpus—Saxophones

They've gone through many personnel changes through the years, beginning as a trio at the end of 1969 when singer/guitarist Tom Johnston, drummer John Hartman, and bass player Greg Murphy, calling themselves Pud, began playing northern California night spots. By mid-1979, with John Hartman gone, none of the original trio remained, but their sound remains strong. Every personnel change has freshened the band with new musical talent and perspective. Through the years the Doobie Brothers have retained the warmth and honesty, the melodic and rhythmic smoothness that captivated the country and sent almost all their albums spinning to gold or platinum status.

The early group was shaky, with Greg Murphy soon leaving to be replaced by Dave Shogren. Pat Simmons joined the band, bringing with him a background in bluegrass and folk music, an influence that was a perfect balance for the band's harder sound. This quartet recorded *The Doobie Brothers,* their first album; though not a smash, it won excellent reviews and led to major tours throughout 1971 and 1972.

Dave Shogren left the group and was replaced by Tiran Porter, whose husky vocals became a trademark. After Michael Hossack joined the group as a second drummer, the band recorded *Toulouse Street,* a fantastic success that included the classic singles "Listen to the Music" and "Jesus Is Just Alright." From their third album, *The Captain and Me,* came the hit songs "China Grove" and "Long Train Runnin'." Mike Hossack left and was replaced by Keith Knudsen, whose percussion work provided a stinging complement to John Hartman's drumming. Their next album, *What Were Once Vices Are Now Habits,* was another huge seller and included the two-million-selling single "Black Water."

Late in 1974 Jeff Baxter joined the group, bringing his pedal steel guitar to *Stampede,* the album that included the single "Take Me In Your Arms (Rock Me)" and marked the beginning of a movement to jazz and R & B for the band. Michael McDonald, pianist, vocalist, and songwriter, joined the band in 1975; his heavy R & B background was a strong force in their next disk, *Takin' It to the Streets,* which contained the smash title single as well as "It Keeps You Runnin'."

In 1977 their album *Livin' on the Fault Line* was a top-ten hit for two months. By this time Tommy Johnston had left the band to go out on his own, but the Doobies continued touring, appearing on television, and creating unique events, including the Doobie Brothers Golf Classic and Concert for the United Way, which featured the first reunion of the cast of "Leave It to Beaver" and a concert with Dinah Shore. In January of 1978, they appeared in a two-part episode of "What's Happening!", capturing a television audience of 34 million. At the end of 1978 they held the third annual Doobie Brothers Christmas Party for the Children's Hospital at Stanford in Palo Alto, California, and have hosted other charitable events.

Their latest album, *Minute by Minute,* was a number-one smash, quickly won platinum sales, and contained the number-one gold single "What a Fool Believes." In the summer of 1979 Hartman and Baxter left the band and were replaced by Chet McCracken on drums and vibes and John McFee on guitar and violin. Cornelius Bumpus was added on saxophone. On the Fourth of July the Doobies confirmed their status as a preeminent American band when 180 FM stations simultaneously broadcast their concert from California's Uni-

versal Amphitheatre—the largest radio network ever to broadcast a live event.
1978/79 Discography: *Minute by Minute*

BOB DYLAN

During his 1978 tour, Bob Dylan, one of rock's few living legends, shocked his fans by tampering with such classic songs as "Ballad of the Thin Man," "Maggie's Farm," and "Like a Rolling Stone," blasting them out with a flashy new wave fervor that often obscured lyrics and rendered familiar melodies unidentifiable. It was not the first time Dylan has shaken up his fans. In 1965, after four years of establishing himself as the leading contemporary folk composer and performer, he stunned his audience at the Newport Folk Festival by performing with the Paul Butterfield Blues Band and introducing his electric guitar. Although they booed and hissed then, there was no way fans could prevent the inevitable changes that Dylan had sensed.

In the late sixties, after a near-fatal motorcycle accident, Dylan temporarily retired. When he came back, it was with another surprise—his rough-edged voice was newly mellowed on the bleak, apocalyptic album *John Wesley Harding*. That was followed by *Nashville Skyline*, an album with a country flavor. Out of the seventies came his remarkably solid performance as Alias in Sam Peckinpah's movie *Pat Garrett and Billy the Kid*. Dylan also wrote the film's score, and from it came "Knockin' on Heaven's Door," a hit single. In the first two months of 1974 Dylan's tour with the Band produced the invigorating LP *Before the Flood*. *Blood on the Tracks* and *The Basement Tapes* were released in 1975. The same year, he toured the United States with the Rolling Thunder Revue, an assortment of rock performers that included Joan Baez, Roger McGuinn, Joni Mitchell, Mick Ronson, and Ronee Blakley. Parts of the tour were filmed and later used in Dylan's mysterious 1978 movie, *Renaldo and Clara*.

In 1978 Dylan was again out on the road, his sizzling performances combined with a new concern for his audiences. He enjoyed touring so much that he extended his schedule from early fall to the end of the year. At the end of 1978 word came out that he was looking for talent for his own label, Accomplice, distributed by CBS. His 1979 albums were *Bob Dylan at Budokan*, a live album containing vibrant reworkings of his old songs as well as new material, and *Slow Train Coming*, a compelling collection of strong new music.
1978/79 Discography: *Bob Dylan at Budokan*
Slow Train Coming

EARTH, WIND & FIRE

Maurice White—Vocals, kalimba, drums

Verdine White—Vocals, bass, percussion

Philip Bailey—Vocals, congas, percussion

Larry Dunn—Piano, organ, Moog synthesizer

Al McKay—Guitars, percussion

Johnny Graham—Guitars

Andrew Woolfolk—Flute, tenor and soprano saxophones

Fred White—Drums, percussion

Ralph Johnson—Vocals, drums, percussion

"We are a free entity in life," announces Maurice White, founder of Earth, Wind & Fire, the dazzling supergroup whose positive vision of a world uplifted by music has led them to fabulous commercial and artistic success. All eight of their albums are gold; six have achieved platinum sales, four are double platinum, and four of their singles are gold. They won a Grammy for best R & B performance by a vocal group for the song "Shining Star." They've also won two Rock Music awards and an American Music award. The 1979 album *The Best of Earth, Wind & Fire, Volume 1*, their first release on their own ARC label, shipped platinum. Teamed with the Emotions, their driving song "Boogie Wonderland" became a gold-winning 1979 smash and their first disco hit. Their second 1979 LP, the fiery *I Am*, was another swift platinum and contained the hit single "After the Love Has Gone."

At the center of the band is Maurice White, who began singing and playing music as a child. After touring with Ramsey Lewis's band for several years, White began to want his own group, one whose music would help transform people's lives. He gathered together some top-quality musicians in 1971, including Ronnie Laws, Ronald Bautista, and Jessica Cleaves, and this band recorded *Last Days and Time*, E, W & F's first album. In 1973, after the departure of Laws and Bautista and the addition of ace guitarists Al McKay and Johnny Graham and horn player Andrew Woolfolk, came *Head to the Sky*. In 1974 *Open Our Eyes* was released, and in early 1975 White's youngest brother, Fred, became the final addition to the band. *That's the Way of the World*, the soundtrack album for the movie of the same name, came out in 1975; late that same year the group released *Gratitude*, their first, long-demanded live album. In 1976 came *Spirit*, and in 1977, *All 'n All*. In 1978 they were one of the brighter spots in the RSO film *Sgt. Pepper's Lonely Hearts Club Band*, and their pell-mell version of the Beatles' "Gotta Get You Into My Life" was the only cut from the soundtrack to sell gold.
1978/79 Discography: *The Best of Earth, Wind & Fire, Volume 1*
I Am

ELECTRIC LIGHT ORCHESTRA

Jeff Lynne—Guitar, vocals

Bev Bevan—Drums

Richard Tandy—Keyboards

Mik Kaminski—Violin

Hugh McDowell—Cello

Kelly Groucutt—Bass

The most breathtaking rock extravaganza of 1978 was the Electric Light Orchestra's awesome stage set. Each ELO concert on their international tour began with a mammoth saucer-shaped spaceship covering the stage. The saucer lifted up to reveal the band, enmeshed in a constantly shifting web of piercing laser lights.

From its beginnings in 1972 the band has always aimed to create a fusion of diamond-hard rock and lush classical sounds. Guitarists Roy Wood and Jeff Lynne from the Move and drummer Bev Bevan and cellist Hugh McDowell came together and created the experimental album *The Electric Light Orchestra*. Although record buyers had never heard anything quite like it, the disk was successful in Britain. Late that same year, however, Wood and McDowell left the band, putting Lynne and Bevan back at square one. They collected a total of nine musicians with eclectic backgrounds, and this hot combination recorded *ELO II*, from which came their enthusiastic rendering of Chuck Berry's classic "Roll Over Beethoven." The eventual discovery of direct amplifiers allowed the band to achieve a balance between the orchestral strings and the more powerful rock instruments, paving the way to successful live performances.

The band won more fans with their third album, *On the Third Day*, and their fourth, *Eldorado*. *Face the Music*, with its hit single, "Evil Woman," was their first gold-seller; *Olé ELO*, a collection of their greatest hits, came next and quickly became their first platinum-winner. It was followed by *A New World Record* and 1977's *Out of the*

Elvis Costello

The Crusaders

Neil Diamond

Dave and Sugar

John Denver

The Doobie Brothers

Bob Dylan

Blue, also platinum achievements.

In 1979, despite back and forth lawsuits between them and a record label they enjoined from distributing copies of *Out of the Blue,* they had new success with the release of the gold-winning *Discovery* and the top single "Shine a Little Love."
1978/79 Discography: *Discovery*

ENGELBERT

In 1967 an unknown, black-haired singer with smoldering eyes appeared on the popular British television show "Saturday Night at the London Palladium." He sang a romantic ballad called "Release Me," and in households throughout the nation women sat spellbound. After he left the stage, switchboard operators at the television station were besieged by calls. The response was so enormous that the singer was asked to come back the following week as the show's headliner.

That performer was Engelbert Humperdinck, and since that early triumph he has been known as the musical "King of Romance," a fantasy heartthrob to millions of women all over the world. The Engelbert Fan Club has more than two hundred chapters. Engelbert knows that he owes his success to these fans. "My audiences are very important to me," he says. "I never want anyone to see me perform and then walk away unsatisfied. I always try to do my very best whenever I'm onstage."

In 1977, ten years after that memorable television appearance, Engelbert made a series of radical and personal changes, shedding sideburns, pounds, his last name, and his original manager, Gordon Mills. He moved his family from England to America, and under the direction of his new manager, British impresario Harold Davison, switched to Epic Records and released his first album for them, *After the Lovin'.* The album and the title single became his first platinum success.

In 1978 he thrilled the world on his SRO tour, which included sensational performances in Australia, New England, Switzerland, Hong Kong, Manila, Singapore, Kuala Lumpur, England, and the United States. He also won the American Guild of Variety Artists award as male singing star of the year. Engelbert suffered years of frustration, however, before he won his first fame. Born Arnold George Dorsey in Madras, India, to British parents, he moved to England with his family when he was young. He discovered his interest in music when he was eleven and began playing the saxophone. When he was eighteen, he turned to singing; while working days in a boot factory, he spent weekends performing in local clubs. After winning a talent competition on the Isle of Man, he decided to make singing his career. Throughout the 1960s he struggled to be heard above the sound of rock until his fortuitous television appearance rocketed him to his first fame. "Release Me" began selling 100,000 copies a day after his appearance, and since then he has sold a staggering 125 million records with such songs as "The Last Waltz," "A Man Without Love," "Love Is All," "Winter World of Love," "We Made it Happen," "Sweetheart," and "Another Time, Another Place." In 1979 "This Moment in Time," from the album of the same name, was a number-one easy-listening hit.
1978/79 Discography: *This Moment in Time*

EXILE

J. P. Pennington—Lead guitar, vocals

Jimmy Stokley—Lead vocals

Buzz Cornelison—Keyboards, vocals

Marlon Hargis—Keyboards, vocals

Sonny Lemaire—Bass, vocals

Steve Goetzman—Drums, vocals

With a sexy love song called "Kiss You All Over," a group called Exile burst onto the music scene in late 1978. The tune was a gold-winning smash, and their album *Mixed Emotions,* a tight, imaginative collection of songs, also won gold. For Exile, a group of hard-working Kentucky boys who began in 1965 as the Exiles, the success of "Kiss You All Over" was the payoff for years of struggle.

When Buzz Cornelison, Jimmy Stokley, and J. P. Pennington got together to make music in high school they never dreamed it would lead to a career. With J. P. on bass, Jimmy singing lead, and Buzz on piano, the boys played soul and R & B on the weekends in local clubs. "We were a weekend band, just having a good time," Buzz says about those early days. But agent Peggy Rogers heard them, loved their sound, and got them a steady job playing on the "Dick Clark Caravan."

The Exiles appeared on the New York club and discothèque circuit throughout the late sixties, playing songs of such New York groups as the Vagrants, Vanilla Fudge, and the Rascals. When they brought these songs to their southern audiences, fans were at first a little confused by the switch from R & B to hard rock. The band kept at it; soon the southern fans were loving them for their hard-playing, dynamic performances, and in 1978 a nationwide audience followed suit.
1978/79 Discography: *All There Is*

F

FABULOUS POODLES

Tony de Meur—Vocals, guitar, harmonicas

Bobby Valentino—Mandolin, guitar, vocals

Bryn B. Burrows—Drums, back-up vocals, screams

Richie C. Robertson—Bass guitar, vocals, lead guitar

With *Mirror Stars* high on the pop album charts, Britain's Fabulous Poodles, known to their fans as the Fab Poos, have succeeded in transplanting their wacky Frank Zappa-esque combination of slapstick and deft musicianship to America. As Jonathan Barrett describes them in the *New Musical Express,* "Like Zappa, the Poodles combine mature musicianship with gross juvenile humor."

The band, which came together in 1974, plays a wide range of music: aggressive hard rock, Buddy Holly style rock and roll, reggae, and British music hall. This variety comes naturally out of their backgrounds. Tony de Meur left school at sixteen and bounced back and forth between such fascinating music gigs as back-up guitar for the Chantelles and Tom Jones, and boring work at the Tate Gallery and the British Museum. Clark Gable look-alike Bobby Valentino played in country, folk, and jazz groups and attended York University for two years before the Poodles. Bryn Burrows played trumpet in his school band and then became a member of the Royal Engineers Army Band; after three months of hating army life, he quit and landed a job in advertising. He then went on to play with Howard Werth and the Moonbeams. Richie Robertson, who began playing guitar to Buddy Holly records when he was ten, worked at such odd jobs as dishwashing, selling encyclopedias, and digging potatoes until he realized that what he wanted to do was join a band. After three weeks with a reggae band, the Gaylords, he was called by the Poodles to become their bassist.
1978/79 Discography: *Mirror Stars*

th, Wind & Fire

Engelbert Courtesy Epic Records

e Electric Light Orchestra Courtesy Epic Records

Exile Courtesy Warner Brothers Records

The Fabulous Poodles Courtesy Epic Records

Firefall Courtesy Atlantic Records

101

FIREFALL

Rick Roberts—Guitars, vocals

Jock Bartley—Guitars, vocals

Mark Andes—Bass, vocals

Larry Burnett—Guitars, vocals

Michael Clarke—Drums

David Muse—Reeds, keyboards

At its core Firefall is a rock band, but its six members bring with them years of experience in a wide variety of musical forms, including jazz, folk, pop, R & B, and country. Together they create Firefall's crystal-clear blend of voices and the supercharged musicianship that has earned them three out of three gold albums—*Firefall, Luna Sea*, and *Élan*—and a series of hit singles including "Livin' Ain't Livin'," "You Are the Woman," "Cinderella," "Just Remember I Love You," "So Long," and 1979's "Goodbye I Love You."

Firefall began in the summer of 1974 when folksinger/songwriter Rick Roberts, the spark of the post-Gram Parsons Burrito Brothers, and guitarist Jock Bartley, late of the Denver/Boulder band Zephyr and a Gram Parsons band alumnus, got together for an informal series of acoustic and electric jam sessions at Roberts' home in Boulder. They were soon joined by Mark Andes, an original member of the underrated late 1960s San Francisco band Spirit and founder of Jo Jo Gunne. Those jam sessions began to take shape, and singer/songwriter Larry Burnett was invited to join. By September of 1974 the quartet was stirring audiences around the Boulder area. Chris Hillman, an early booster, suggested just the right powerhouse drummer: Michael Clarke, charter member of the Byrds.

During 1975, with the wisdom born of experience, the band had no desire to rush into a six-figure contract and grind out an overnight album. Shrewdly deciding to give themselves the time to let their five disparate personalities mesh together, they continued to give concerts in the Denver/Boulder area. The band members also continued to honor previous musical commitments, but Firefall was clearly their future. Finally, in October of 1975, they began to rehearse for their first LP. They spent five weeks at Miami's Criteria Studios. Realizing as they worked that they wanted a greater musical depth, they called in keyboard and reed player David Muse, who helped them complete *Firefall* by January of 1976. The album soared to gold sales just as Firefall began its first national tour, playing larger halls all the time. *Luna Sea*, released late in July 1977, was a swift gold. That year also included a major tour with Fleetwood Mac and closed with a series of hard-rocking performances.

1978/79 Discography: *Élan*

FLEETWOOD MAC

Christine McVie—Keyboards, vocals

Lindsey Buckingham—Guitar, vocals

Stevie Nicks—Vocals

John McVie—Bass

Mick Fleetwood—Drums

In the middle of 1979 radio listeners were treated to the haunting strains of a John Stewart song called "Gold." Weaving in and out of that song was the unmistakable, smokey voice of Stevie Nicks. After a year and a half of silence, the mighty Mac machine was starting to move. Following the fabulous success of *Rumours*, their eleven-million-selling, multiple-award-winning 1977 album, the band took a

much needed rest throughout most of 1978, swinging out only for a summer tour. But 1979 saw them back in the studio again, working to make their next album a worthy follow-up to that earlier monster.

Fleetwood Mac's story is not one of a smooth, speedy climb to fame. From 1967, when guitarist Peter Green, bass player John McVie, and drummer Mick Fleetwood got together as Peter Green's Fleetwood Mac, the band has always had a hard core of devoted and faithful fans. They were critically respected and had turned out several modestly successful albums, including *Kiln House, Future Games, Bare Trees, Penguin, Mystery to Me*, and *Heroes Are Hard to Find*. But it wasn't until 1975 and the album *Fleetwood Mac* that the group began to achieve real success. That album sold more than 4 million copies, and from it came three smash singles, "Rhiannon," "Over My Head," and "Say You Love Me." The band had already suffered through more than its share of trials, including the loss of original members Peter Green, Jeremy Spencer, and Danny Kirwan, the existence of a spurious group that toured under their name, and the departure of Bob Welch, who had stepped in as a temporary replacement for Jeremy Spencer but had become almost indispensable to the group. In 1975, however, the band added Stevie Nicks and Lindsey Buckingham. The two new members clicked into the Fleetwood family as if they had been born for the roles, providing the spark that sent the band's fortunes soaring.

1978/79 Discography: *Tusk*

FOREIGNER

Mick Jones—Lead guitar, vocals

Ian McDonald—Guitars, keyboards, horns, vocals

Lou Gramm—Lead vocals

Al Greenwood—Keyboards, synthesizer

Ed Gagliardi—Bass, vocals

Dennis Elliott—Drums

The top new group of 1977 continued to slam out blistering hard rock in 1979. When Foreigner released their first pounding singles, "Feels Like the First Time" and "Cold as Ice," from their debut album, *Foreigner*, rock aficionados around the world recognized the British-American blend as a powerhouse new entry in the rock sweepstakes. In 1978 their second album, *Double Vision*, shipped platinum; "Hot-Blooded" was *the* hard rock song of summer 1978, and the title song was solid gold.

The band's seemingly instant success comes out of the experience of the two founding members—Mick Jones from Spooky Tooth and Ian McDonald from King Crimson. When their guitars shot sparks off each other, and when Lou Gramm, Al Greenwood, Ed Gagliardi, and Dennis Elliott added rhythm, keyboards, and sharp vocal harmonies, both band and listeners were excited by the sound. Although confident of success, they played for months before recording their first album—both for the sheer joy of playing and also because it was important to them to be an ace live band as well as a fine recording band. Ecstatic critics and fans prove they've achieved their goal. In the summer of 1979 Rick Willis replaced Ed Gagliardi.

1978/79 Discography: *Head Games*

PETER FRAMPTON

With his chart-climbing album *Where I Should Be* and his hit single "I Can't Stand It No More," Peter Frampton is back from a terrifying car accident. The recovered Frampton is playing a firmer, more emphatic rock and roll with a style and vigor guaranteed to gladden fans who have been waiting since his multimillion-selling 1976 winner *Frampton Comes Alive* to hear their hero play the guitar riffs they love so much.

Frampton's musical career began in the late sixties, when he whipped out stinging guitar licks with the British band the Herd. When they broke up, Frampton and Steve Marriott formed another hard-rocking band, Humble Pie. In 1971 Peter left them to go out on his own. After working on album sessions for such top performers as George Harrison, Harry Nilsson, and John Entwistle, he released four solo albums: *Wind of Change, Frampton's Camel, Something's Happening,* and *Frampton.* Although they weren't big sellers, they helped build Frampton a loyal army of fans.

Even his most devoted admirers, however, were unprepared for the dizzying success of *Frampton Comes Alive,* the first album to capture the electric sting he radiated onstage. The album blasted to the top of the charts, sparkled in the number-one spot for four and a half months, and didn't slow its momentum until some eight million copies had been sold. Some critics say even Frampton wasn't ready for this peak. His next album, the self-produced *I'm in You,* was much quieter and more reflective, and, though a million-seller, did not reach the heights of *Alive.* During 1977 Peter toured the United States, Europe, and Japan and appeared in the ill-received Robert Stigwood epic *Sgt. Pepper's Lonely Hearts Club Band.* A few weeks before the film opened, Peter was in a serious automobile accident in the Bahamas, suffering a broken arm, broken ribs, and cuts and bruises. Fully recovered except for a damaged muscle that prevents him from straightening his right arm, Peter spent part of 1979 on the road again, touring to promote his new album.
1978/79 Discography: *Where I Should Be*

G

JAMES GALWAY

In the summer of 1978 a powerful flutist blew a fresh breeze through New York City's immensely popular Mostly Mozart festival. Elegant Avery Fisher Hall shimmered with the brilliant silver tones of James Galway, whose recording of John Denver's "Annie's Song," from Galway's album of the same name, was a top-five pop hit in Great Britain. Remarkably spanning classical and pop, the album was also the top classical best-seller in America for four months. Galway, whose twinkling Irish eyes radiate almost as much warmth as his music, is so much in demand that during one hectic season he played as a soloist with all four major London orchestras.

Galway's first choice of an instrument was the violin, but he soon discarded it in favor of the wind instrument. By the time he was fourteen, when he won a scholarship to go to London and study flute full time, he knew that he was a musician for life. His first professional job was with the Wind Band at the Royal Shakespeare Theatre in Stratford on Avon, followed by stints with the Sadler's Wells Opera Company, the Royal Opera House Orchestra, and the BBC Symphony. In the mid-1970s he was appointed principal flutist with the London Symphony and the Royal Philharmonic Orchestra. For six years he held the honored position of first solo flute of the Berlin Philharmonic Orchestra under the direction of maestro Herbert von Karajan.

He left the Berlin in 1975, and, in his first season as a soloist, the dedicated musician cut four records for RCA, appeared on more than twenty television shows, and gave one hundred and twenty concerts on four continents. Galway has won several silver disks and a Grand Prix du Disque for his recording of the Mozart flute concertos.
1978/79 Discography: *Annie's Song*

LEIF GARRETT

With his second album, *Feel the Need,* winning gold certification at the end of 1978, Leif Garrett fulfills the promise he showed in his first outing, *Leif Garrett,* also a gold-winner.

The blond skateboarder from California, whose sparkling updates of "Surfin' USA" and "Runaround Sue" sold a million copies each, has been an actor since he was five, making his premiere performance in the film *Bob and Carol and Ted and Alice.* That was followed by roles in *Macon County Line,* the *Walking Tall* series, and appearances on many television shows.

But the young actor, who starred in the Universal picture *Skateboard,* has always been a music fan. In the mid 1970s he began listening to the Rolling Stones and Led Zeppelin more carefully, hoping he could learn to make music the way they did. Friend and fellow soccer fan Rod Stewart graciously gave Garrett advice and encouragement; Leif went into the studio to cut that first album with confidence and came out with a winner.

In 1979 Leif released the single "I Was Made for Dancing," had his own televison show, "The Leif Garrett Special," featuring Pink Lady, the top Japanese singing duo, and toured Spain during the summer.
1978/79 Discography: *Feel the Need*

MARVIN GAYE

Here, My Dear is Marvin Gaye's first studio album in more than two years; with its frank and revealing look at love, marriage, and divorce, drawn from his own painful experiences, it continues in the Gaye tradition of transforming life into high art.

He puts his heart and soul into everything he does, his energy and ambition pushing him to give his all. "Being the best," he says, "isn't for public recognition. When you're the best it means you have done your best, and that's what counts."

Born in Washington, D.C., Gaye's musical talents began to emerge in the choir of a church where his father, the Reverend Marvin Gaye, Sr., was pastor. By the time he was twelve Marvin was playing the organ and piano.

His professional career began in the 1950s when he sang with a popular group called the Rainbows. After a stint in the Air Force he sang with Harvy Fuqua's Moonglows and toured the country with them, learning for the first time the joys of performing before a large public. Performing in Detroit, Gaye was spotted by Berry Gordy, head of Motown Records, who immediately offered him a contract to record as a solo artist. Gaye gave Gordy a string of solid-gold smashes with such songs as "Ain't That Peculiar," "How Sweet it Is," "I Heard it Through the Grapevine," "Too Busy Thinking 'bout My Baby," "What's Going On," "Mercy, Mercy Me," and "Inner City Blues." During those years he worked with such female singers as Mary Wells, Kim Weston, the late Tammi Terrell, and Diana Ross.

Today he boasts a collection of six gold and platinum albums, including the 1977 smash *Marvin Gaye Live at the London Palladium,* from which came the good-time single "Got to Give it Up."
1978/79 Discography: *Here, My Dear*

CRYSTAL GAYLE

In 1979 Crystal Gayle scored on the country charts with her album *When I Dream;* the title single and "Why Have You Left the One You Left Me For?" were both number one on the country charts. The year was an exciting follow-up to 1978, when her album *We Must Believe in Magic* sold more than a million copies and her single "Don't it Make My Brown Eyes Blue" was one of those ubiquitous background songs, its sweet melody lingering everywhere. That song won her a Grammy and awards as top female vocalist from both the Academy of Country Music and the Country Music Association. The CMA also voted it song of the year.

Success is no stranger to Crystal, whose very first single, sister Loretta Lynn's song "I've Cried (the Blue Right Out of My Eyes)," was a top-twenty country winner in 1970. For the next few years Crystal toured the county fair and festival circuit with Loretta. In 1973 Crystal signed with United Artists. Her first album for them was *Crystal Gayle*, and from it came the hit single "Restless." Her second album, *Somebody Loves You*, yielded her first number-one country song, "I'll Get Over You." In 1975 she was voted the most promising female vocalist of the year award by the Academy of Country Music, and, although she has gone on to achieve pop success, her heart remains in country.

1978/79 Discography: *Miss the Mississippi*

GLORIA GAYNOR

Crowned Queen of the Discos in 1975, Gloria Gaynor has grown far beyond the title. Her soaring performance of 1979's platinum smash "I Will Survive" elevated disco to a new level of emotional intensity. As a measure of her success, she began a Spring 1979 tour as opening act for the Village People, but by the beginning of June she had left that tour to go out on her own as a headliner.

She started developing her powerhouse voice when she was eight years old, challenged by hearing the beautiful singing of her sister and five brothers. By age thirteen, she was certain that singing was going to be her life. Unable to afford lessons, she would spend hours listening to the records of her favorites—Nat King Cole, Sarah Vaughan, and Marvin Gaye—playing them over and over and studying their diction, phrasing, and nuances of feeling.

At eighteen that self-training paid off when she was offered her first job singing, in Canada. "I'd never been out of Newark, but I quit my job as an accountant and told everybody I was going to be a big star. We were there two weeks. Then I worked one week in New Jersey and that was it for my career for almost three years." Then came one of those rare strokes of fairy-tale good luck. One night, at a Newark club, a friend of Gaynor's persuaded the band to call the singer to the stage. They were so impressed with Gaynor's voice and stage presence that they hired her that night. Her three years away from the stage were over. She traveled through the Midwest with that band and then formed City Life, her own group. For the next two years she worked six shows a night, six nights a week, a nonstop ride into her first album, *Never Can Say Goodbye*, a seamless flow of music that discos played full tilt. It zipped Gloria to world fame. Boogiers in France, Spain, Italy, Germany, Belgium, and England clapped for Gloria's scorching singles like "Reach Out, I'll Be There" and "Cassanova Brown." Her subsequent albums, *Experience Gloria Gaynor, I Got You, Glorious*, and 1979's platinum *Love Tracks*, were all commanding hits.

Today Gloria spends nearly half her time touring the world, showing her respect for her fans by learning the language of each country she visits. She also shows her devotion with her music, saying, "I just want to help them forget all their problems and just be alive."

1978/79 Discography: *Love Tracks*

ANDY GIBB

He began 1979 with his single "Our Love—Don't Throw it Away," a top easy-listening hit and a gold-winner. But to Andy Gibb, youngest brother of the fabulous Bee Gees, gold and platinum come easily. His first two albums, 1977's *Flowing Rivers* and 1978's *Shadow Dancing*, were both platinum disks, and every one of his singles—"I Just Want to Be Your Everything," "(Love Is) Thicker than Water," "Shadow Dancing," and "An Everlasting Love"—has sold more than a million copies each.

The dynamic Andy, at the ripe old age of twenty-one, has been a professional performer for years. Born March 5, 1958, in Manchester, England, Andy moved with his family to Australia when he was only six months old. After the family moved back to England in 1967 and the Bee Gees began to achieve fame, Andy would come home from school and have to fight his way through the crowds of his brother's fans.

After three years in England, the peripatetic Gibbs were on the move again, this time to Ibiza, a tiny island off the coast of Spain. When Andy was twelve, older brother Barry gave him his first guitar. A year later Andy made his performing debut at a local tourist bar. He enjoyed it, his audience loved it, and Andy became a regular, occasionally joined by an older brother or two.

In 1973 the family moved to the Isle of Man. After forming a band with some local boys and playing regularly at the island's major clubs, Andy decided it was time to give himself a real trial; he headed back for Australia, planning to work in front of audiences reputed to be the world's most critical. He expected to remain there, honing his craft, for five or six years. Australian concertgoers, however, felt that Andy was more than ready, and in a year he was appearing regularly in large halls. His first single, his own composition called "Words and Music," was a top-five hit in Australia.

Robert Stigwood then arranged for Andy to fly to Miami's Criteria Studios to record some demonstration tapes. Barry went along to help, and the two wrote several new songs. The tapes generated thunderous excitement, and Andy recorded his first album with coproducers Albhy Galuten and Karl Richardson, a lineup of top musicians, and Barry Gibb as executive producer.

Since then the Gibb career has sparkled with many television performances, tours, and Grammy nominations.

NICK GILDER

Nick Gilder, long dancer's legs flying, leaps and gyrates to the front of the stage. Thousands of young girls surge out of their seats, shrieking "Nick," with swooning adoration. Twenty or thirty of the boldest crowd the lip of the stage, reaching out their hands to their idol, who stands coolly above their forest of arms, exuding aristocratic magnetism. In 1978 more than two million people bought his tantalizing, sultry "Hot Child in the City."

It's not only Nick's mesmerizing sexuality that attracts his fans; it's also his empathy for them and understanding of their world. "Hot Child," he says, "was a definite Los Angeles experience. This is the city. There are a lot of lost girls out there. You wonder why they ran away and you see them being taken advantage of. That's kind of sad. So I wrote about it."

Nick's burgeoning career has been anything but sad. With multiple appearances on "American Bandstand," Don Kirshner's "Rock Concert," and "Midnight Special," his fame and popularity continue to grow. Although he spent most of his career performing with groups, Nick always stood out. Growing up in Vancouver, he loved to sing, and as a teenager joined with a group of friends in a combo called Throm Hortis. Although their first gig, in a small battle of the bands just outside of Vancouver, was fumbling, Nick's magnetic stage presence caught the eye of guitarist Jim McCulloch, who led a band called Rasputin. Nick soon joined the group as their lead singer.

At Nick's suggestion they changed the name of the band to Sweeney Todd. In the early 1970s in Vancouver, Sweeney Todd experimented with wild costumes, heavy makeup, flash pots, dry ice—every visual gimmick to help communicate the supercharged excitement they all felt. Their first important gig was a half-hour spot in a concert headlined by Chuck Berry. In their first moments onstage they raised the crowd of eight thousand to its feet and kept it there throughout the entire set. The band had a huge hit in Canada with the song "Roxy Roller" at the end of 1975, but no matter how much attention the rest of them won, it was always Nick who was the center.

In 1976 he left the group to go out on his own and was snapped up by Chrysalis Records. His first two albums for them, *You Know Who You Are* and *City Nights*, began to build a large audience in the United States, and "Hot Child" was his breakthrough to national fame.

1978/79 Discography: *Frequency*

G Q

Emmanuel Rahiem LeBlanc—Vocals, guitar

Keith "Sabu" Crier—Bass

Herb Lane—Keyboards

Paul Service—Drums

Known first as Sabu & the Survivors, then Sons of Darkness, then the Third Chance and Rhythm Makers, the group that today calls itself G.Q. is another of those overnight successes whose performing calendar dates back half a lifetime. The sleek elegance of their gold-winning sensations, the single "Disco Nights (Rock Freak)" and the album *Disco Nights*, has its roots more than a decade ago on the front stoop of a building on the edge of New York's South Bronx. There eleven-year-old Emmanuel Rahiem LeBlanc sat strumming Sly Stone's "Sing a Simple Song" on his guitar. Neighbor Keith "Sabu" Crier wandered by, stopped to listen, and within seconds decided to join his musical talents with LeBlanc's, a partnership that has lasted eleven years.

The first ten of those years were mostly lean ones, beginning with a slew of neighborhood dates. The duo played clubs, parties, bars—anything short of street corners where they would find an audience. They played with other musicians who drifted in and out of the band until they clicked with Herb Lane and Paul Service. By this time they were working for a small, independent label, where they spent a frustrating six years—young, inexperienced, growing gradually, but buffeted by their ignorance. "We were all about fifteen or sixteen when we signed," Rahiem recalls, "and in those years we learned a lot about writing, about the studio, and about the business. Now we're ready for whatever happens next."

All this time, although their records were getting little exposure, they were building a reputation as a dynamite live band. Their fortunes changed lightning fast when Tony Lopez became their manager and Beau Ray Fleming their producer. Beau Ray, Rahiem explains, was instrumental in persuading Arista Records to see them. Arista executive Larkin Arnold watched them play in a tiny basement in the South Bronx, and within two weeks G.Q. was in the studio cutting *Disco Nights*, the disk that swiftly propelled them into the national limelight at last.

1978/79 Discography: *Disco Nights*

HERBIE HANCOCK

Jazzman extraordinaire Herbert Jeffrey Hancock, born and bred on Chicago's South Side, has been a daring jazz pioneer since the 1960s, when his brilliant explorations with Miles Davis and on his own albums resonated through the decade, restructuring the jazz idiom.

Hancock's musical career began when he was seven and became interested in the piano "because," as he puts it, "a friend of mine had one." By the time he was eleven, he was performing the Mozart D Major Piano Concerto with the Chicago Symphony. Classical music was his only love until he was a sophomore in high school, when he heard jazz for the first time at a school talent show. He instantly leaped at the challenge of improvisation, realizing that, despite all his classical training, it was a technique he hadn't learned. He taught himself to analyze harmony and rhythms by listening to Oscar Peterson or George Shearing records for days on end, until he learned to play every solo. Although he enrolled at Grinnell College intending to major in engineering, he couldn't stay away from music.

Before long he was arranging and composing for his own seventeen-piece concert band. He soon changed his major to music composition.

After college, Herbie played in the rhythm sections of various orchestras until Donald Byrd needed a good pianist in a hurry. Herbie's first performances with Byrd were electrifying, and when Byrd returned to New York, Herbie went with him as a regular member of the band. In 1963 Hancock recorded his own first album, *Takin' Off*, featuring his classic song "Watermelon Man."

For the rest of the 1960s Hancock turned out a series of classic jazz albums for Blue Note, including *Maiden Voyage, Inventions and Dimensions, Empyrean Isles, Speak Like a Child*, and *The Prisoner*. In addition to his solo work, Hancock was part of the titanic Miles Davis Quintet, did session work with such top artists as Wes Montgomery, Quincy Jones, Sonny Rollins, and Freddie Hubbard, and composed jingles for Chevrolet, Eastern Airlines, and Standard Oil. His music was featured in Michelangelo Antonioni's film *Blow Up* and on Bill Cosby's television special "Hey, Hey, Hey, It's Fat Albert."

After leaving Miles, Herbie recorded *Mwandishi*, which means "composer" in Swahili. A daring leap, this first album with his own sextet was the first jazz album to include electronic sounds. From there he went on to even deeper electronic exploration in *Crossings* and *Sextant*, but his music became less accessible. "I would see many people leave the club with a heavier weight on their shoulders than when they came in," he later said. "They had to work to listen to my music. I was, in effect, just creating another problem for them."

He loosened up in the album *Headhunters*, which contained the popular single "Chameleon," one of the spearheads of the jazz crossover revolution.

In 1976 he made another dazzling turnaround, reuniting the Miles Davis Quintet under the name V.S.O.P. and returning to classical jazz. In 1978 he and Chick Corea toured triumphantly with an all-acoustic piano duet show, and on his 1978 album, *Sunlight*, he experimented with a new vocal synthesizer. In 1979, *Feets Don't Fail Me Now* was a top jazz LP.

1978/79 Discography: *Feets Don't Fail Me Now*

GEORGE HARRISON

It is one of the music world's many minor and amusing coincidences that George Harrison and John Lennon attended the Dovedale Primary School at the same time. They never met while there, and George's musical talents didn't emerge until he was thirteen, when he bought a cheap acoustic guitar from a friend and allowed himself to be seduced by its soothing sound.

In 1958 Harrison and Paul McCartney, schoolmates at the Liverpool Institute, began to play Lonnie Donegan material together. Before long the two had become members of John Lennon's group, the Quarrymen. After completing school, George worked briefly as an apprentice electrician, but, after the Quarrymen disbanded in November of 1959, he was delighted to go along with John and Paul when they changed their name to Johnny and the Moondogs. The band finally renamed itself the Silver Beatles; played dates in Scotland, England, and Germany; cut a record; and were discovered by manager Brian Epstein, beginning the most phenomenal success story of the century.

Between the years 1960 and 1970, the life span of the Beatles, George was a vital part of that success, contributing his fine guitar work and hauntingly melodic songs. The names of those songs evoke the texture of the sixties, beginning with "Don't Bother Me," from *With the Beatles*, and including "I Need You," from *Help*; "Think for Yourself" and "If I Needed Someone," from *Rubber Soul*; "Taxman," "Love You To," and "I Want to Tell You," from *Revolver*. In 1966 George traveled to India with Ravi Shankar to study sitar and yoga. His songs on the last Beatles albums— "Within You, Without You," "Blue Jay Way," "While My Guitar Gently Weeps," "Long Long Long," "Savoy Truffle," "Only a Northern Song," "All Too Much," "Something," and "Here Comes the Sun"—reflect the blossoming of his natural mysticism that occurred during the Indian journey.

The demise of the Beatles seemed to free George, spurring him on to a wide variety of successful creative and business ventures. In November, 1970, his three-record set, *All Things Must Pass,* was released. From it came the international smash "My Sweet Lord." In addition to his eight gold solo albums, including 1979's *George Harrison,* he masterminded the two legendary Bangladesh benefit concerts in July 1971. The following year he was executive producer for the award-winning film *Little Malcolm.* He founded the Material World Charitable Foundation; began his own record company, Dark Horse Records, with offices in Los Angeles, London, and Rotterdam; sponsored the Ravi Shankar Music Festival; toured; and appeared on a segment of "Saturday Night Live" that won the largest viewing audience in the program's history. In addition to appearing in the Eric Idle Beatles spoof, "All You Need Is Cash," he was executive producer of the Monty Python film *Life of Brian.*

In the fall of 1978 he and former Beatles press agent Derek Taylor began work on *I, Me, Mine,* a book about George's songs and songwriting. In 1979 "Blow Away" was a top easy-listening song.

His personal life has taken on a new shine, also. In 1978 he married for the second time and became the father of a son—his first. 1978/79 Discography: *George Harrison*

HEART

Ann Wilson—Lead vocals, flute

Nancy Wilson—Guitars, mandolin, keyboards, vocals

Roger Fisher—Lead guitar

Steve Fossen—Bass

Michael Derosier—Drums

Howard Leese—Keyboards, guitar, vocals

Onstage, Heart is clearly an irresistible force, with Nancy Wilson, the beautiful blond sister coaxing piercing wails from her guitar and Ann Wilson, the equally beautiful raven-haired sister, stalking the stage, flinging her awesome voice with abandon. Roger Fisher and Steve Fossen masterfully blend guitar and bass, Howard Leese commands the keyboards, and Michael Derosier shatters the air with his drumming. That onstage bite is captured in their records, each of which has sold more than a million copies. *Dreamboat Annie, Little Queen, Magazine,* and *Dog and Butterfly*—with such clear hard rockers as "Crazy on You," "Magic Man," "Dreamboat Annie," "Barracuda," and "Kick it Out"—all capture that ferocious live energy.

Neither Nancy nor Ann, who compose all the band's music, wanted a musical career. Ann originally intended to write and illustrate books of poetry, and Nancy planned to study art. But Ann learned music early and formed Heart in 1970. Nancy, who had played acoustic guitar for thirteen years, quickly picked up the electric guitar, blues harp, mandolin, keyboards, and vocals when she joined the band in 1974. Heart's present lineup came together by 1975.

After years of playing small clubs in the Pacific Northwest, slowly building a strong local audience, the band signed with Mushroom Records. The label was delighted by the dedication of the hard-driving band, who, by staying with the grindstone of the road, sent audiences rushing to record stores to buy more than three million copies of *Dreamboat Annie.* International favorites, the band will always remain loyal to their hometown fans of Seattle.

INSTANT FUNK

Kim Miller—Guitar

Scotty Miller—Drums

Raymond Earl—Bass

Dennis Richardson—Piano

Charles Williams—Congas

James Carmichael—Percussion, lead vocals

Larry Davis—Trumpet

Johnny Onderline—Saxophones

Eric Huff—Trombone

George Bell—Guitar

The overnight success of the ten-man dynamo called Instant Funk actually began in 1972, when a Philadelphia group called the TNJ's had a top soul single and album called *Get Down With the Philly Jump.* They disbanded after two years, but guitarist Kim Miller, drummer Scotty Miller, and bass player Raymond Earl, the collective heart of the band, stayed together. Soul singer Bunny Sigler recruited the trio to become part of his back-up band, and for the next five years they performed and recorded with Sigler as well as such soul and disco stars as Lou Rawls, the O'Jays, the Pips, Evelyn "Champagne" King, Barbara Mason, Archie Bell and the Drells, Loleatta Holloway, and the Salsoul Orchestra.

In 1977, however, with the addition of pianist Dennis Richardson and conga player Charles Williams, the band stepped out on its own as Instant Funk. They added players James Carmichael, Larry Davis, Johnny Onderline, Eric Huff, and George Bell, and at the beginning of 1979 released "I Got My Mind Made Up (You Can Get It Girl)," a soul climber that topped the charts for three weeks, won gold, and nudged their debut album, *Instant Funk,* to gold as well. In 1979 they triumphed in New York City—May 22 was declared Instant Funk Day and was capped with a successful concert at Avery Fisher Hall. 1978/79 Discography: *Instant Funk*

ISLEY BROTHERS

Ronald Isley—Lead vocals

Rudolph Isley—Vocals

Kelly Isley—Vocals

Ernie Isley—Guitar, drums

Marvin Isley—Bass

Chris Jasper—Keyboards, ARP

Costumes flashing, voices shouting, Ernie Isley's drums pounding out a powerful pulse, the fabulous Isley Brothers have been churning out towering R & B since 1959, when brothers Ronald, Rudolph, and Kelly recorded their relentlessly driving "Shout." Throughout the years they've scored with such arresting songs as "(Who's) That Lady," "Twist and Shout" (recorded by the Beatles), "It's Your Thing," "Take Me to the Next Phase," and 1979's "I Wanna Be With You," from such aggressively titled albums as *Live it Up, The Heat Is On, Go for Your*

Courtesy Warner/Reprise

Fleetwood Mac

Courtesy Atlantic Records

Mick Jones, Foreigner

Courtesy A&M Records

Peter Frampton

James Galway Courtesy RCA Records

Courtesy Scotti Brothers Records

Courtesy United Artists Records

Garrett

Marvin Gaye Courtesy Motown Records

Crystal Gayle

Guns, 1978's platinum *Showdown,* and 1979's gold *Winner Takes All.*

At the end of 1978 they recorded *Timeless,* a brilliantly conceived album of such classic songs as "Fire and Rain," "Lay, Lady Lay," "It's Too Late," "Love the One You're With," and "Spill the Wine."

In the early sixties the brothers learned their trade by studying every musician they could see and hear, including the legendary Jimi Hendrix. In 1966 they signed a contract with Motown, and there, in addition to the experience they gained touring and recording, they learned about the business of songwriting, producing, and financing. At the end of the decade, they emerged from that apprenticeship with enough business savvy to form their own label, T-Neck Records. The addition of brothers Ernie and Marvin and brother-in-law Chris Jasper made the group wholly a family affair.

1978/79 Discography: *Winner Takes All*
Timeless

J

JACKSONS

Michael Jackson—Lead vocals

Jackie Jackson—Lead vocals, guitar

Tito Jackson—Guitar, vocals

Randy Jackson—Vocals

Marlon Jackson—Vocals

In 1969, in Gary, Indiana, Joseph and Katherine Jackson and their five sons began to sing together as the Jackson Family. Mr. and Mrs. Jackson soon left the music-making to the boys—Marlon, Michael, Jermaine, Tito, and Jackie—whose infectious enthusiasm and natural talent soon burst out of Gary's confines. Wherever they appeared they transformed normal, everyday audiences into bouncing, hand-clapping, grinning screechers. By 1970 they had appeared in New York's Apollo and Philadelphia's Uptown. Word of their fame spread to Detroit, where Berry Gordy took one listen and signed them to Motown.

From then on there was no stopping the Jacksons, and hits followed like wildfire: "I Want You Back," the Grammy-winning "ABC," "The Love You Save," and "I'll Be There." Their albums, including *Diana Ross Presents the Jackson 5, ABC, The Jackson 5's Greatest Hits,* and *Moving Violation,* were also pop smashes.

Guided always by the shrewd managerial hand of father Joseph, the boys were shining examples of respect and genuine good nature; they received commendations from Congress in 1972 for their contributions to American youth.

In 1975, when they signed with Epic Records, brother Jermaine chose to remain with Motown. The band worked with Gamble and Huff for *The Jacksons* and *Goin' Places,* on which the brothers began to write and produce their own music—"Do What You Want" and "Different Kind of Lady." Their third Epic album, *Destiny,* a gold-winning, top soul disk, was conceived, written, performed, and produced by the Jacksons. From that album came two smash hits, "Blame it on the Boogie" and "Shake Your Body." In February of 1979 the boys enjoyed a triumphant series of performances in London.

1978/79 Discography: *Destiny*

BOB JAMES

With its clairvoyantly triumphant title, *Touchdown,* Bob James's late 1978 album floated easily to the top of the jazz charts and remained in the number-one spot for months. After spending most of his musical career arranging other people's music, this was immensely satisfying for James. Of *Touchdown* he says, "I decided to stick with my own compositions, with each tune representing a particular kind of mood in which I felt particularly comfortable."

The man whom many people credit with jazz's immense popularity in the 1970s began playing piano when he was four. The Missouri-born James put together his first jazz trio when he was at the University of Michigan. Quincy Jones heard them play at the Notre Dame Jazz Festival in 1962, was delighted by their sound, and signed them to Mercury Records. James's first album, *Explosions,* which included heavily electronic compositions and live improvisations, was followed by a four-and-a-half-year stint as Sarah Vaughan's musical director. He then arranged music for such song stylists as Dionne Warwick, Roberta Flack, Aretha Franklin, and Morgana King. Quincy Jones introduced him to Creed Taylor, and Bob worked for Taylor's CTI label until 1976, arranging and composing for such jazz greats as Hubert Laws, Eric Gale, Stanley Turrentine, Hank Crawford, Ron Carter, Johnny Hammond, and Grover Washington, Jr. He wrote, arranged, and conducted several songs for Washington's gold-winning crossover albums *Mister Magic* and *Feels So Good.* At CTI he also squeezed in four of his own albums, and the public responded well to his crisp style.

In 1976 James moved to CBS as director of progressive A & R, a job that gave him the chance to work with pop artists. He orchestrated Paul Simon's Grammy-award-winning "Still Crazy After All These Years," scored Neil Diamond's platinum *A Beautiful Noise,* and arranged and produced Kenny Loggins's first two solo disks, the gold-winning *Celebrate Me Home* and the platinum *Nightwatch.*

At the beginning of 1977 he began his own label, Tappan Zee Records, featuring such artists as Mark Colby, Wilbert Longmire, Richard Tee, Howard Johnson, and Mongo Santamaria. His own first album for Tappan Zee, *Heads,* was a top jazz LP in 1978. The success of his own records has not led him to abandon producing. In 1978 he produced the Kenny Loggins/Stevie Nicks smash, "Whenever I Call You Friend."

1978/79 Discography: *Touchdown*

RICK JAMES AND THE STONE CITY BAND

Disco hasn't been the same since Rick James let loose his thundering, flamboyant brand of punk/funk. His first album, 1978's *Come and Get it,* a double-platinum monster, and its fierce gold single "You and I" helped him win awards from *Cash Box* and *Record World* as top new male vocalist for rhythm and blues albums. He finished 1978 with "Mary Jane," a top-five soul single, and in 1979 he followed with the platinum-winning *Bustin' Out of L Seven,* a blazing collection combining rebellious funk and soft ballads.

This authoritative success started out playing in Buffalo rhythm and blues bands in his early teens. He joined the navy reserves when he was fifteen, but when he was called up he had a change of heart and moved to Toronto, Canada. There, his impeccable taste led him to join up with neophyte musicians Neil Young and Bruce Palmer, who would soon go on to form part of the Buffalo Springfield, and Goldie McJohn, founder of the smash sixties band Steppenwolf. The four called themselves the Mynah Birds.

When the Mynah Birds flew their separate ways, Rick was hired by Motown as a staff writer. Despite some small successes, he felt limited as a writer and returned to Canada, where he could once again build his own group. The resulting band, White Cane, was an eight-piece jazzrockfunk combo that recorded an MGM album and toured America with B.B. King.

The dramatic James, sporting his Masai African warrior hair style, took his Rick James Stone City Band Magical Funk Tour on a knockout cross-country jaunt in 1979; James, as always, pulled out all stops. As he describes himself, "I'm into theatrics and having people remember what I say and lay down. I'm very energetic. I'm not your organic, laid-back tree."

1978/79 Discography: *Bustin' Out of L Seven*

Charlyn Zlotnik

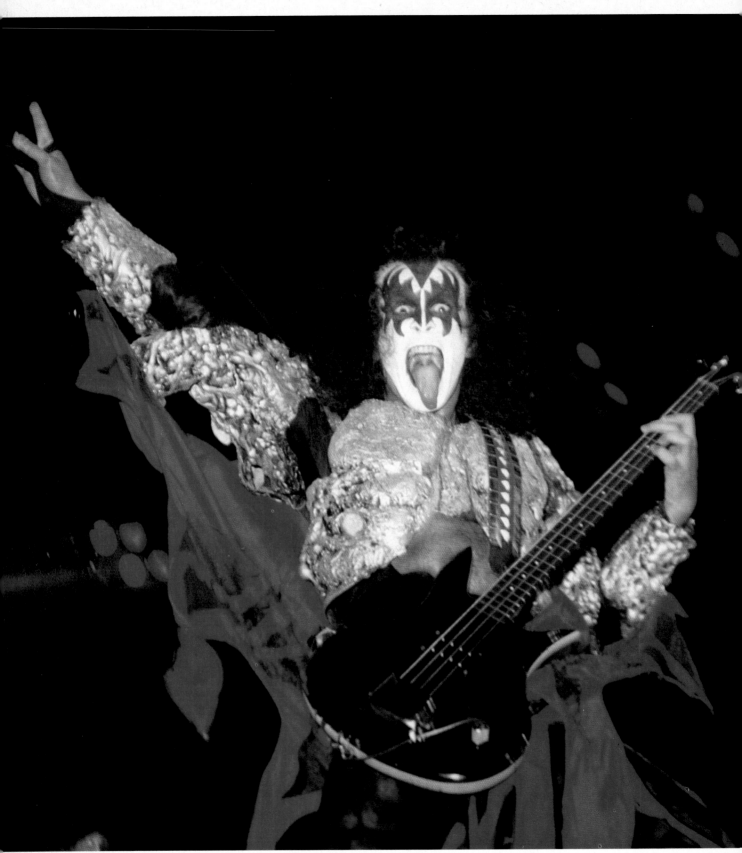

Chuck Pulin

Preceding page: *Rod Stewart's 1979 joy came from both his career and new wife and daughter.* Opposite: *Although Cher has cooled their romance, Gene Simmons of Kiss stays as sweet as ever.* Above: *Ryan O'Neal and Barbra Streisand show off muscular physiques in* Main Event. Right: *Van Halen's David Lee Roth puts on an energetic show.*

Opposite: *Winsome Dolly Parton reigned as the Country Music Association's entertainer of the year throughout 1979.* Below: *Gloria Gaynor's big voice sent "I Will Survive," her soaring disco anthem, to platinum sales.*

Opposite: *In 1979 Paul McCartney's informal performance with George and Ringo at Eric Clapton's wedding celebration led once more to Beatle reunion rumors.* Right: *Crystal Gayle was voted top female vocalist by the Country Music Association.* Below: *Angela Lansbury and Len Cariou won Tony awards as best actress and actor in a musical for Sweeney Todd. Seen also are Tom Conti and Carole Shelley, who won best actor and actress Tonys for drama.* Bottom: *The Oak Ridge Boys were voted vocal group of the year by the CMA.* Following page: *Grammy-winner Anne Murray cut a string of smash hits in 1979.*

AL JARREAU

The awesome power of Al Jarreau's voice, its range, versatility, and flexibility, puts him in a class all by himself. In 1979 his growing recognition reached a new pinnacle, as his sparkling album *All Fly Home* won him a Grammy for best jazz vocal performance, and his thrilling performance at the eighth Tokyo Music Festival won him the silver prize. Since 1975, when his first album, *We Got By*, slowly gathered an impressive roster of accolades, Al Jarreau's international fame has grown steadily. In Europe his unclassifiable talents were more readily accepted than in America. His first four-week tour of Europe in 1976 stretched into eight weeks and won him a German Grammy as the best new international pop vocalist, his own ninety-minute special on German television, and acclaim at the Eurovision festival as "the American triumph."

American critics soon recognized his talents, as Leonard Feather in the *Los Angeles Times* and *Cash Box* both named him number one jazz vocalist for 1976. In 1977 he won a Grammy as best jazz male vocalist.

By 1977 and the release of *Glow*, Jarreau was gaining more listeners in America, his performances on the "Dinah Shore Show" and "Saturday Night Live" introducing his vocal talents to an enormous national audience.

Jarreau was born in Milwaukee and won a masters degree in psychology from the University of Iowa. During the late 1960s, while working in San Francisco as a rehabilitation counselor for the state of California, he began singing with George Duke's piano trio in local clubs. He soon quit his counseling job and went to Los Angeles seeking a big break, which came on his last night as a support act for Les McCann at Doug Weston's Troubadour, a club noted for introducing new talent. Several Warner Brothers executives were in the audience, and they needed only a few minutes of listening to his voice to know they had made a real find; they signed Jarreau to a recording contract the next day.

After the success of his first two albums, Jarreau made a major swing throughout Europe, recording sixteen sold-out concerts in the major European capitals, resulting in a live double LP, *Al Jarreau*. His sparkling 1979 effort, *All Fly Home*, was a top jazz LP.
1978/79 Discography: *All Fly Home*

JEFFERSON STARSHIP

Grace Slick—Vocals, keyboard

Paul Kantner—Vocals, guitar

Marty Balin—Vocals

Craig Chaquico—Lead guitar

David Freiberg—Vocals, keyboards, bass

John Barbata—Drums

Pete Sears—Bass, keyboards

By this time as much an institution as a band, the Jefferson Starship surprised no one when their 1979 release, *Jefferson Starship Gold*, rapidly became a gold-seller. Containing such memorable songs as "Miracles," "With Your Love," "Runaway," and "Count on Me," the disk shimmers with their unmistakably vibrant vocal harmonies sung out against a complex instrumental background.

As the Jefferson Airplane, the standard-bearers of the revolution in consciousness of the 1960s, the band created ten eccentric albums that included such songs as "White Rabbit," "Plastic Fantastic Lover," "Volunteers," and "Wooden Ships." In their psychedelic fervor they seemed an indivisible unit. At the beginning of the 1970s, however, the band went through an internal crisis. Marty Balin, whose searing vocal duets with Grace Slick had been the heart of the

Airplane's sound, left the group. Guitarist Jorma Kaukonen and bass player Jack Casady began devoting much of their energy to their new band, Hot Tuna. Grace Slick and Paul Kantner recorded several solo albums. Although Airplane albums appeared, they were weak; it appeared that the Airplane was finished.

In 1974, however, a new lighter-than-air band, calling itself the Jefferson Starship, emerged from the ashes of the Airplane. Featuring Grace Slick, Paul Kantner, and a new rhythm section, their first album, *Dragonfly*, contained a song, "Caroline," by Marty Balin. In 1975 Balin brought his talents back to the group full time, and with him they cut their first superseller, *Red Octopus*, which was devoured by more than two-and-a-half million fans and was their first number-one LP. The band's next two albums, *Spitfire* and *Earth*, sold more than a million copies each.

In 1978 the band was once more in turmoil, with Grace Slick suffering ailments; in 1979 there were rumors that she was leaving the band. When the Starship played a surprise free concert in Golden Gate Park on May 13, neither Slick nor Balin appeared onstage. Early 1979 rumors that Grace would be replaced were denied by the band and at this writing there is no official word on their future.
1978/79 Discography: *Jefferson Starship Gold*

WAYLON JENNINGS

"I was raised in the suburbs of a cotton patch" is the way Waylon Jennings drily describes his home town of Littlefield, Texas. But from those prairie beginnings, Jennings has grown into a towering country superstar, the first to make a million-selling country album with 1976's historic *The Outlaws*. He now has three platinum albums as well as seven gold ones. In 1978 his *I've Always Been Crazy* became the first country album ever to ship gold. With the gold success of his *Greatest Hits* album, his and Willie Nelson's Grammy for best country vocal performance by a duo or group for their 1978 smash, "Mamas Don't Let Your Babies Grow Up to Be Cowboys," and his hit country singles "Don't You Think This Outlaw Bit's Done Got Out of Hand" and "Amanda," 1979 is another winning year for this individualist who has reached the peak of his profession by doing things his way.

Music has been the main love of Waylon's life since he was a child. He began his musical career as a disk jockey, and from the time he was twelve until he was twenty-one he spun records, hosted local talent shows, and sang.

After he moved to Lubbock, Texas, Buddy Holly heard him sing and play bass and asked Jennings to join with him and the Crickets. Waylon worked with Holly through 1958. For some reason, he declined to accompany Holly and the band on the ill-fated plane ride in 1959 that ended in tragedy, taking the lives of Buddy Holly, J. P. Richardson (The Big Bopper), and Richie Valens.

Waylon put his shattered life together and worked again in Lubbock as a disk jockey. He formed a group called the Waylors, and they moved to Phoenix, Arizona, where, at a club called J. D.'s, Waylon sang and experimented with every kind of music, developing his unique guitar style. In 1965 Chet Atkins signed Waylon to an RCA recording contract, and Jennings moved to Nashville, where he quickly won the Stockman's Association of the Greater Southwest's Pioneer Award as the top new country-and-western act of 1965.

Never one to follow a crowd, Waylon raised eyebrows in Nashville by recording songs of such urban folks as Bob Dylan and Gordon Lightfoot. During those years he had a string of hits with such songs as "The Taker," "Mississippi Woman," "Cedartown, Georgia," and "Good Hearted Woman." But he was mismanaged, and despite his successes he found himself broke and more than half a million dollars in debt. "It just looked like it was all over," he says of that time. But with the help of drummer and coproducer Richie Albright, new manager Neil Reshen, and good friend Willie Nelson, Waylon was able to recover and pour himself back into his music. He found a group of young songwriters, mainly Billy Joe Shaver, Steve Young, and Lee Clayton, who introduced him to the cowboy sound that was to become known as Outlaw music, the sound that Waylon made his own.

The songs that signaled the beginning of this movement were 1972's "Ladies Love Outlaws" and "Lonesome, On'ry and Mean." The following year, the movement began to spread out from Texas with 1973's album *Honky Tonk Heroes*. In 1976, RCA put together *The Outlaws*—featuring Waylon, Willie Nelson, Waylon's wife Jessi Colter, and Tompall Glaser—which turned into the legendary first million-selling country LP. In 1977 Waylon earned his own gold record for the album *Dreaming My Dreams*, and *Ol' Waylon* won him his second platinum disk. In 1978 he and Willie Nelson received a platinum album for *Waylon and Willie*.

BILLY JOEL

"I'll always be a musician. Since I was four years old I've been a musician," Billy Joel says. And in every one of his songs, his shrewd musicianship captures a universal aspect of life that's never been musically examined before; 1979's "Big Shot," for example, which he calls "a great hangover song," is a condensed portrait of the morning after, a biting reminiscence of half-forgotten, outrageous behavior. "Honesty" refreshingly conveys that unstylish trait. Both songs come from his 1978 album, *52nd Street*, his latest platinum disk. In 1979 Joel won a Grammy for his tender ballad "Just the Way You Are," named record of the year.

It was at the age of four that the parents of William Martin Joel noticed he responded to the music of Mozart. They began giving the toddler classical piano lessons, which he took until age sixteen, when he discovered rock and roll. From then on, it was roll over Beethoven as Billy joined with a band called the Echoes and helped support his mother (his father had left home when Billy was seven) by working as a keyboard musician throughout his teenage years. By 1968 he had left the Echoes to play with a band called the Hassles. Then he and the Hassles' drummer formed a duo called Attila and made one forgettable album for Epic records. After working at various 9-to-5 jobs to keep body and soul together, Billy signed with Family Productions in 1971 and recorded his first solo album of original songs, *Cold Spring Harbor*. The album created legal problems, so Billy decided to pack up; with his girlfriend (now wife), Elizabeth, he moved to North Hollywood where he indulged in the California life-style. He played at piano bars as Bill Martin and began to write some new songs. "Captain Jack," a song he had written during his last days in New York, had become an underground hit on the East Coast, and Columbia Records tracked Billy down in Los Angeles, signing him in the late spring of 1973. His first single was the instant hit "Piano Man," an autobiographical sketch of his months at the piano bar. The album of the same name was released one week later and stayed on the charts during the first six months of 1974, becoming a million-seller. *Streetlife Serenade*, his second album, was released in October 1974, and at the end of the year Billy won *Cash Box*'s award as best new male vocalist. He also began to headline on tours, selling out Carnegie Hall and Lincoln Center in New York, the Kiel Opera House in St. Louis, and Massey Hall in Toronto.

In 1975 Billy moved back to New York, gathered together a group of top New York musicians, and released *Turnstiles* in May 1976, a musical tribute to his home town. Throughout the rest of 1976 and into 1977, Billy toured, selling out all of 108 concerts, the grand climax of the tour coming during three sizzling sold-out nights at Carnegie Hall.

In September 1977, Billy released *The Stranger*; produced by Phil Ramone, the album quickly became a platinum-winner and yielded the outstanding singles "Movin' Out (Anthony's Song)," "Just the Way You Are," "Only the Good Die Young," and "She's Always a Woman."

ELTON JOHN

It's been Elton's year to slam out there and slay 'em in the aisles once again. After a performing hiatus that lasted from 1976 to mid-1979, broken only by a few small gigs, the outrageous singer/songwriter conquered Russia with a spectacular concert at the end of May. In September he came back to conquer the States in a forty-city tour called Back in the USSA. From his hit album *The Thom Bell Sessions*, produced by noted producer/arranger/songwriter Thom Bell, came the song "Mama Can't Buy You Love," a bouncy rocker in the tradition of such great Elton John smashes as "Crocodile Rock," "Saturday Night's Alright for Fighting," "Bennie and the Jets," "Island Girl," "Honky Cat," and "Don't Go Breaking My Heart." These songs come from a string of such hit albums as *Tumbleweed Connection*; *17 - 11 - 70*; the soundtrack to the movie *Friends*; *Madman Across the Water*; *Honky Chateau*; *Don't Shoot Me, I'm Only the Piano Player*; *Goodbye Yellow Brick Road*; and *Blue Moves*.

Elton's extraordinary success—he's sold out every concert for seven straight years, and he's had six number-one singles in the seventies, more than anyone except the Bee Gees and Wings—has its roots in the British four-year-old who sat down at a piano and taught himself to play. By the time he was fourteen he was with his first band, Britain's well known Bluesology. After he left that group, his career faltered until, in the late 1960s, he was introduced to lyricist Bernie Taupin. The two formed a dynamic partnership that continues to this day. At first, however, as salaried writers to music publisher Dick James, they struggled for years trying to churn out top-forty, middle-of-the-road songs.

They finally realized they were wasting their time trying to force themselves to write ballads when their real love was rock and roll. They cut two albums of their own songs, *Empty Sky* and *Elton John*. To promote the latter, the first album to be released in the United States, Elton brought his boundless energy to a rave-up show at Los Angeles's Doug Weston's Troubadour Club, famed for breaking new stars. Critics were bowled over by the John juggernaut, adoring his whole-body piano playing and nonstop boogie.

Top albums poured out through the years, and in 1975 Elton made his film debut as the Pinball Wizard in *Tommy*, Ken Russell's flamboyant film spectacle based on the Who's rock opera. Since that time John has headed his own record company, Rocket.

1978/79 Discography: *Solitary Man*
The Thom Bell Sessions
Victim of Love

QUINCY JONES

Known to his friends as "Q," Quincy Jones is a towering musical talent, a prolific composer, an imaginative conductor, producer, and arranger, a shrewd businessman, and a seemingly nonstop machine who has packed a prodigious amount of musical expression into his twenty-five-year career. He won an Emmy for the music of 1977's "Roots"; he has won five Grammy awards, the most recent in 1979 for his instrumental arrangement of the main title theme for the film *The Wiz*. In addition, he's won three Oscar nominations, one Emmy nomination, twenty-two Grammy nominations, *Downbeat* magazine's critics' and readers' polls, the Brazil International Song Festival, two Golden Globe nominations, and two Dutch Edison awards. He also somehow finds the time for involvement in a number of black organizations, from the Black Expo, a business exposition for blacks, to the Reverend Jesse Jackson's Operation PUSH (People United to Save Humanity), to his own Quincy Jones Workshop.

Chicago-born, Seattle-raised Jones was playing trumpet for Billie Holiday and composing and arranging with Ray Charles when he was only fourteen. Jones was ready to tour with Lionel Hampton, but Mrs. Gladys Hampton spotted him on the tour bus and yelled, "Get that child out of here. Let him finish school!"

School was the famed Berklee College of Music in Boston, where Jones, on scholarship, took an incredible ten courses a day and then played in strip joints at night to pay for rent and food. His name was buzzed around jazz circles as far away as New York, and he began to travel there on weekends, playing with such jazz titans as Art Tatum, Thelonius Monk, Charlie "Bird" Parker, and Miles Davis. After Berklee, Quincy finally did tour with Hampton, and after one of his European

Gloria Gaynor

Andy Gibb

Nick Gilder

G.Q.

The Herbie Hancock Group

George Harrison

tours decided to make Paris his home. There, he worked at Barclay Disques as musical director and studied classical composition with the legendary Nadia Boulanger. During his years in Paris he won awards from nearly every European country as best new arranger and composer.

Returning to New York in 1961, Quincy began a seven-year stint at Mercury Records, where he recorded his own music and arranged and produced for such artists as Sammy Davis, Sarah Vaughan, Frank Sinatra, Andy Williams, Johnny Mathis, Glen Campbell, B.B. King, Count Basie, and Tony Bennett. He also became the first black vice-president of a major white record label and the first black man to compose for films, beginning with Sidney Lumet's *The Pawnbroker.* He has since scored more than thirty major motion pictures and television shows.

In the late seventies his collaboration with George and Louis Johnson helped propel those two previously unknown musicians to international fame. His early 1978 album, *Sounds and Stuff Like That,* featuring the work of such premier talents as Hubert Laws, Herbie Hancock, Ashford and Simpson, and Chaka Khan, rocketed to gold sales, his third gold LP. He surpassed that later in the year with the platinum-awarded, two-record set of the film score for *The Wiz.*

After the hectic work schedule of 1978, Jones zipped right into 1979, producing Michael Jackson's solo album, a new Brothers Johnson disk, and forming his own record label, Qwest.
1978/79 Discography: *The Wiz*

KANSAS

Kerry Livgren—Guitar, keyboards

Robby Steinhardt—Violins, vocals

Steve Walsh—Keyboards, vocals

Phil Ehart—Drums, percussion

Dave Hope—Bass

Rich Williams—Guitars

In 1979, *Monolith,* Kansas's sixth album, thundered onto *Billboard's* charts in its second week, striking gold instantly. Its swift success was a repeat of the winning pattern Kansas established with their 1977 monster *Leftoverture,* their first breakthrough, which sold more than two million copies. That was followed in 1978 by *Point of Know Return,* another double-platinum. From these albums came their haunting singles, "Carry on Wayward Son" and "Dust in the Wind."

Kansas began making their combinations of pulsing rock rhythms and classically influenced melodies when they were schoolmates in Topeka, Kansas. For two years they braved the midwestern and southern small-club circuit, exposing their bold vision to rough and rowdy audiences in nonstop touring. Don Kirshner eventually heard them and signed them to his label. From that signing at the end of 1972 until the success of *Leftoverture,* the band created three underrated albums—*Kansas, Song for America,* and *Masque.* A late 1977 and early 1978 whirlwind tour of fifty-four American cities was a triumph, as was their March tour of Europe and their June 29 concert at New York's Madison Square Garden.
1978/79 Discography: *Monolith*

KENDALLS

Royce Kendall—Vocals, guitar

Jeannie Kendall—Vocals

After seven years of consistent if not sensational country music success, the father-daughter duo of Royce and Jeannie Kendall finally hit fame and glory with a song that had originally been tucked away on a B side, 1977's smash "Heaven's Just a Sin Away." The song won them a Grammy for best country vocal performance by a duo, and their 1978 hit, "It Don't Feel Like Sinnin' to Me," won a Grammy in 1979 as country single of the year. It also won the Country Music Association's award as country single of the year and won them *Billboard's* award as number one country vocal duo.

Royce picked up his first guitar when he was only five, and by the time he was eight he and his brother Floyce were singing and strumming on a local radio station. However, although he toured with both the merchant marine and army bands, he didn't feel music offered enough stability. He settled down in St. Louis, where he and wife Melba ran a barbershop/beauty salon.

When his daughter Jeannie was a teenager, the two began singing at home for their own pleasure and discovered their voices blended perfectly. They began to play local engagements and were heard by a St. Louis disk jockey who encouraged them to contact Nashville producer Pete Drake. Drake immediately signed them to his tiny STOP Records, and the first song they made for him, a country version of John Denver's "Leavin' on a Jet Plane," reached the top twenty on the country charts. The Kendalls packed away their tonsorial equipment and moved to Nashville.

Over the following several years, they moved from label to label, achieving only moderate and sporadic success. Their second single for Ovation Records, "Live and Let Live," was getting respectable airplay when deejays began to report that the playing of the B side, "Heaven's Just a Sin Away," caused the phones to start ringing off the wall. Ovation wisely made that side the A side, and the song took off like a flash, becoming a firm number-one country single for weeks.

In addition to the award-winning "It Don't Feel Like Sinnin' to Me," the Kendalls' hits in 1978 and early 1979 included "Pittsburgh Stealers," "Sweet Desire," "I Had a Lovely Time," and "Just Like Real People," the title song of their 1979 album. In March of 1979 they became heroes in their hometown when St. Louis held a Kendalls Coming Home Celebration.
1978/79 Discography: *Just Like Real People*

EVELYN "CHAMPAGNE" KING

One of the surprises of 1978 was a disco, R & B, and pop smash called "Shame," performed with dazzling expertise by a newcomer named Evelyn "Champagne" King. The surprise was not only the magnitude of the song's success, but the authority and professionalism of the singer, who, when her first single was declared gold, was one day shy of her eighteenth birthday. The young lady with the beautifully inflected voice proved immediately that "Shame's" success was no fluke when her first album, *Smooth Talk,* also became gold. Since then, her second single, "I Don't Know if It's Right," has sold gold, and when *Music Box,* her second album, was released early in 1979, it had advance orders of more than half a million copies, making it an instant gold-winner.

Evelyn feels she owes much of her success to her father, Erik, who sometimes stood in with vocal combos at the Apollo Theatre in New York, and to her uncle Avon Long, who was the original Sportin' Life in *Porgy and Bess* and recently starred in *Bubbling Brown Sugar.* Both encouraged Evelyn when she was a child. But her story is truly a Cinderella tale. In 1976 she was cleaning bathrooms in the Gamble and Huff studios in Philadelphia, singing as she worked. Writer/producer/musician T. Life remembers being impressed with her vocal power. "She had very big pipes for a kid," he recalls. He gave her

Heart Courtesy Columbia Records

Instant Funk

The Isley Brothers Courtesy Epic Records

The Jacksons Courtesy Epic Records

Bob James

Rick James Courtesy Gordy Records

some new songs, coached the rough spots out of her naturally dynamic voice, and produced her first album.

The album may have been a little slow getting started, but "Shame" was a fireball, leading Evelyn to a slew of appearances on the top television music and talk shows, from "The Mike Douglas Show" to "Soul Train" and "Hot City." She toured with the O'Jays and on her own, her performances radiating the same commanding presence she displays on her records. As one critic exclaimed after her performance at New York's Felt Forum in 1978, "My God! What'll she be like when she's twenty!"

1978/79 Discography: *Music Box*

KISS

Paul Stanley—Guitar

Ace Frehley—Guitar

Gene Simmons—Bass

Peter Criss—Drums

When Neil Bogart, president of Casablanca Records and Filmworks, announced in 1978 that not only was he releasing one solo album by each of the members of Kiss, but that he was issuing those disks simultaneously and was going to spend two million dollars promoting them, industry observers once again thought he was mad. As Bogart told *Los Angeles Times* pop music critic Robert Hilburn, "Three weeks ago, the word around the industry was that I had flipped my wig again, but they say that about me every couple of years." If Bogart was mad when he made his decision, it was lunacy touched with genius—each of Kiss's solo albums easily sold a million copies. And, to show that fans had not been the least confused by the solo LPs, Kiss's first album together after a year of not recording as a group, *Dynasty*, soared into the top twenty of the pop charts and became their tenth gold disk minutes after its release. In 1979, rock's most flamboyant stage act became the subject of a series of pinball machines from Bally manufacturing; the games play "I Want to Rock 'n Roll All Night." Kiss was also the subject of a July Home Box Office special.

Rock's thunder and lightning bad boys have been fabulously successful since 1973, when they became the first band to put together a slick, dramatic, all-costumed and made-up stage show, complete with fright tactics guaranteed to send delightful shivers up and down the spines of their young audiences.

The band began in a club called Coventry, in Queens, New York. They were already experimenting with make-up and costume when television producer/manager Bill Aucoin saw their potential and signed them to Casablanca Records. Their first three albums—*Kiss, Hotter than Hell*, and *Dressed to Kill*—sold well, but it was *Alive*, their first live recording, that sparked them into multimillion sales, selling well over 2 million copies in the United States alone.

After that the Kiss Army snapped up increasing numbers of their idols' albums: *Rock and Roll Over, Love Gun, Alive II*, and *Double Platinum* sold millions. Kiss's fans bought Kiss products—from warm-up suits to bubble gum cards to T-shirts to Kiss dolls—also in the millions.

1978/79 Discography: *Dynasty*

KRIS KRISTOFFERSON

"Like a lotta you out there, I had a handicap," Kris Kristofferson deadpanned to his audience on a "Saturday Night Live" segment. "I was a college graduate with degrees in literature an' creative writin', and I couldn't get arrested. Then how did I write songs that made me a legend in my own time?" Not only did the well-loved singer/songwriter/actor earn a college degree, he also won a Rhodes scholarship and studied at Oxford for two years. His gentle self-spoof shows how

well aware he. is that such a background puts him in a different universe from other winning country stars. His career, since those early academic days, has been the envy of many who didn't start out with his "handicaps."

After a temporary stop in Nashville turned into a five-year stay, he hit paydirt in 1969 with the song "Me and Bobby McGee," which first swept the country in Janis Joplin's memorable posthumously released recording. By 1970 the *New York Times* was calling him "the hottest thing in Nashville." "Me and Bobby McGee" underlined his top position when it won the country music song of the year award and won him the songwriter of the year award from the Nashville Songwriter's Association. He has hit with such songs as "Sunday Mornin' Comin' Down," "Help Me Make it Through the Night," "Loving Her Was Easier (Than Anything I'll Ever Do Again)," "Josie," and "The Pilgrim, Chapter 33." At the end of 1978 his *Songs of Kristofferson* won a gold album.

Kristofferson's acting career has included one well-done role after another. Since his debut in *Cisco Pike*, he has been featured or starred in such movies as *Alice Doesn't Live Here Any More, Pat Garrett and Billy the Kid, Bring Me the Head of Alfredo Garcia, Blume in Love, Vigilante Force, The Sailor that Fell from Grace With the Sea, A Star is Born, Semi-Tough*, and *Convoy*.

He and Rita Coolidge married in 1973, and the two of them thrill audiences with supercharged live shows and spellbinding album work. In 1979 they appeared together on "A Gift of Song," the Bee Gees' UNICEF benefit, and at Havana Jam, the live concert sponsored by CBS records in Havana, Cuba. At the beginning of the year he and Rita released their latest album as a duo, *Natural Act*.

1978/79 Discography: *Natural Act* (with Rita Coolidge)
Shake Hands with the Devil

L

NICOLETTE LARSON

With her waist-length braids, perky smile, and big-as-all-outdoors voice, Nicolette Larson has easily sashayed to instant success on her first outing. Her debut single, Neil Young's poignant "Lotta Love," was a number-one easy-listening hit; her first album, *Nicolette*, was a gold-winner; and her 1979 concerts were packed. Combining country, Latin, and rockabilly influences, Nicolette has arrived.

Although *Nicolette* is her first solo album, her voice has brightened the albums of such stars as Waylon Jennings, Neil Young, John Stewart, Jesse Winchester, Arlo Guthrie, and the Doobie Brothers. From them she has received unprecedented support and encouragement.

Nicolette's musical heritage is in her genes, as her mother always wanted to be a professional singer. When her large family (she's one of six children) settled in Kansas City, Nicolette grudgingly took piano lessons and loved the Beatles but never thought of music as a career. In 1974, however, she moved to San Francisco, where she worked as a production secretary for the Golden State Country/Bluegrass Festival. She met many bay area bands, and by 1975 she was singing in bars and clubs with David Nichtern (who wrote "Midnight at the Oasis," Maria Muldaur's hit) and the Nocturnes. Later that year she moved to Los Angeles and worked with Hoyt Axton as a back-up singer. Through the next few years she worked in the Commander Cody Band, added her voice to the sessions of other major recording artists, and met and became close friends with Emmylou Harris, Linda Ronstadt, and Mary Kay Place.

Long pursued by several record companies, Nicolette finally decided to sign with Warner Brothers, and the result was almost instant stardom.

1978/79 Discography: *Nicolette*

LITTLE RIVER BAND

Glenn Shorrock—Lead vocals

Beeb Birtles—Vocals, guitars

David Briggs—Lead guitar

Graham Goble—Vocals, guitars

George McArdle—Bass

Derek Pellicci—Drums, percussion

One of the best-loved Australian bands to splash down in America is the Little River Band, whose 1978 album, *Sleeper Catcher*, rode to platinum in 1979, and whose song "Reminiscing" was a top-five single at the end of 1978.

The leader of the group is Glenn Shorrock, whose professional musical career began in the 1960s when he started a group called the Twilights. After seeing that band through several hits, and after a short stint with a new group called Axiom, in 1972 Shorrock went to England and joined a twelve-piece classical/rock band called Esperanto. In the meantime, Graham Goble, Beeb Birtles, and Derek Pellicci were members of an Australian band called Mississippi; that group's self-titled first album was named best group album of 1972 by Australia's Federation of Commercial Broadcasters. When Mississippi broke up in 1975, Glenn Wheatley, the band's manager, suggested that they get together with Shorrock to form Little River Band, a name inspired by an Australian road sign. Briggs and McArdle joined soon after, and the band was ready to rock and roll.

Their first LP, *Little River Band*, was named album of the year by the Australian Record Industry Association, which also gave their first single the award for best performance by a group on record. Audiences swept into their concerts, delighted by LRB's complex and bubbling arrangements. In 1976 they toured Europe, Canada, and the United States and saw their single "It's a Long Way There" shoot into the top thirty of the American charts.

In June 1977 the peripatetic band took off for an even longer tour—six months this time—to support their next album, *Diamantina Cocktail*. Named after a potent Australian drink, the album included the best of their songs from earlier Australian albums. It became their first gold-winner and spawned several top twenty singles. This first gold award came just as the band heard the news that they had made a clean sweep of the First Australian Rock Awards, winning every award given.

Returning home from their gruelling six months on the road, they were given a hero's welcome when they performed for more than seventy thousand at the annual Festival of Sydney, setting a new attendance record for outdoor music events in Australia.

In 1979 the band filmed some of their concerts in Adelaide, Australia, where they were backed by the eighty-piece Adelaide Symphony Orchestra.

KENNY LOGGINS

"*Nightwatch* is the best work I've done yet," Kenny Loggins announced soon after he completed his second solo album. In October of 1978, barely five months after its release, *Nightwatch* justified his confidence by becoming the first solo million-seller for this gentle, intelligent singer/songwriter/guitarist. From late 1970 he and Jim Messina worked together as a duo, steadily turning out hit records. At the end of 1976 they split up, mutually deciding to pursue the solo careers that each had originally wanted.

Born in Everett, Washington, Kenny was raised in California. He was in college as a telecommunications major when he had a stunning revelation. "One day it dawned on me that I wanted to be a musician but that I was spending 90 percent of my time learning

something to fall back on if I didn't make it as a musician." He left school and started working in bands, auditioning his music for anyone who would listen. When a friend introduced Kenny to Bob Todd at ABC/Wingate Publishing, Todd was bawling out a writer who was receiving one hundred dollars a week but who hadn't produced a song in two years. Kenny eagerly broke in, "For a hundred a week I'll give you a song a week," he exclaimed.

Todd took him at his word. One of his songs was "House at Pooh Corner," which became a hit for the Nitty Gritty Dirt Band and which led to a contract for Kenny with Columbia Records. Jim Messina, formerly of Poco, had admired Loggins's tunes and was delighted when he was assigned to produce Kenny's first album. He contributed so much that the album was called *Kenny Loggins with Jim Messina "Sittin' In."* After that million-seller, they stayed together for six years and produced seven more albums, of which two were platinum and five gold.

Kenny Loggins' first solo album was *Celebrate Me Home*. At the end of 1978, in addition to the shimmering success of *Nightwatch*, Loggins saw his single "Whenever I Call You Friend" become a top-five hit.

L.T.D.

Arthur Lorenzo Carnegie—Saxophones

Henry Davis—Bass, flute, saxophone, piano

Jake Riley, Jr.—Trombone

Abraham Joseph "Onion" Miller, Jr.— Saxophones

Carle Vickers—Trumpet, fluglehorn, saxophones, flute

Johnny McGhee—Guitar

Jeff Osborne—Lead vocals, drums

Billy Osborne—Lead vocals, percussion, keyboards

Jimmy "J.D." Davis—Piano

Melvin Webb—Percussion

With *Togetherness* a platinum-winner and "Holdin' On" a top-three soul single, 1978 closed on a buoyant note for the hard-working L.T.D., a band that doggedly kept believing in itself, continuing to make soulful music despite rejections from almost every record company in America.

It's been a long trip for L.T.D. The ten-man group began in 1968 in North Carolina, wanting to play a horn-rich rhythm and blues that would appeal to a wide range of soul fans. They worked tirelessly up and down the East Coast in miniscule clubs the size of which made it easy for audiences to give unknown bands a hard time. In 1970 the band packed up and headed for the Golden West to try their luck in California. But the state didn't shine its light on them, and before too long it was back to poor-paying gigs to keep a roof over their heads.

At the end of 1971, the band went to Japan for ten weeks; there they found, to their relief, that Japanese audiences loved them. Buoyed by their enthusiastic reception, the band confidently returned to the United States and won a contract with A & M Records. They made a small impression with their first two albums, *Love, Togetherness and Devotion* and *Gittin' Down*, but they began to tour with such top bands as the O'Jays, Average White Band, Bob Seger, Aerosmith, and Harold Melvin and the Blue Notes. These tours gave them experience and the opportunity to polish their act.

Their first number-one R & B hit, "Love Ballad," came from their third album, *Love to the World*. Unexpectedly, the success caused the first real friction within the band. They weren't used to hit songs or

Al Jarreau

Jefferson Starship

Waylon Jennings

Billy Joel   Courtesy Columbia Records

Elton John

Quincy Jones   Courtesy A&M Records

the pressures brought on by a best-selling record, and the group almost split apart. Arranger/producer Bobby Martin pulled them back together and produced their first gold album, *Something to Love*, from which came the number-one gold single "Back in Love Again."
1978/79 Discography: *Devotion*

CHERYL LYNN

Hard though it may be to believe, singer/composer Cheryl Lynn won her recording contract with CBS as a result of appearing on Chuck Barris's "Gong Show." Of course, Cheryl Lynn's talent towers above most "Gong Show" contestants. Not only did she win the highest possible score of thirty points, but the tough judges who rated her were lavish in praise of her performance. J.P. Morgan called her a "fabulous singer"; Rex Reed prophetically said, "Singers with gold records can't do half as well as Cheryl Lynn"; and Elke Sommer said, "She gave me goosebumps." Chuck Barris himself wrote, "Of the four thousand acts I've seen, Cheryl Lynn was the all-time great."

Cheryl was thrilled by this praise and by the subsequent army of record labels that began courting her. She had just finished performing in the road production of *The Wiz*, playing the part of the Wicked Witch of the West, and had decided to stop singing and pursue other goals. Former singing partner Delbert Langston was shocked by her decision. He told her she was too talented to consider not singing and arranged for the "Gong Show" appearance. Langston and Eric Kronfeld, now her managers, played a ninety-second video cassette of her "Gong Show" performance for CBS Records' President Bruce Lundvall, who agreed that she had a formidable talent and signed her to CBS Records. With her first single, "Got to Be Real," a top soul and disco charter and a million-seller, and with *Cheryl Lynn* a top-five soul album and a gold disk as well, Cheryl herself finally agrees that she's too good a singer to stop.
1978/79 Discography: *Cheryl Lynn*

BARBARA MANDRELL

For sparkling Barbara Mandrell 1979 has been a year of special triumph. She swooped up the Academy of Country Music award as top female vocalist of 1978. She saw her songs "Sleeping Single in a Double Bed" and "(If Loving You Is Wrong) I Don't Want to Be Right" both reach number one on the country charts. She appeared in the English Leather Pro-Am Ski Tournament which was televised in March on ABC's "Wide World of Sports," and she was an honored guest at the Statler Brothers tenth annual Happy Birthday U.S.A. Celebration.

The bubbly country superstar began her musical career as a child in California, where she grew up. Her house was always full of music, with her father, Irby, singing and playing guitar, mother, Mary, playing piano, sister Irlene playing drums, and sister Louise singing. Barbara learned to play steel guitar, bass, banjo, and saxophone as well as to sing. Her father formed the Mandrells, and they toured U.S. military bases in Europe and Asia. It was on this tour that Barbara met drummer Ken Dudney, who later became her husband.

In 1968 Irby moved his family to Nashville. Within four months Barbara was signed to Columbia Records for whom she made a string of hits, including "Treat Him Right," "Tonight My Baby's Coming Home," and "Midnight Oil." She appeared on many country radio shows, on the club and concert circuit, and recorded three albums. In 1972 she joined the Grand Ole Opry.

In 1975 she changed record companies, moving to ABC. She has since had a number of top-ten singles, culminating with 1979's number-one winners.
1978/79 Discography: *The Best of Barbara Mandrell*
Just for the Record

CHUCK MANGIONE

In addition to gladdening the hearts of flugelhorn manufacturers around the world with his radiantly warm, soaring music, Chuck Mangione has also brought musical joy to his millions of fans. In 1979 he won his second Grammy award, this one for best instrumental performance on his 1978 album, *Children of Sanchez*. His first Grammy, won in 1977, was for best instrumental composition, for *Bellavia*. In 1979 *Children of Sanchez* sold a gold-winning half million copies, and his 1978 jazzpop winner, *Feels So Good*, racked up platinum sales and the award for best-selling jazz album from the National Association of Record Manufacturers.

Chuck Mangione grew up in a family that loved music. Often, as Chuck remembers, "We would go hear somebody like Dizzy Gillespie. Father would walk up to them like he knew them all his life, and he'd say, 'Hi, Dizzy! My name is Frank Mangione, these are my kids, they play.' And before you'd know it, my father would be talking to this guy and would invite him over for spaghetti and wine, and we'd wind up having a jam session in the living room." Some of those who ate spaghetti in the Mangione kitchen were Art Blakey, Kai Winding, Cannonball Adderley, Jimmy Cobb, and Chuck's greatest hero, Dizzy Gillespie. Gillespie was so impressed with fifteen-year-old Chuck's playing that he sent the boy one of his horns.

Chuck had chosen the trumpet when he was a starry-eyed ten-year-old, impressed by the movie *Young Man with a Horn*. When he was in high school, he and his brother Gap formed a quintet called the Jazz Brothers and cut several albums for Riverside Records. At the famed Eastman School of Music, Chuck abandoned the trumpet for the flugelhorn. With its darker, mellower tone he felt it suited his personality better. At Eastman he also composed "Feel of a Vision" for classmate Lew Soloff, one of the original trumpeters with Blood, Sweat & Tears.

Chuck stayed on at Rochester for a year, teaching music, and in 1965 he traveled to New York to see what success he could have in the big city. At the end of 1965 he was tapped by one of his boyhood idols, drummer Art Blakey, who offered him the trumpet spot in his Jazz Messengers, newly re-formed to include Keith Jarrett, and later, Chick Corea. For the next two and a half years Chuck played in that exalted company. Blakey's flowing melodies and African and Latin rhythms influence Mangione's work even today.

In 1968 Chuck returned to Rochester where he wrote for the Outsiders, a Cleveland-based rock group. When they disbanded he taught at Rochester's Hochstein School of Music and, later, at Eastman. At Eastman he put together his own quartet, playing piano as well as flugelhorn for the first time.

Late in 1969, because he wanted to hear a performance of his own music, he hired fifty musicians to play his composition *Kaleidoscope*, a work scored for orchestra and soloists. Although *Kaleidoscope* was not financially successful, it attracted the attention of Tom Iannaccone, manager of the Rochester Philharmonic. He invited Chuck to guest-conduct the Philharmonic in a concert of Chuck's music. Called *Friends and Love*, the sold-out concert was a smash success, was videotaped, and finally became the first of many Mangione albums, leading to a Grammy nomination and a phenomenal musical career that's been studded with successful albums by the Chuck Mangione Quartet, television appearances, and awards.
1978/79 Discography: *Live at the Hollywood Bowl*

BARRY MANILOW

For Barry Manilow 1979 was another year of dazzling high points. The jovial singer/songwriter reaped one fabulous accolade after another and would have been hard pressed to choose the pinnacle. Perhaps most thrilling was winning a Grammy for best male vocal performance on his 1978 song "Copacabana (At the Copacabana)." Although in the 1960s he was coproducer and arranger of Bette Midler's Grammy-winning LP The Divine Miss M, this was Barry's first Grammy as a performer. Or, perhaps the high point was the sales figures of "Copa" or "I Can't Smile Without You" or "Even Now," which together have sold more than 4 million copies. Perhaps Barry got his greatest satisfaction from the early 1979 easy-listening success of his song "Somewhere in the Night." Maybe it was the platinum award won by his Greatest Hits album, which included such memorable songs as "Mandy," "Weekend in New England," "Tryin' to Get the Feeling Again," and "Looks Like We Made It." Was he most pleased at being voted favorite male vocalist by Seventeen Magazine? Did his greatest enjoyment come from the relaxed "The Third Barry Manilow Special," on which he and John Denver cavorted through a mellow medley of sugar-sweet Everly Brothers songs? Or was he most moved by the warm glow that remained from 1978 when he contemplated the triple-platinum success of his album Even Now, which stayed on the charts for fifty-two consecutive weeks?

Thrilling as they are, these honors are nothing new to Manilow, who has been winning them throughout his professional life. Brought up in Brooklyn, in a house full of music, he enjoyed accordion lessons as a child. While attending night school, he suffered through a brief stint in advertising that showed him his life belonged to music. Accordingly, he switched from the City College of New York to the New York College of Music and finally to Juilliard. In fairy-tale tradition he was going to school at night and working during the day in the CBS mailroom when he was tapped by a director to arrange some music for a TV show. From there Barry sailed into a stint as Bette Midler's musical director, arranger, and pianist and then out on his own with sensational songs, fabulously successful albums, acclaimed television specials, and a limited engagement on Broadway that won him a special Tony.

STEVE MARTIN

From the nine-year-olds who adopt daffy grins and sinuous horizontal arm movements to the adolescents who refer to their best friends as "wild and cra-a-a-azy guys" to the adults who put on a bland, blank stare after tossing off a good one-liner, the whole country has clasped Steve Martin, the handsome, blond, California comic, to its heart and its funny bone. At the end of 1978, with his marvelous "King Tut" spoof a gold-winning single and his second album, A Wild and Crazy Guy, selling more than a million copies, Martin's position as premiere American funny man was assured. In 1979 he clinched the crown when A Wild and Crazy Guy won a Grammy as the comedy album of 1978 and the National Association of Record Manufacturers award as the best-selling comedy album of 1978. He also appeared in a gloriously funny, all-too-short cameo role as a lederhosen-clad waiter in The Muppet Movie. His book, Cruel Shoes, was published in the summer of 1979 and quickly made the best-seller list.

Of course, Grammy-awarded platinum albums are not new to Martin. His first LP, Let's Get Small, achieved the same distinction, and Martin's loony, apolitical humor has appealed to audiences since he was a sixteen-year-old, billed as "Mouth and Magic," appearing at Disneyland's Golden Horseshoe Revue. Those early appearances led to his stint writing comic routines for the Smothers brothers' television series and "The Glen Campbell Good-Time Hour." After two weeks of that program he quit because he thought it was dumb and went on to write for Ray Stevens, Sonny and Cher, Pat Paulsen, John Denver, and Dick Van Dyke. Seeing others perform his material was frustrating. "I did a couple of summer shows and then I realized . . . I gotta get back to performing."

For several years Martin tried out his routines on the toughest audiences he could find—rock fans. He put his very life on the line working as an opener for rock acts, trying to break through the sullen

wall of inattention that met his attempts. In 1973 Martin moved to Santa Fe, where he lived with a girl friend for a year, and then settled in Aspen. He adopted his well-known white suit, swore he would never be an opening act again, and began to work clubs. By the end of 1975 he was packing them into San Francisco's popular Boarding House, and in the fall of 1976 national audiences saw him on a Home Box Office special and in his first guest-host appearance on "Saturday Night Live."

1978/79 Discography: Comedy Is Not Pretty

McFADDEN AND WHITEHEAD

Gene McFadden—Vocals

John Whitehead—Vocals

If ever a song was prophetically titled it's McFadden and Whitehead's infectious "Ain't No Stoppin' Us Now," one of the biggest-selling twelve-inch singles ever. Effervescent Whitehead and straight-man McFadden have known each other since they were three-year-old toddlers in the North Philadelphia ghetto. They've written more than two hundred songs together, many of them successful, but it wasn't until Philadelphia International released "Ain't No Stoppin' Us Now" that they attained a glittering peak as performers.

Their career has been studded with lucky breaks. In the tenth grade they formed a group called the Epsilons. One day, while McFadden was standing on a street corner holding some Otis Redding albums, Redding's bandleader approached and asked McFadden if he wanted to meet Redding. McFadden didn't have to be asked twice; that evening he and the Epsilons sang their hearts out for their hero, who asked them to be part of the Otis Redding Revue.

In 1969 McFadden and Whitehead were signed as performers by Kenny Gamble and Leon Huff, but their first few singles were not successful, and it looked as if their career was stalled at the start. But, feeling they could write songs as well as sing, they sat down together one evening and turned out "Back Stabbers," the first monumental hit for the O'Jays. Since that time McFadden and Whitehead have won more than twenty gold records and a number of Grammy nominations.

Although their songwriting career was flourishing, the duo wanted to record their own songs. Gamble and Huff were reluctant to turn them loose as singers again until their crackerjack producing job on Melba Moore's debut album convinced their bosses that the boys had finished their musical education. McFadden and Whitehead were given the opportunity to record, and, in addition to the smash of "Ain't No Stoppin' Us Now," McFadden and Whitehead, their soulful debut LP, became a top-twenty charter.

1978/79 Discography: McFadden and Whitehead

MEAT LOAF

Meat Loaf—Lead vocals

Jim Steinman—Piano

Karla Da Vito—Vocals

As befitting a man of his stature, Meat Loaf's first album, 1977's Bat Out of Hell, was a debut hit of gargantuan proportions. Sales of that roaring assault of unleashed rock and roll have now soared far past double-platinum. In 1979 the disk won the National Association of Record Manufacturers award for best-selling album by a new group (sharing that honor with albums by Toto, the Cars, and Gerry Rafferty). Hit singles from the album included the gold-winning ballad "Two Out of Three Ain't Bad," the dynamic "Hot Summer Night," and the classic teenage tale "Paradise by the Dashboard Light."

Kansas Courtesy Epic Records

The Kendalls Courtesy Ovation Records

Evelyn "Champagne" King Courtesy RCA Records

Kris Kristofferson Courtesy Columbia Records

Little River Band Courtesy Harvest Records

Nicolette Larson Courtesy Warner/Reprise

127

Kenny Loggins

Cheryl Lynn

Barbara Mandrell   **Chuck Mangione**   **Barry Manilow**

128

Steve Martin

Meat Loaf was born in Dallas into a family of gospel singers. Today he continues to sing just as hard as any revivalist preacher, throwing body and soul into every performance, sometimes collapsing after a show and requiring oxygen.

After touring with several West Coast bands and pulling out all stops as lead singer on Ted Nugent's blasting LP *Free for All,* he met writer/arranger/pianist Jim Steinman during "The National Lampoon Show," and the two found they worked together well. After a year of honing their act, they performed at Carnegie Hall, where their supercharged show rocked the sedate venue to its rafters. Todd Rundgren produced that first monumental album, which featured blond singer Ellen Foley on vocals. In Meat's live act, he and dark-haired Karla Da Vito generate sizzling sparks.

1978/79 Discography: *Bad for Good*

ZUBIN MEHTA

It's hard to believe that Zubin Mehta, conductor of one of the world's most respected orchestras, the New York Philharmonic, was encouraged by his father to abandon music and to study medicine. But for Bombay-born Mehta, who had been, as he puts it, "brainwashed with classical music from the cradle," medicine could never take the place of music. "Every time I sat down to write an exam or cut up a dog-fish," he recalls, "there I was with a Brahms symphony running through my head." So when he was sixteen, despite his father's fears that India held little promise for a musician captivated by Western music, he went to Vienna, where he absorbed everything he could learn about piano, string bass, composition, and—what was to become his deepest love—conducting.

Mehta's father can perhaps be excused for his negative attitude. As founder of the Bombay Symphony, if anyone was familiar with the problems a Western musician faced in India, it was he. But he hadn't counted on his son's determination or the love of music that he himself had implanted in Zubin, who began studying violin and piano when he was only seven and who was helping his father with the Bombay Symphony when he was eleven.

It was Mehta's determination and talent that led him, at the age of twenty-six, to his position as music director of the Los Angeles Philharmonic Orchestra, a job he held for fifteen years. He won the First International Conductors' Competition in Liverpool, England, in 1958; has performed or recorded in such a variety of places as the Salzburg Festival, the front line during the 1973 Middle East war, and at a southern California men's prison; conducted the London Royal Opera House production of *Die Fledermaus,* the first opera to be transmitted by satellite from Europe to the United States; and has conducted the Metropolitan Opera. In 1977 and 1978 he led the Los Angeles Philharmonic at the Hollywood Bowl in a series of laser-sliced concerts called *Music from Outer Space.* On September 24, 1978, he conducted the New York Philharmonic and Vladimir Horowitz in a performance of the Rachmaninoff Third Piano Concerto, telecast live from Lincoln Center by ABC television.

PAT METHENY

Pat Metheny was born into a musical family in rural Lee's Summit, Missouri, on August 12, 1954. Although his father and brother played the trumpet, Pat was inspired to pick up a jazz guitar by a dazzling Gary Burton Quartet concert. "My family was into band music, marches—John Sousa and that sort of thing," he recalls. "When the time came that I was getting into music, the guitar was the one instrument they didn't want me to play. So, being a rebellious fourteen-year-old, that was the one I definitely wanted to play."

Despite Pat's resistance to those early marches, his own invigorating compositions swing with the same brisk directness. On his first solo disk, the top jazz LP *New Chautauqua,* his sparkling playing brings together the improvisations of jazz with the bold rhythms of rock, fusing them wholeheartedly in a glide toward a new guitar idiom.

Pat's entire career has been marked by the same breezy ease as his music. Soon after he began playing in 1968, he won a *Downbeat* scholarship at the jazz magazine's National Stage Band Camp. Two years later he was teaching there. When he graduated high school in 1972, he applied to the University of Miami. A few months later, he was on the faculty there, teaching guitar. By the time he was twenty, only six years after the Gary Burton Quartet showed him his musical direction, Pat was a member of Burton's band, having already played with such jazz masters as Hubert Laws, Clark Terry, Louis Bellson, Paul Bley, and others. He toured Europe and the United States with Burton's group, appeared on three of his albums, and then recorded two disks as a leader: *Bright Size Life* and *Watercolors.*

He recently formed his own combo, the Pat Metheny Group, with co-composer and pianist Lyle Mays, bass player Mark Egan, and drummer Danny Gottlieb. Their first recording, the top-five jazz LP *Pat Metheny Group,* is a vivid and vital statement, combining electric and acoustic instruments in completely new ways.

1978/79 Discography: *Pat Metheny Group*
                       New Chautauqua

FRANK MILLS

With a tinkling, graceful melody called "Music Box Dancer," Canadian Frank Mills won the ears and hearts of the American public in 1979. The million-selling title song from the gold-selling album rocketed Mills to fame and fortune in the United States.

In Canada, Mills has been a successful and respected musician for years. When he graduated from Montreal's McGill Conservatory of Music he worked with a group called the Bells, who earned a Canadian gold single with their hit "Stay Awhile" and toured throughout Canada and into the United States. Although he enjoyed being part of the Bells, Frank wanted to record his own material and broke away from the band. His very first solo effort, "Love Me Love," earned a gold record in Canada and has become a classic MOR hit there. He also recorded his own version of "Poor Little Fool," which became another winner. As a songwriter, Mills shares his instinctive love of people with his audience. "I understand people," he explains. "I know their problems—they're no different from mine. I listen to them, I hear what they're saying, even when they don't say it out loud, and I understand." He has turned his understanding into eight albums of songs in just six years, combining his heavy recording schedule with personal appearances throughout North America, television guest spots on "American Bandstand," and composing for television and film including the score for the movie *Ski East.*

RONNIE MILSAP

"The only music I heard for the first six years of my life was country," explains Ronnie Milsap. "It's hard to get away from those early influences. I have played, and can play, any kind of music, but you must do what your heart feels is right, and to me, that's country." By following what his heart feels is right, Ronnie Milsap has achieved outstanding success in a breathlessly short time. In 1974, only two years after he had begun singing country music professionally, the Country Music Association voted him male vocalist of the year. They repeated the honor in 1976, and in the fall of 1977 Ronnie Milsap swept the awards, winning entertainer of the year, male vocalist of the year, and album of the year for his 1977 winner, *Ronnie Milsap Live.* His album *(I'm a) Stand by My Woman Man* won him a Grammy as the best male country vocalist in 1977, and in 1978 he won his first gold album with *It Was Almost Like a Song,* which also won him the Country Music Association's award for album of the year.

The blind musician, who attended the State School for the Blind in Raleigh, North Carolina, was a violin virtuoso by the age of seven, played the piano at eight, and had mastered the guitar by the time he was twelve. The school taught the classics, and while Milsap loved Bach and Mozart, he often sneaked away to pound out a little Jerry Lee Lewis or Elvis Presley, much to the dismay of school officials. Milsap was suspended more than once for blasting out hot licks instead of cool fugues. But the school finally realized there was no way to subdue Milsap's strong talent and encouraged him to form his own rock group with three fellow students. They called themselves the Apparitions and performed frequently at local high school and college assemblies.

Although Ronnie studied pre-law at Young-Harris Junior College in Atlanta and won a full scholarship to study law at Emory University, he gave it up for music. In 1966 he formed his own band who regularly appeared in clubs and colleges. In 1969 he and the band moved to Memphis where they experimented with all kinds of music at T. J.'s, a popular Memphis club. He hit with pop songs like "Denver" and "Loving You Is a Natural Thing," but he still wasn't satisfied with his creations. He finally realized it was country music that he wanted, and he and his wife moved to Nashville in the early 1970s. He signed with RCA Records, settled down to the country songs he loved best, and began churning out hits, starting with a two-sided smash "(All Together Now) Let's Fall Apart" and "I Hate You." This was followed by a firecracker string of country smashes, including "The Girl Who Waits on Tables," "Pure Love," "Please Don't Tell Me How the Story Ends," "Legend in My Time," "Daydreams About Night Things," and "Let My Love Be Your Pillow."

In 1979 his hit country singles included "Let's Take the Long Way Around the World," "Back on My Mind Again/Santa Barbara," and "Nobody Likes Sad Songs." He appeared in the NBC made-for-television movie "Murder in Music City" and on ABC's "Wide World of Sports/Harlem Globetrotter's Special."

EDDIE MONEY

Eddie Money projects a fierce will in his singing, a drive that propelled him from the Queens and Brooklyn street corners where he sang harmonies as a kid to the spotlight on national tours, television appearances, a top-ten single in "Two Tickets to Paradise," and two gold-winning albums—1978's *Eddie Money* and, his latest, *Life for the Taking.*

Although music was a vital part of Money's childhood, he initially followed in the footsteps of his grandfather and father, who were policemen. But life as one of New York's finest did not satisfy Money's ambitions, and after a year he decided that the call of the stage was too great to resist.

He moved to San Francisco, where he blasted out feverish, white-hot performances in bay area rock clubs. He formed his own band, called Eddie Money, and, as if singing alone could not contain his irrepressible energy, he occasionally took over keyboards, harmonica, or saxophone. In March 1977 he appeared in the play *Bakk Tracks,* a one man tour de force about a ninety-year-old former rock star who is the last remaining man on earth after the holocaust. Money's performance won critical praise and fueled his growing need to win such praise for his singing. He approached noted vocal coach Judy Davis, well known for her work with such stars as Frank Sinatra, Barbra Streisand, Sammy Davis, and Grace Slick. Davis saw his potential and agreed to take him on. Bill Graham, who also knows a star when he sees one, signed him as the first artist with Wolfgang Productions.
1978/79 Discography: *Life for the Taking*

ANNE MURRAY

With her warm smile, gentle manner, and rich voice, Anne Murray continues to shine brilliantly. In 1979 her radiant presence dominated award ceremonies, the television screen, radio playlists, and record counters, as one after another of her beautiful song interpretations hit the country, easy-listening, and pop charts.

She won a Grammy for best female vocal performance for "You Needed Me," 1978's top-five easy-listening and pop single. The achingly beautiful song was also named song of the year by the Academy of Country Music. *Let's Keep it That Way,* a platinum-winner, was 1978's best-selling album by a female country artist. Her 1979 LP, *New Kind of Feeling,* was a top-three country album and won her another gold disk. In 1979 every one of her songs became hits. "I Just Fall In Love Again" was a top easy-listening and country single, and "Shadows in the Moonlight" topped the easy-listening charts for weeks, was a top-three country single, and rose high on the pop charts as well.

But there was a time when Anne deliberately turned her back on her career. After the birth of her first son in August, 1976, she decided she wanted to be a full-time mother and abandoned the career she had begun with trepidation years before. Although she had sung all her life, played piano, and enjoyed all kinds of music, a career as a singer was the furthest thing from her mind. "Singing was something you did in the bathtub and around bonfires. I felt there was no security in singing," she recalls. She thought her family and friends were crazy when they urged her to leave teaching, but she finally allowed them to talk her into cutting *What about Me,* her first album, for a miniscule Canadian label.

Just as her friends had predicted, the album attracted the attention of a major record company. Capitol of Canada signed her up, and in 1970 her single "Snowbird" became an international smash. For the next few years her albums and singles won thousands of listeners. She was bitten hard by the performing bug, spending eight months of each year on the road. She turned out such hit songs as "He Thinks I Still Care," "Love Song," and "Danny's Song" and such albums as *Country, Highly Prized Possession,* and *Keeping in Touch.* She won five years' worth of Canada's Juno award as best female vocalist, a Grammy in 1974 for best performance by a female country singer (for "Love Song"), and has earned many international awards as well.

For Anne, 1979 was also a year of children. Not only did she give birth to a baby girl, Dawn Joann, on April 16, she also was national chairwoman for the Save the Children Fund in Canada and, at the end of 1978, recorded a Christmas album for children called *There's a Hippo in My Tub,* released in the United States as *Anne Murray Sings for the Sesame Street Generation.*
1978/79 Discography: *New Kind of Feeling*

N

WILLIE NELSON

Listening to the legendary Willie Nelson voice today, transforming every song it touches to gold or platinum, it's hard to believe that back in the 1950s Nashville pundits advised him he'd never make it as a singer. Nelson, however, knew they were wrong and set out to prove it, forging for himself an unequalled career as singer and songwriter, blazing a trail of powerhouse hits that grows more impressive with each passing year. In 1979 the beloved country star surpassed himself once again, easily topping his staggering achievements of the previous year. In 1979 not only did his 1978 LP *Stardust* reach the million copy mark, but *Willie and Family Live* was a gold-winning, number-one country album, hanging in near the top of the country charts for half the year. His album with Leon Russell, *One for the Road,* zipped up the country charts as did the first single from the album, "Heartbreak Hotel." "All of Me" and "Sweet Memories" were top-five country singles.

The music industry honored him by awarding him two Grammys, one for best country male vocal performance, for his version of "Georgia on My Mind." His rendition of Georgia's official state song is the one now used by the state. He and Waylon Jennings also won a Grammy for best country vocal performance by a duo or group for the 1978 song "Mamas Don't Let Your Babies Grow Up to Be Cowboys."

For Willie, these impressive achievements crown a career that began when he was a precocious ten-year-old, playing rhythm guitar for a Bohemian polka band in a tiny Texas town. After his marriage in 1950 he was faced with the reality of having to support himself, his wife, and daughter. He worked at a variety of odd jobs to feed and clothe his family, but music was his real love, and he sang and played whenever he got the chance.

In San Antonio he silver-tongued his way into a disk jockey job, which he performed skillfully, spinning well-chosen disks during the day. At night he performed in small clubs. He was inspired by the music he heard and found song lyrics and melodies flowing out of him.

Before long he made the move to Nashville, where he performed at a famed songwriters' hangout, Tootsie's Bar. Pamper Publishing signed him to write songs, and they were immediate hits. "Hello Walls" was a smash for Faron Young, and "Crazy" was a knockout success for Patsy Cline. "Night Life" and "Funny How Time Slips Away" were monsters for Ray Price, part-owner of Pamper Publishing and leader of Ray Price and His Cherokee Cowboys. Willie could only grin as song after song of his was performed by such greats as Aretha Franklin, Little Anthony and the Imperials, Stevie Wonder, Frank Sinatra, Elvis Presley, Perry Como, and many others. In 1973 he was named to the Hall of Fame by the Nashville Songwriters Association.

Although he loved songwriting, Willie chafed at what he felt was Nashville's limited definition of country. In the early 1970s he broke away from Nashville, a rift that was not healed until 1979 when he was at last named entertainer of the year by Nashville's powerful Country Music Association. In 1976 his singing career finally began to take off when The Outlaws, recorded with Waylon Jennings, Jessi Colter, and Tompall Glaser, became the first country album ever to sell a million copies. In 1978 he scored platinum with Waylon and Willie and Red Headed Stranger, while The Sound in Your Mind sold gold. From Stardust, a number-one country album for many weeks, came "Georgia on My Mind," and "If You Can Touch Her at All."

In 1979 Willie celebrated America's birthday with his Seventh Annual Willie Nelson Fourth of July Picnic in Austin, Texas.
1978/79 Discography: Willie and Family Live
                    One for the Road (with Leon Russell)

OLIVIA NEWTON-JOHN

The lovely blond Australian who first captured America's heart with her Grammy-winning version of "Let Me Be There" proved in 1979 that her fragile looks are deceptive. Battling a one-hundred-three-degree fever, she ignored her doctors' advice in true trouper style and appeared at the Academy awards presentation, singing her Oscar-nominated smash hit "Hopelessly Devoted to You." She paid for her courage, however, spending a week in the hospital, exhausted, frightened, and in pain.

Olivia's collapse may have been a result of her frenetic pace during 1978 when she traveled more than 200,000 miles, performing all over the world and touring to promote the movie Grease. She was also under the pressure of back and forth law suits between her and MCA, her record company, each claiming the other had failed to live up to certain contractual obligations. Olivia admits that she has always suffered intense stage fright before every performance, and, although she is better able to control that paralyzing fear, she is certain that years of stress have taken their toll on her body.

Olivia has always been devoted to music, even to the point of defying her parents when they asked her to stop performing. With Max Born, the Nobel-prize-winning physicist as a grandfather, and Professor Brin Newton-John, headmaster of Ormond College in

Melbourne for a father, Olivia was reared in a household where music was considered an enjoyable if frivolous pastime. When she and three school friends formed a group called the Sol Four, her parents asked that Olivia give up the quartet to devote more time to her schoolwork. In the time-honored tradition of teenagers everywhere, Olivia didn't listen.

When she was sixteen she won a trip to England, first prize in her very first talent contest. For the next two years she and Pat Carroll, another Australian, performed as a duo in cabarets and on many BBC television shows. Pat returned to Australia when her visa expired, but Olivia remained in England. As her first solo single she cut Bob Dylan's "If Not for You" and watched with delight as it became an international smash. Her next single, "Banks of the Ohio," was another blockbuster, winning her the English Silver Disk and the Australian Gold Disk.

Olivia's conquest of America was equally immediate. After winning her first Grammy as best country vocalist, for "Let Me Be There," in 1974 she swept up another Grammy for best pop female vocal performance, for "I Honestly Love You," which was also voted record of the year. The Country Music Association voted her top female vocalist of the year for that record also.

Since that spectacular beginning, Olivia has continued in stellar fashion with five platinum and three gold albums, one platinum and seven gold singles. In 1978 she starred in the movie Grease, and hit with three singles—"You're the One That I Want," "Hopelessly Devoted to You," and "Summer Nights"—from the film's soundtrack. In 1979 she scored with the gold-winning "A Little More Love" and the steamy "Deeper than the Night."
1978/79 Discography: Totally Hot

TED NUGENT

If you are what you eat Ted Nugent must eat nails and broken glass. Nothing softer could power the aggressive rock frenzy that snarls from his guitar, an unleashed dynamite charge that inspires his audiences to explosive responses. "If they ain't foaming at the mouth after ten minutes then I've screwed up," explains Ted, who's spent more than half of his thirty-one years blasting out twenty-one-gun salvos from rock stages and recording studios around the world.

A Detroit native, Ted was just fourteen when he became a member of a Detroit band, the Lords. At sixteen he formed the original Amboy Dukes; the group sweated through two hundred rowdy concerts a year for years, winning out of all that struggle two minor but legendary hits, "Baby Please Don't Go" and "Journey to the Center of Your Mind." Although midwestern audiences kept coming back for more, the Amboy Dukes' four albums were underpromoted and the band never achieved the national fame they lusted after.

In 1975, however, Ted woke up to the power of his own name. He dropped the Dukes, signed with Epic Records, and released one screamingly successful record after another, all gold-winners: Ted Nugent, Free-for-All, and Cat Scratch Fever. Double Live Gonzo, the first live album, was his first platinum-winner. It was followed by 1978's Weekend Warriors, also platinum. In 1979 his new LP, State of Shock, was an instant gold-winner. His brutal touring pace has slackened little. In 1977 he took his band of metal men to Europe, where he wiped out the British with his musical assaults. As he himself described Double Live Gonzo, in words that fit all of his music, "If you want something mellow, this ain't it."
1978/79 Discography: State of Shock

O

OAK RIDGE BOYS

Bill Golden—Vocals

Duane Allen—Vocals

Richard Sterban—Vocals

Joe Bonsall—Vocals

They've got it all, this dynamic quartet, in 1978 even winning the Country Music Association award as vocal group of the year, the first time in six years that award hasn't gone to the Statler Brothers. The association also named their back-up band top instrumental group of the year. The Academy of Country Music voted them top vocal group of the year and their 1978 album, *Y'All Come Back Saloon*, album of the year. At the end of 1978 "Cryin' Again" was a top-five country single, and in 1979 "Come On In" and "Sail Away" were top-five country singles, while their album *The Oak Ridge Boys Have Arrived* was a top-five country LP.

All this is pretty impressive for a band that lost $114,000 in 1975 and was so desperately in debt that they offered to sell their publishing companies to Johnny Cash. Cash pointed out to them that they would be very unhappy one day if they sold the rights to their songs and offered to lend them as much money as they needed. The band decided that if they could believe in their future as much as Cash did, they would make it.

The group dates back to the 1940s, when four singers called the Oak Ridge Quartet sang gospel songs for workers at the atomic energy plant in Oak Ridge, Tennessee. Although the current Oak Ridge Boys were not members of that original group, baritone Bill Golden joined the Quartet fourteen years ago; lead singer Duane Allen became part of the group thirteen years ago; and tenor Joe Bonsall and bass Richard Sterban became part of the group in 1971. This quartet continued to record gospel hits, and for many years they were extremely successful. But when their winning streak ended, it ended with a thud.

Their luck turned quickly, however, thanks to Johnny Cash and booking agent/manager Jim Halsey who saw them perform one night in 1975 and was swept off his feet by their spontaneous revivalist stage show, sex appeal, and complex vocal arrangements. Halsey immediately set to work to translate that onstage blaze onto vinyl. It was not an easy task. Halsey had to battle the pessimism of ABC Records executives, the initial reluctance of producer Ron Chancey, the need to forge a unique sound for the Boys, and their own resistance to a new musical idiom.

Halsey persisted, and finally the boys recorded "Y'All Come Back Saloon," which was a thunderous success. The album also was a smash, as was "You're the One," the album's second single. *Room Service*, their second outing, was a top-ten country charter and produced the number-one country single "I'll Be True to You." The boys closed 1978 by winning the award as best country group at Britain's famed Wembley Festival of Country Music. They made many top television appearances and toured as well. To add to their country success, in 1978 they won a Grammy for best traditional gospel performance, for "Just a Little Talk with Jesus."

1978/79 Discography: *The Oak Ridge Boys Have Arrived*

P

PAILLARD CHAMBER ORCHESTRA

One of the most durable classical best-sellers of the past two years is the *Pachelbel Kanon: Two Suites; Fasch: Two Symphonies*, performed by the renowned Paillard Chamber Orchestra. The album has been on the classical charts for more than 126 weeks. Under the direction of Jean-François Paillard, the ensemble has made more than 250 records, performs an average of 120 concerts a year, has won twenty major international record prizes, and consistently receives the highest praise from critics around the world.

Conductor and founder Paillard, a noted musicologist, studied with Igor Markevitch and is a winner of the first prize for conducting the National Conservatory in Paris. Since he brought together the thirteen-member orchestra in 1953, they have spearheaded the revival of seventeenth- and eighteenth-century music. Their luminous treatment of the baroque includes both well-known and long-neglected early French music. In addition, the orchestra performs a great deal of contemporary music, much of which is written especially for them by such composers as Marcel Landowski, Charles Chaynes, and Marc Carles.

PARLIAMENT—FUNKADELIC

Sixty-one thousand funkified Geepies wiggled in outrageous ecstasy as George Clinton, Doctor Funkenstein himself, led his crack musical henchmen in their headline appearance at 1979's twelve-hour World's Greatest Funk Festival. And although Parliament-Funkadelic's latest gold-winning album, *Motor Booty Affair*, didn't succeed in raising Atlantis and reconnecting the continents, it did add another gilded disk to the team's collection, a blinding array of gold and platinum that includes *Funkentelechy Vs. the Placebo Syndrome* and Funkadelic's 1978 LP, *One Nation Under a Groove*, both platinum.

For Clinton, the outrageously costumed King of Funk, coming up with continual toppers has been a challenge. To follow the smash success of 1978's outrageous Mothership Connection Tour, Clinton decided 1979 was a year to go deeper. The scenario for the Motor Booty Affair took his show underwater where dedicated funksters once again battled Sir Nose d'Voidoffunk and his evil sidekick, Rumpofsteelskin, this time bumping and jiving in the underwater Emerald City of Atlantis.

Events for Clinton were much more earthly back in the late 1950s, when out of a barbershop near Newark, New Jersey, grew a group called the Parliaments. After years of hard scrabbling, they finally cut a towering hit single for Revilot Records, 1967's smash boogie "(I Just Wanna) Testify." Revilot folded in 1968 and took the Parliament name as one of its assets. Clinton, who by this time had discovered the liberating ecstasies of LSD, staked out new territory in the black pride world of funk, renaming his band the Funkadelics and restructuring them into costumed zanies who always turned out a whomping good show. When the Parliament name again became available, shrewd businessman Clinton signed his band to Casablanca as the Parliaments and to Warner Brothers as Funkadelic.

Despite his onstage lunacy, Clinton was stung by the accusation of frivolity leveled at him in 1978 by Communicators with a Conscience. To prove his social conscience, in addition to donating fifty cents for every concert ticket sold in August and September 1978 in

Dallas, Chicago, St. Louis, and L.A. to the United Negro College Fund, he contributed an additional twenty-five cents to the fund for every concert ticket sold on his five-month 1979 national tour.
1978/79 Discography: *Motor Booty Affair*

DOLLY PARTON

She's a hot one, this blond bombshell. And every year, just as her career seems ready to peak, she rises even higher. In 1979 her 1978 platinum smash "Here You Come Again" won her a Grammy award for the best country female vocal performance. The Country Music Association named her entertainer of the year; *Billboard* voted her number-one female artist. Her biography, published by Grosset and Dunlap, was excerpted in *Good Housekeeping*. Her 1978 LP *Heartbreaker* sold gold; the title single was a number-one country song, as was "I Really Got the Feeling/Baby I'm Burning," which made forays into the pop and disco charts as well. Her European tour at the end of 1978 was a ringing success, and her song "You're the Only One," from her 1979 album *Great Balls of Fire,* was a number-four country single its second week on the charts. She and Carol Burnett sparkled in a sweet Valentine's Day treat called "Carol and Dolly in Nashville," shown on CBS-TV.

The only sour note in her year was the three-million-dollar lawsuit for breach of contract brought against her by Porter Wagoner, the country star who gave her her first chance back in 1967. Dolly had not been in Nashville long when Wagoner asked her if she would join his show, and she eagerly accepted. She had come to Nashville when she was eighteen with a cardboard suitcase full of songs and a heart full of hope. She had been singing and writing music since she was a little girl, and she was fiercely determined to succeed. With Porter Wagoner's group she shone, but she knew that with her voice and songwriting talent and her sensational looks played to the hilt she could easily burst out of the country compound and achieve success in the much vaster and more profitable pop world.

She cut her first solo album, the well-received *Jolene,* in 1974, but it wasn't until 1976 that she felt she was ready to go out on her own. She left Wagoner, fired the ragtag group of friends and relatives that made up her band, and cut her first pop-oriented album, *New Harvest, First Gathering,* which won the American Music award as 1977's favorite country album. The Academy of Country Music named her entertainer of the year. She won gold in 1978 with the title song from the platinum-winning *Here You Come Again,* which was a top-ten easy-listening and pop hit as well. *Best of Dolly Parton* became her second gold LP in June of 1978.
1978/79 Discography: *Great Balls of Fire*

LUCIANO PAVAROTTI

"God has kissed his vocal chords," wrote *New York Times* music critic Harold C. Schonberg of Luciano Pavarotti. But the unchallenged king of contemporary lyric tenors, who has appeared with every great opera house in the world, is adored for more than the beauty of his voice. Audiences cheer Pavarotti for his enormous warmth, boundless joy, and buoyant charisma.

Born in Modena, Italy, Pavarotti had a naturally beautiful tenor voice even as a child. But he didn't want to sing professionally, preferring the life of a teacher instead. After two years of teaching, he realized that he was denying himself great experience and pleasure by not using his voice, so, to the joy of his father, who had always urged Luciano to become an operatic tenor, young Pavarotti decided to sing.

After studying with two of the leading Italian vocal teachers, in 1961 he made his debut in *La Bohème*. His performance received thunderous applause, and for the next two years he sang throughout

Italy. By 1963 word of this remarkable young talent had spread through Europe. Luciano appeared as Edgardo in *Lucia di Lammermoor* in Amsterdam and then traveled with the role throughout the Netherlands. In Vienna and Zurich he raised bravos, and in September of 1963, when he substituted for an ailing star at London's Covent Garden, he thrilled the British with his performance in *La Bohème*. He began to broaden his audience even further, making his first television appearances and closing the year by singing in Spain, Poland, Hungary, and Czechoslovakia. Wherever he went, opera fans were mesmerized by his powerfully sweet voice and magnetic personality.

Throughout 1964 and 1965 Pavarotti continued to conquer the world. He made his North American debut in 1965 and then toured Australia with Joan Sutherland. Australian critics compared his voice favorably with the great historical tenors. When he returned home, he was awarded the Principessa Carlotta prize for his contribution to the arts by his hometown of Modena. By 1966 he was ready to take on the mantle of the world's foremost lyric tenor. Not only did he make his debut at Milan's famed La Scala, but Herbert von Karajan chose him to sing the tenor part in a performance of the Verdi *Requiem* to celebrate the hundredth anniversary of the birth of Toscanini. In 1966 the city of Parma, home of the world's most critical opera-goers, awarded him the prestigious Verdi d'Oro prize.

Since the mid-1960s Pavarotti's career has continually grown. In addition to *Lucia* and *La Bohème*, his repertoire includes the great tenor roles in *Tosca, Rigoletto, Il Trovatore, La Traviata, Ballo in Maschera, Turandot, Fille du Regiment,* and *La Favorita*. He won a Grammy in 1979 for best classical solo vocal performance on *Hits from Lincoln Center*. He released Puccini's *Tosca,* recorded with the National Philharmonic, and Mascagni's *Cavalleria Rusticana* with Leoncavallo's *Pagliacci* as his two 1979 albums.
1978/79 Discography: *Cavalleria Rusticana and Pagliacci*
                            Tosca

PEACHES AND HERB

The hottest duo of 1979 was Peaches and Herb, whose double-platinum album *2 Hot* sizzled to the top of the R & B charts and spun there for weeks, throwing off sparks with the singles "Shake Your Groove Thing" and the smash "Reunited." "Reunited" whisked to the top of the singles charts where it nested comfortably for weeks.

For old-timers the name of the duo is familiar, as Peaches and Herb had a string of monster hits in the mid 1960s, including "For Your Love," "Love Is Strange," "Close Your Eyes," "United," and "Let's Fall in Love." During that period, "Herb" was Herb Fame and "Peaches" was Francine Barker, former lead singer for a group called the Sweet Things. They broke apart when Francine decided to marry and retire from show business. Herb returned to his hometown of Washington, D.C., and became a policeman. Herb enjoyed serving his community, but whenever he was on duty at a concert or a show he was overcome by the desire to be back onstage. He finally decided to find a new partner and try again. After auditioning prospects for months, he found Linda Greene, a sparkling singer whose talents have helped make Peaches and Herb household words to a new generation of fans.
1978/79 Discography: *2 Hot*

TEDDY PENDERGRASS

In two short years Teddy Pendergrass established himself as a soulful solo singer with a highly demonstrative female following. Not only do his ladies shriek and wail at his concerts, they also go out and buy his records—one million each of 1977's *Teddy Pendergrass,* his first solo album, and 1978's *Life Is a Song Worth Singing,* and half a million of 1979's *Teddy,* snapped up as soon as it was released. His 1979 appearances, including a benefit concert at the California Institute for

Meat Loaf and Jim Steinman Courtesy Epic

McFadden and Whitehead

Zubin Mehta

Pat Metheny Courtesy ECM Records

Frank Mills Courtesy Polydor Records

Ronnie Milsap Courtesy RCA Records

Women at Chino, California, overflowed with turned-on women, charmed by sexy Teddy's magnetism.

Philadelphia born and raised, Teddy had already packed in a staggering amount of musical experience by the time he finished school. The precocious Pendergrass began singing when he was two, was an ordained minister at ten, and had taught himself the drums by the time he was thirteen. He sang in Philadelphia's McIntyre Elementary School Choir and the All-City Stetson Junior High School Choir. In his teens he sang lead with a local R & B group. He was so eager for a singing career that he let a smooth con man talk him into paying for a demo record. The fast talker took the record, Teddy's money, and, with tantalizing promises of a major recording contract, disappeared with both. Soured on singing for the moment, he became drummer for another Philadelphia group, the Cadillacs, which eventually became the back-up band for Harold Melvin and the Blue Notes.

During a 1970 tour of the West Indies, the Blue Notes split apart. They needed a new singer, and Teddy stepped in. "I Miss You," their first single with him as a vocalist, was a smash and was followed by a succession of gold-winning singles featuring his sensual, throaty voice. Blue Notes fans thrilled to "If You Don't Know Me by Now," "To Be True," "The Love I Lost," and "Bad Luck," from such albums as *To Be True* and *Wake Up Everybody*.

From his instantly successful solo albums came "I Don't Love You Any More," "You Can't Hide From Yourself," "The More I Get the More I Want," "Close the Door," and, 1979's winner, "Turn Off the Lights." 1978/79 Discography: *Teddy*

POCO

Rusty Young—Pedal steel guitar, vocals

Paul Cotton—Lead guitar

Charlie Harrison—Bass

Steve Chapman—Drums

Kim Bullard—Keyboards

Since 1968, when former Buffalo Springfield members Jim Messina and Richie Furay joined forces with Rusty Young, George Grantham, and Randy Meisner, the band named Poco has displayed more than a little pluck and tenacity. The band has gone through many changes since its first album, 1968's *Pickin' Up the Pieces*, was released but has always maintained its fresh, melodic, western style. In 1970 Paul Cotton was brought in to replace Jim Messina, and for the next eight years, through several more personnel changes, Cotton and Young remained the core of the band. In 1979, with Britishers Charlie Harrison and Steve Chapman on bass and drums and Kim Bullard on keyboards, Poco has reemerged with a new gold-winning album, *Legend*. From that album came a song called "Crazy Love" that soared to the top of the easy-listening charts and stayed at number one for more than six weeks. The song was also a pop hit, their first in eleven years and fourteen albums. They followed that with "Heart of the Night," another easy-listening winner.

Perhaps the spark is the result of the rock flavor added by Harrison and Chapman, who also have been playing together for eight years, recently having toured with both Leo Sayer and Al Stewart. Kim Bullard is from Atlanta and comes to Poco after touring the States with Crosby, Stills and Nash. All the new members have the common goal of wanting to be one band, not sidemen but a solid unit creating distinguished and distinguishable music. 1978/79 Discography: *Legend*

POINTER SISTERS

Ruth Pointer—Vocals

Anita Pointer—Vocals

June Pointer—Vocals

It's a long way from 1940's thrift-shop dresses to rolled-up pants, and it's even further from a childhood of church music to Bruce Springsteen's sexy song "Fire," but the Pointer Sisters have made both transitions in high style, talking fast, staying close, laughing through their career like adolescents at an amusement park.

Born of minister parents in Oakland, California, the four sisters (Bonnie has since left to pursue a solo career with Motown Records) spent their early childhoods singing in church; it wasn't until they were in high school that they discovered there was more to music than hymns. Combining their fine voices with such new (to them) and enormously appealing musical forms as rock and roll and rhythm and blues was a natural step, and in 1969 Bonnie and June billed themselves as the Pointers—a Pair and played small clubs and parties in the bay area. At the end of the year Anita joined them. Anita's boyfriend believed that their future lay in Texas and somehow convinced them that they could become famous there. The girls packed up and left for Houston, only to find two months down the road that the Lone Star state was far from the promised land.

Low on funds and too embarrassed to call on mom and dad to help, they frantically phoned producer David Rubinson, a friend of a friend, who kindheartedly sent them tickets home. When they returned, they plunged themselves into music, singing back-up for anyone who would hire them. In 1971 they signed to Atlantic Records and recorded two unsuccessful singles. After Ruth joined the group in 1972, Rubinson stepped in and moved them from Atlantic to Blue Note, where they recorded an album of 1940's songs done in their silky smooth harmonies. The album, *The Pointer Sisters*, supported by their stylish, tightly choreographed stage show, was a hit.

They made a few more records in the 1940s mold, but it wasn't their only musical persona. Anita and Bonnie won a Grammy award for best country song of 1974 with "Fairy Tale." After a few years the bloom was off the forties' rose, and their fifth album for Blue Note, *The Best of the Pointer Sisters*, slipped off the trade charts without making much headway. Disappointed, determined to resurrect their careers, they fired Rubinson at the beginning of 1977. During that year they toured; June and Anita cut some solo demos; Ruth had a baby; and Bonnie signed with Motown. In August 1978 June, Anita, and Ruth, ready to record together again, signed with producer Richard Perry's new label, Planet Records. Their first album for him was *Energy*, a rock and roll raver that won them a gold LP. The single from that album, their relentless version of Bruce Springsteen's "Fire," was a top-five gold-winning pop sizzler. 1978/79 Discography: *Priority*

JEAN-LUC PONTY

The shimmering electric violin work of Jean-Luc Ponty grew and ripened through a peculiarly rich musical combination of classical, jazz, and rock influences. Born in the Normandy region of France, Jean-Luc's father taught violin and his mother taught piano. Jean-Luc's classical music training began when he was five and continued until he was seventeen, when he graduated with the highest rating, Premier Prix, from the famed Conservatoire National Superieur de Musique in Paris. Jean-Luc quickly joined the Concerts Lamoureux Symphony Orchestra, but, after three years of playing classical music and jamming with friends at odd hours, he decided that improvisation was more enjoyable and chose to concentrate on jazz.

His first solo album, *Upon the Wings of Music*, was technically brilliant, and it wasn't long before Jean-Luc had absorbed the best of

Eddie Money   Courtesy Columbia Records

Anne Murray   Courtesy Capitol Records

Willie Nelson   Courtesy Columbia Records

Olivia Newton-John   Courtesy MCA Records

Courtesy Columbia Records

Courtesy Mariedi Anders Artist Management, Inc.

Ted Nugent   **The Oak Ridge Boys**   Courtesy MCA Records   **The Paillard Chamber Orchestra**

the European jazz scene. He began to drift out of that mainstream, moving away from unamplified jazz to the electronic dazzle of rock. In 1969 Ponty came to the United States, just when the jazz-rock fusion concept was beginning to bubble up in the West Coast musical stew. He appeared with Frank Zappa and the George Duke Trio at Thee Experience nightclub in L.A., where, as Michael Ross wrote in the Los Angeles *Herald Examiner*, "Jean-Luc Ponty sends electric chills up and down the walls of Thee Experience with a most exciting and personal blending of jazz and rock music."

Ponty returned to Europe, on fire with a thousand new musical ideas. He brought together his own group, the Jean-Luc Ponty Experience, and together they toured Europe and England. After working with Elton John for several years, Ponty moved to America, where he played with the Mothers of Invention throughout most of 1973 and then joined guitarist John McLaughlin's Mahavishnu Orchestra as solo guitarist. Since 1975 he has toured with his own band, appearing initially in clubs and colleges and then on a slew of television shows, including, in 1978, PBS's "Fiddlers Three" with Doug Kershaw and Itzhak Perlman, as well as "The Tonight Show," "The Merv Griffin Show," and "The Dinah Shore Show." With such breathtaking albums as *Aurora, Imaginary Voyage, Enigmatic Ocean, Cosmic Messenger*, and, his latest, *Jean-Luc Ponty: Live*, Ponty has carved a unique niche for himself.

1978/79 Discography: *Jean-Luc Ponty: Live*

CHARLEY PRIDE

Top country star Charley Pride began his career not in music but in sports, as a pitcher and outfielder for the Los Angeles Angels. He had always sung, however, and he spent his evenings playing guitar and singing in small Los Angeles clubs. In 1963, during his third year with the Angels, noted country star Red Sovine caught his act and urged Charley to take his voice to Nashville where he was sure the singer would succeed. Early in 1964 Pride heeded Sovine's advice and traveled to Nashville to cut some demo tapes for Chet Atkins.

Atkins, too, was excited by Charley's dramatic voice and signed him to RCA Records, where Charley's first single, "Snakes Crawl at Night," was a substantial country hit. Since then, Charley has been awarded country male vocalist awards by the Country Music Association, *Billboard, Cash Box* and the Music Operators of America. He's raked in three Grammies as both a country and gospel singer. He appears frequently on such television series as "The Lawrence Welk Show," "The Kraft Music Hall," "Hee-Haw," and "The Johnny Cash Show." Some of his recent hits include 1978's "Someone Loves You Honey" and "When I Stop Leaving (I'll Be Gone)" from his top-ten country LP *Somebody Loves You Honey*. In 1979 he scored with the number-one country single "Where Do I Put Her Memory?" as well as "You're My Jamaica."

SUZI QUATRO

All it took was the shrewd eye of British starmaker Mickie Most to lift young Suzi Quatro from the relative obscurity of her all-girl group Cradle to international pop stardom. Detroit-born Suzi and her siblings had learned music at their father's knee. Jazz bandleader Art Quatro gave all his children the opportunity to play in the Art Quatro Trio, where Suzi learned drums, piano, and guitar. She formed her first rock group with her sisters when she was fourteen, calling the band the Pleasure Seekers.

They eventually changed the name to Cradle, and it was Cradle that Mickie Most caught one fateful night in a small-time Detroit dance hall. The audience was wild about Suzi, and Most asked her to look him up if she ever decided on a solo career. Cradle broke up soon after that meeting, and Suzi took off for London, where she signed to Most's RAK Records. Suzi wrote her first single, "Rolling Stone," but it didn't click. Most brought in successful songwriters Nicky Chinn and Mike Chapman, who created a string of aggressive pop stingers that topped the British charts and sold like gangbusters. They included "Can the Can," "48 Crash," "Daytona Demon," "Devil Gate Drive," and "The Wild One." Suzi's image was rough and rebellious, and England, Europe, Australia, New Zealand, and Japan adored it, jamming her concerts and tuning in to her television specials.

Despite two 1974 American tours, Suzi didn't make it in the States until she was chosen to play the role of rock star Leather Tuscadero on "Happy Days." Leather was originally scheduled to appear in only a special two-part episode, but audiences loved Suzi so much that Leather became a regular. In 1979, Suzi had her first American record hit as well, striking gold with the winsome song "Stumblin' In," a top-five easy-listening and pop charter.

1978/79 Discography: *If You Knew Suzi*

Suzi and Other Four Letter Words

QUEEN

Freddie Mercury—Vocals, keyboards

Brian May—Guitar, vocals

Roger Taylor—Drums, vocals

John Deacon—Bass

According to Queen's touring contract, pinball machines must be backstage at every concert. They also take a full-size pool table with them on the road. They also carry a reputation as the seventies' most varied and melodic heavy metal band, a reputation they've carefully forged since 1971, when Freddie Mercury, Brian May, and Roger Taylor, who had been playing together since 1970, added bass player John Deacon and set themselves the task of creating a show that combined visual flash with high-decibel music. When they felt they were ready, they approached Elektra Records with their polished presentation; Elektra eagerly signed them, releasing *Queen* in 1973. From it came the two smash singles "Keep Yourself Alive" and "Liar," propelling the album to gold sales.

Queen made a monumentally successful tour of England, cut *Queen II*, and then, in 1974, toured America for the first time. The tour was cut short when Brian May became seriously ill, but back in England the band regrouped and turned out their blistering LP *Sheer Heart Attack*, which contained "Killer Queen," a top-ten single. In 1975 they attempted their most ambitious single, a complicated six minute tour de force called "Bohemian Rhapsody," which became their biggest international hit up to that time. It helped *A Night at the Opera*, its parent album, achieve platinum sales. Late in 1976 the album *A Day at the Races* spawned two more smash singles, "Somebody to Love" and "Tie Your Mother Down."

Their fame continued to grow in 1977, when they made a massive tour of the United States. *News of the World* was declared platinum early in 1978. A short time later, "We Are the Champions," the album's smash single, also won platinum. The New York Cosmos soccer club adopted it as their theme song.

At the end of 1978 the band released *Jazz*, which included a titillating, full-color poster of fifty-five young, nude women riding bicycles in a race held in England's Wimbledon Stadium, a race organized for the sole purpose of providing the picture. Although the attractive poster certainly did nothing to diminish sales, it was the high-energy rock and roll on the album that drove it to instant platinum.

In 1979 Queen toured Spain in February and March and released *Live Killers*, a sizzling live recording of such Queen chestnuts as

"Death on Two Legs," "Bicycle Race," "Dreamers Ball," "Love of My Life," and "39."
1978/79 Discography: *Jazz*
Live Killers

R

EDDIE RABBITT

The dark, handsome, bearded singer is tickled pink when audiences of young girls scream and wildly rush the stage. As he described one concert to *Chicago Sun-Times* reporter Mary Ellen Moore, "We couldn't hear what we were playing, it was almost like a Beatles concert, the noise was incredible ... I dig when girls do that....They turn me on."

For Rabbitt, success is still new and tastes as sweet as can be. Since 1973 he's had a firecracker string of eight country hits; his latest, the title single from the vastly popular Clint Eastwood movie *Every Which Way But Loose* was a powerful country winner and top-thirty pop charter as well. "Suspicions," another pop crossover, released in June of 1979, followed easily in the number-one footsteps of such songs as "Forgive and Forget," "Drinking My Baby Off My Mind," "Two Dollars in the Jukebox," "Rocky Mountain Music," "I Can't Help Myself," "We Can't Go on Living Like This," and "Heart's on Fire." His 1978 LP *Variations* was on the country charts for more than a year.

But Eddie wasn't born with a silver guitar in his hands. Unlike almost every other top country music name, Rabbitt was not born in a tiny backwoods town but in Brooklyn, New York. East Orange, New Jersey, where he was raised, is a considerable population center compared with the miniscule dots on the map that spawned most of today's country superstars. However, the twang of country was brought into young Rabbitt's otherwise urban life by Boy Scout leader Tony Schwickrath, a former country singer who taught Rabbitt to play guitar.

Rabbitt took to country music as though he had been born in the mountains of Tennessee, and as soon as he graduated high school he began playing the country bar circuit in New Jersey. He soon realized that this was no way to become a country star, so he scraped together some money and took a Greyhound bus to Nashville, where he took the cheapest, closest lodgings he could find.

Sitting one night in his shabby, rundown room, he wrote the wry song "Working My Way Up to the Bottom," which he sold to singer Roy Drusky. It became a hit, and Rabbitt found himself with a steady songwriting gig, earning a magnificent $37.50 a week plus royalties, which, alas, didn't amount to much. When he wasn't writing, he added pleasure to his meager days by hanging out in bars with a congenial group of other young unknowns, including Kris Kristofferson, Billy Swan, and Larry Gatlin. Like them, Eddie was determined to hang in until his break came.

Although he penned hits for the likes of Elvis Presley and Ronnie Milsap, it wasn't until the mid-1970s that Elektra Records producer David Malloy approached Rabbitt and signed him to sing for Elektra's fledgling country division. From then on it was one hit after another. In 1979 Rabbitt slowly began to make the move to headline performances. His first engagement at the Sahara Tahoe was an SRO smash. To honor that appearance, the Nevada/California border town of Stateline changed its name to Loveline, the title of Rabbitt's fifth album. He also appeared in Bloomingdale's, New York City's most chic department store, at a $1,000-a-plate charity benefit introducing designer Ralph Lauren's line of western clothes.
1978/79 Discography: *Loveline*

JEAN-PIERRE RAMPAL

"The first thing you think of when you say 'Jean-Pierre' is a smile, is a kind of bouncy, jouncy radiance that comes out of the man. ... There's always this almost love of life, this enjoyment of every second, this kind of ecstasy that one is alive and I think that also describes his music making." With this loving tribute to premier flutist Jean-Pierre Rampal, violinist Isaac Stern voices feelings with which millions of listeners all over the world agree. Critics have praised him with such descriptions as a poet, the flute king, the greatest living exponent of the flute, a paragon among flutists.

He is unquestionably the twentieth century's greatest flutist, having mastered every major classical work for the instrument and having recorded the mesmerizing Claude Bolling work *Suite for Flute and Jazz Piano*, a classical best-seller for more than two years. All his recent recordings, including *In Concert, Three Concertos for Two Flutes, Greatest Hits, Sakura, Japanese Melodies for Flute and Harp*, and *Rampal*, have been classical best-sellers, and several of his recordings have won the coveted Grand Prix du Disque. The appeal of his exquisite playing is universal, young and old alike responding to the music he makes. At Lincoln Center's Mostly Mozart concerts, where he made his conducting debut in the early 1970s, Avery Fisher Hall is always overflowing when he is on the podium. He has also conducted the San Francisco Symphony, the Los Angeles Philharmonic, the St. Louis Symphony, and orchestras in Europe and Japan.

Surprisingly, Rampal did not begin playing the flute until he was nearly thirteen years old. Although his father, Joseph Rampal, had long been a professor of the flute at the Marseilles Conservatory, he didn't want his son to be a professional musician and resisted Jean-Pierre's pleas to learn the instrument. Jean-Pierre's mother wanted her son to be a doctor and was afraid that flute lessons would lead him to ignore medicine. Finally, however, only because the enrollment in Joseph's flute class was small one year, he agreed to let Jean-Pierre be his student.

After being denied his desire for years, Jean-Pierre plunged into the study of the flute with passion. Nothing else existed for him, and at the end of two years he won first prize in flute from the Marseilles Conservatory. But he kept to his medical studies and graduated from the University of Marseilles in 1941. He abandoned his medical career when he was called up for service during the German occupation of France. He escaped and hid in Paris, where he studied at the Paris Conservatory, graduating with first prize in flute in a mere five months.

After the war, Rampal played first flute with the Paris Opera and began the then revolutionary practice of giving solo flute recitals. He and prize-winning harpsichordist Robert Veyron-Lacroix met at the conservatory and joined forces, performing and recording together for years. At the conservatory Rampal also met oboist Pierre Pierlot, with whom he organized the French Wind Quintet. In 1958 he toured America and Canada for the first time and now tours North America four months of each year, spending the rest of the year recording, touring other parts of the world, and relaxing in his Corsican villa with his beloved wife, Françoise, his children, and his grandchildren.
1978/79 Discography: *Rampal*
Japanese Melodies for Flute and Harp

CHARLIE RICH

Country rocker Charlie Rich scored at the end of 1978 with "On My Knees," a number-one country duet with singer Janie Fricke. In 1979 he hit the top five of the country charts again with "I'll Wake You Up When I Get Home." The top of the charts is not a new place for the Silver Fox, a two-time Grammy winner who pulled in his awards for 1973's smash "Behind Closed Doors," which was named best country song and earned him the title of best country male vocalist. The single sold gold and the album of the same name won platinum. From the album came his second gold-winning song, "The Most Beautiful Girl."

Although Charlie is now at the top, having forged his own rousing combination of rock and country, it took him a long career to get there. When he was fourteen he was already playing with local bands near his tiny hometown of Colt, Arkansas, and when he was eighteen he worked at refining his keyboard technique at the University of Arkansas. After college he joined the air force and put together the Velvetones, an R & B and jazz group that belted out forceful music on their own weekly television program in Oklahoma.

After the air force, it was back to farming and playing in local clubs to support his family. He wasn't terribly ambitious for great stardom at that time, but he was inspired by his wife, Margaret Ann, herself the author of a handful of country hits, who persuaded him to cut a demo. When Sam Phillips of Sun Records heard the tape he recognized Charlie's flashes of brilliance and steered the singer/piano player toward a harder rocking sound. In 1958 that direction paid off, and Charlie enjoyed his first hit with the song "Lonely Weekends."

A long dry spell followed, and in 1965 Charlie switched to Smash Records, where he teamed with producer Jerry Kennedy, the man who had injected new life into Jerry Lee Lewis's sagging career. Late in 1965 that collaboration paid off for Charlie too, as he turned out the top-seller "Mohair Sam" and followed it quickly with his classic "Big Boss Man."

It wasn't until 1973 that he made his big breakthrough with "Behind Closed Doors"; in 1975 he won gold with his album *Very Special Love Songs*. Another great favorite of his fans is the single "Rollin' with the Flow."

KENNY ROGERS

In 1979 the country singer with the platinum touch was unquestionably Kenny Rogers. As a songwriter and performer he's on a hot streak that began in 1977 with the stunning country and pop success of his song "Lucille" and shows no signs of slowing down. In 1979 he won a Grammy for best country song, for "The Gambler," his number-one country chart winner. The Academy of Country Music named him entertainer of the year and for the second year in a row voted him the top male vocalist. He and Dottie West were named duo of the year by the Country Music Association; his album *The Gambler* was the number-one country album from the beginning of February to the end of June, selling more than a million copies. His other singles, "Anyone Who Isn't Me Tonight" and "All I Ever Need Is You" (with Dottie West), topped the country singles charts, and "She Believes in Me" was a country, easy-listening, and pop smash. His album with Dottie West, *Classics,* was a number-three country album. In addition to his recording and performing successes, Kenny coauthored *Making it With Music*, a clear and complete guide to the challenges and potential pitfalls that await the neophyte musician.

Of course, Kenny's been on a hot streak since the very beginning of his career, when the Scholars, a high school band he organized, cut a single called "Crazy Feeling," a million-seller in the early sixties. Kenny went on to sing with the Bobby Doyle Trio and then the New Christy Minstrels. In 1967 he began singing with a new group called the First Edition, who smashed immediately with an ironic commentary on states of altered consciousness called "Just Dropped In to See What Condition My Condition Was In." He and the First Edition stayed together through a string of seven number-one hits, years of touring, and their own television series, "Rollin," but in the mid-seventies Kenny decided he had been a group member long enough. As he puts it, "I guess I always had it in the back of my head that I would be a solo performer. Maybe that's why I always stood in front or apart when I was with groups."

His first single as a solo performer, "Love Lifted Me," and the album of the same name, made inroads on the country charts, but Kenny really hit it big in 1977 with the smash success of his invigorating waltz "Lucille." That country and pop gold-winner earned him an armload of awards. It propelled the album *Daytime Friends* to gold and won him a Grammy for best country vocal performance, the single of the year award from the British Country Music Association, the American Music award for favorite country single, the American Country Music Association awards for single and song of the year, and the Academy of Country Music awards for record and song of the year. The Academy also gave *Daytime Friends* the top prize of album of the year.

In 1978 his *Ten Years of Gold* became his first platinum album. He won gold with *Love or Something Like It,* and his album with Dottie West, *Every Time Two Fools Collide,* also rose high on the country charts.

In 1979 he debuted at the Versailles Room in the Las Vegas Riviera, where he roused audiences with a slick, polished combination of rockers and ballads. He toured in March with Dottie West and the Oak Ridge Boys and appeared on his own television special in April.

1978/79 Discography: *The Gambler*
Classics (with Dottie West)
Kenny

ROLLING STONES

Mick Jagger—Vocals, guitar

Keith Richards—Guitar, vocals

Ron Wood—Guitar

Bill Wyman—Bass

Charlie Watts—Drums

For seventeen years now the core quartet of Mick Jagger, Keith Richards, Bill Wyman, and Charlie Watts, joined by a small, select succession of semipermanent guitarists and occasional sidemen, have been turning out flaming rock classics. Such pile-drivers as "Satisfaction," "Get Off My Cloud," "Let's Spend the Night Together," "Paint it Black," "Jumpin' Jack Flash," "Sympathy for the Devil," "Street Fightin' Man," "Honky Tonk Woman," "Midnight Rambler," "Brown Sugar," "It's Only Rock 'n' Roll," "Miss You" and occasional ballads such as "Ruby Tuesday" and "Midnight Mile," sound perennially fresh.

Throughout the 1960s the Stones were black to the Beatles' white, revelling in their reputation as Britain's bad band, taking drug busts and outrage in stride. Perhaps, however, they were more shaken than they cared to admit by two shocking events that climaxed the sixties for them. One was the never fully explained drowning of guitarist Brian Jones, who had been with them since the beginning and who was found dead in his pool on July 3, 1969, less than a month after he left the band. The other was the murder of a black concertgoer, not fifty feet from the stage where the Stones were performing at California's jammed Altamont Speedway. Jagger's ineffective pleas to the audience to cool it are unforgivingly captured in the Maysles brothers' film *Gimme Shelter*.

Although the Stones produced two more intense albums, *Sticky Fingers* and *Exile on Main Street*, their next three LPs, *Goat's Head Soup, It's Only Rock 'n' Roll*, and *Black and Blue*, did not measure up to their earlier works. A tour of the United States in 1975 suffered from lackluster performances; Richards' heroin bust raised the unthinkable picture of the Stones without him. By the end of 1975 the band was in a bad slump, and whispered rumors that they were finished ran rampant through the music world.

However, a 1976 tour of Europe, climaxing in six blistering performances at London's cavernous Earl's Court, was a resounding success. Their 1977 shows in Toronto's 350-seat El Mocambo Club almost blasted that venue into orbit, and in 1978 they satisfied themselves and their American fans by playing small halls as well as vast arenas throughout the country. Their eerie disco single "Miss You" swooped instantly from record stores to a million turntables across the country, and *Some Girls*, the album it came from, was also a million-seller.

In 1979 the best news for the Stones was the dropping of drug charges against Keith Richards, who spent part of the year on the road with Ron Wood, Ian McLagan, Stanley Clarke, Ziggy Modeliste, and Bobby Keyes, an aggregation called the New Barbarians.

LINDA RONSTADT

From 1964 to 1979, the sensational career of Linda Ronstadt, the beautiful singer from Tucson, Arizona, scaled one height after another. In 1979 she made extramusical headlines with her on-again, off-again romance with California Governor Jerry Brown, frustrating photographers by insisting on a modicum of privacy during a mid-spring African jaunt. Although there were strong rumors that the two would marry in Kenya, they returned separately.

Despite cavils from critics who wished she would stop reworking rock and roll classics, her late 1978 album *Living in the USA* was her fifth platinum plus, a top-five country and pop disk from which came her hit versions of "Ooh, Baby, Baby," "Just One Look," and the title track. She was voted favorite female singer in Dig It Radio Broadcasting's Rock Radio awards and she scooped up *Billboard's* awards as number-one pop female singles artist, top album artist, top record artist, and top vocalist. She closed 1978 with two sensational sold-out shows at Los Angeles's Forum, where she was joined by Smokey Robinson in "Ooh, Baby, Baby," the song he co-wrote.

From the beginning, Linda's powerful voice and tenacity have fueled her nonstop ride to the top. From 1964, when she formed the Stone Poneys and enjoyed the success of "Different Drum" the lone smash out of three albums, she was determined to be more than just another girl singer with a group. In 1969 she left the Poneys to go out on her own. *Hand Sown, Home Grown,* her first solo album for Capitol records, was full of country songs and began attracting fans to Linda's meltingly rich voice and sultry stage presence. Her second album, 1970's *Silk Purse,* contained her first solo hit, "Long, Long Time," which earned her her first Grammy award nomination.

By 1971 her image had begun to change. She put together a band that included incipient Eagles Glenn Frey, Don Henley, and Randy Meisner; those three added a charging rock pulse to *Linda Ronstadt,* her third album. *Don't Cry Now* was her first album for her new label, Asylum, and her touring schedule began to heat up as the album began to spread the Ronstadt voice and name.

The turning point in her career came in 1974 when Peter Asher became both her manager and record producer. Her first album with him, *Heart Like a Wheel,* was a platinum-winner, containing the singles "You're No Good" and "I Can't Help It If I'm Still in Love With You," which won her a Grammy for best female country vocal.

From that point on hits exploded from her in emphatic versions of such songs as "Heat Wave," "That'll Be the Day," "Blue Bayou," "It's So Easy," "Poor, Poor Pitiful Me," and "Tumbling Dice," and "I Never Will Marry," from her unbeatable platinum-winning LPs *Prisoner in Disguise, Hasten Down the Wind, Linda Ronstadt's Greatest Hits,* and *Simple Dreams.*

ROSE ROYCE

Kenji Chiba Brown—Lead guitar, vocals

Kenny "Captain Gold" Copeland—Trumpet, vocals

Gwen Dickey—Lead vocals

Freddie Dunn—Trumpet

Henry "Hammer" Garner—Drums, vocals

Lequeint "Duke" Jobe—Bass guitar, vocals

Michael Moore—Saxophone, vocals

Mike Nash—Keyboards

Terral "Powerpack" Santiel—Percussion, vocals

They slammed onto the funksoul scene with a thunderous jet roar, a mighty eight-man, one-woman aggregation who scored platinum with their first two albums, *Rose Royce* and *In Full Bloom,* had number-one soul singles with "Do You Dance, Part One" and "Ooo Boy," and racked up awards by the wagonload in 1976. *Cash Box* voted them number-one new R & B group of the year and number-one pop group of the year; they won the Golden Disco award as the number-one new group of the year. For the soundtrack from the movie *Car Wash* they won the Grammy for best original soundtrack as well as awards for the best soundtrack of the year from the Cannes Film Festival and from *Record World. Record World* also named them both the number-one top vocal group and number-one top new vocal group of the year.

Although they first came together as Rose Royce in 1976, the band members already had years of experience. At the beginning there were two bands, with Kenji Brown, Duke Jobe, and Victor Nix in one and Henry Garner, Kenny Copeland, Freddie Dunn, Michael Moore, and Terry Santiel in the other. When the Garner group invited the Brown group to a rehearsal, the two bands hit it off and have played together ever since. Calling themselves Total Concept, they won raves as backup artists for the Temptations, Edwin Starr, and Yvonne Fair. Making music was terrific, but they soon felt they wanted to be more than merely background for bigger stars.

Fate stepped in in the form of hit-maker Norman Whitfield, then one of Motown Records' stellar producers. He saw that the band could have a considerable future as headliners and took them under his wing for polishing. They began to tour and realized their need for a strong female voice at about the same time that Gwen Dickey came west to audition for another band on Whitfield's newly formed label. Rose Royce loved Gwen's arresting stage presence and soulful voice and signed her on. The last change in the group lineup came when keyboard player Victor Nix took sick after completion of the first album and Michael Nash joined to replace him.

At the end of 1978 they had a top-five soul LP with *Rose Royce Strikes Again* and a top-five soul single with "Love Don't Live Here Any More."

1978/79 Discography: *Rose Royce Strikes Again*

DIANA ROSS

Throughout her entire life Diana Ross has set herself one challenge after another, meeting every one with the same steely, street-toughened will and determination. She grew up a poor, skinny kid on the harsh streets of Detroit. When she wasn't playing baseball with a local boys' team, she would sing with classmates Mary Wilson and Florence Ballard. Their own enjoyment of the music and the excited reactions of listeners convinced the teenage trio that they were no ordinary high school singing group. Under the leadership of Diana they set their sights on a professional career, polishing their act and then auditioning for Berry Gordy, who was just beginning Motown

Parliament

Dolly Parton

Luciano Pavarotti

Peaches and Herb

Teddy Pendergrass

Poco

Records. Gordy was as excited by their potential as their friends and relatives, and he hired them on the spot to be a back-up group for some of Motown's already established stars, such as Marvin Gaye and Mary Wells.

As the Supremes, the girls toured for the first time as soon as they had graduated high school. Audiences loved them, and "Where Did Our Love Go?" their first single, zipped to the top of the pop and soul charts. That was just the beginning. Throughout the 1960s the Supremes were synonymous with memorable songs, their tight, sinuous harmonies sparking such unforgettable hits as "Baby Love," "Stop! In the Name of Love," and "Come See About Me."

The girls could do no wrong. It looked as though their future would be one sensational smash after another; and then Diana Ross stunned the music world by announcing she was leaving the group. The usual cynics waited for her to fall on her face, but they hadn't counted on the Ross superdrive.

She starred in the first of her solo TV specials, "Diana," which won a huge viewing audience and excellent reviews. She headlined in Europe, Las Vegas, and New York, working the cabaret circuit as well as major arenas, and won the same adulation for her concerts. In the mid-1970s she appeared in her first film, *Lady Sings the Blues*, the story of Billie Holiday, which won her an Academy Award nomination. In 1976, she appeared in the film *Mahogany*, and the poignant song from that movie, "Do You Know Where You're Going To?" won an Academy award nomination.

Throughout 1977 and 1978 Diana's career surged along full throttle. She scored with her albums *An Evening with Diana Ross* and *Ross* and the singles "Baby It's Me," "Gettin' Ready for Love," and "You Get It." She starred as Dorothy in *The Wiz*, and in 1979 took a fifty-piece orchestra, thirteen singers, and nine dancers out to twenty-eight cities in a splashy show called Diana Ross Tour '79, which won raves from critics and cheers from audiences. She also had a disco hit in 1979 with "The Boss," from the album of the same name.

1978/79 Discography: *Ross*
The Boss

S

SANTANA

Carlos Santana—Guitar, vocals

Greg Walker—Lead vocals

Graham Lear—Drums

Chris Rhyne—Keyboards

Raul Rekow—Congas, bongos

Armando Peraza—Percussion

Pete Escovedo—Timbales

David Margen—Bass

Chris Solberg—Rhythm guitar

It's been ten years since the exotic, haunting rhythms of *Santana* and *Abraxas*, led by the authoritative, crystalline guitar of Carlos Santana, awed a generation of rock fans with their sizzling power.

Born in Autlan, Mexico, in 1947, Carlos Santana was tempered in the steamy cauldron of Tijuana's red-light district, where he spent his late teens playing guitar in sleazy night clubs, one eye on his strings, the other on his rowdy, sometimes murderous, audiences. At the height of the flower-power movement, he moved to San Francisco,

where he was discovered and promoted by starmaker Bill Graham. He was something very special in those psychedelic days, an unheard of blend of insistent Latin rhythms and ultrasophisticated guitar.

In 1972, after three very successful albums, Carlos became a disciple of Sri Chinmoy, a noted spiritual guru. He also began his experimentation with more cerebral music, recording *Love, Devotion, and Surrender* with John McLaughlin and *Illuminations* with Alice Coltrane. Santana's fans were not prepared for such sounds, and his popularity waned in the United States. Although he consistently drew huge crowds in Europe, Australia, New Zealand, and Japan, his American appeal remained low until 1976, when he recorded *Amigos*, a return to rhythmic, accessible music. He continued in this direction on his latest albums, 1977's *Festival* and *Moonflower*, with its stinging version of the Zombies' 1965 song, "She's Not There," and 1978's *Inner Secrets*, which won gold certification at the end of 1978.

The year 1979 has seen Santana touring the United States, winning the title musician of the year from San Francisco's bay area artists, and releasing *Devadip*.

1978/79 Discography: *Inner Secrets*
Devadip

RENATA SCOTTO

Tough, determined, never willing to settle for second best, Renata Scotto and her thrilling voice have knifed their way to the top of the bitterly competitive operatic world. Perhaps the greatest singing-actress in opera today, Miss Scotto has sung in nearly all the great opera houses of the world and for the past three years has reigned as the Metropolitan Opera's *prima donna assoluta*.

Born in Savona, Italy, Miss Scotto began studying voice, piano, and violin when she was fourteen. Two years later she decided to concentrate on singing and moved to Milan, where she could study with such great teachers as Ghirardini, Merlini, and finally with Mercedes Llopart, who transformed Scotto from a mezzo-soprano to a soprano. In 1953 Scotto won a national competition which resulted in her formal debut at Milan's Teatro Nuovo.

The next season she triumphed at La Scala in the secondary role of Walter in Catalani's *La Wally*. But when the company offered her other supporting roles, she chose instead to perform at smaller Italian houses where her glorious voice guaranteed her the lead. Between 1954 and 1957 she starred in *L'Elisir d'Amore*, *La Bohème*, and *Don Giovanni* in opera houses throughout Italy. Her big chance came in 1957 during the La Scala tour to the Edinburgh Festival; called on to replace Maria Callas in Bellini's *La Sonnambula*, she won raves from the critics.

During the 1960s Scotto performed throughout the world. She made her Covent Garden debut in what has become her signature role, that of Cio-Cio San in Puccini's *Madama Butterfly*. Eight days later she brought the house down with her vocal pyrotechnics as Mimi in *La Bohème*. She made her American debut during the 1960 season at the Lyric in Chicago. On October 13, 1965, she debuted at the Metropolitan Opera in *Madama Butterfly*, a bountifully praised performance.

While maintaining a performing schedule that regularly includes appearances with the San Francisco, Miami, Cincinnati, Dallas, and Houston operas as well as appearances in Rome, Parma, Paris, and Florence, her career continues to be studded with firsts. In June 1975 her Met concert performance of *Madama Butterfly* in Central Park attracted an estimated 100,000 listeners, the largest audience in the history of the Met's park concerts. In 1976 she became the first Metropolitan Opera soprano to sing all three heroines in Puccini's *Il Trittico*. In 1977 she starred in *La Bohème* on the first live television broadcast from Lincoln Center, a performance that won television's prestigious Peabody Award. Her performance on the Met's recording of *Otello* helped make that album a classical best-seller. Her performance in *Adriana Lecouvreur* helped that record win *Stereo Review's* record of the year award, and a 1978 recording of *Butterfly* with Lorin Maazel conducting won the Grand Prix du Disque in 1978.

During the 1979–80 season the tireless Scotto made her first concert tour of Australia and debuted in the title role of *La Gioconda* at the San Francisco Opera, the first live worldwide telecast from the United States. She also sang the *Verdi Requiem* with the Los Angeles Philharmonic, made a recital tour of the United States, sang her first *Manon Lescaut* with the Dallas Civic Opera, taught master classes at the Manhattan School of Music, and performed *Otello* in Florence and *Norma* in Vienna.

1978/79 Discography: *Otello, Verdi Requiem, Cavalleria Rusticana, I Pagliacci, Le Villi,* and *Norma*

BEVERLY SILLS

In January of 1978 the vivacious Beverly Sills announced she would retire from singing in 1980 to become codirector with Julius Rudel of the New York City Opera. However, when Mr. Rudel announced that he intended to retire as director at the end of June 1979, the indefatigable Miss Sills announced that she would become full director July 1, 1979, while maintaining her already busy performing schedule.

Since announcing her decision to retire from the stage, the ebullient redhead almost seems to be trying to fill in any gaps in her already overflowing career. Rather than slowing down during her last months as a singer, Miss Sills, if anything, has speeded up. In June 1978 she sang for the first time—and later recorded—the role of Norina in *Don Pasquale* with the Opera Company of Boston. In the fall of 1978 she sang another first, the role of Donna Fiorilla in *The Turk in Italy* with the New York City Opera, a performance later seen on PBS television. In December 1978 and January 1979 she repeated her Norina role with the Metropolitan Opera, also televised. In June 1979 she created the role of Joan, the mad Queen of Spain, for the world premiere of Gian-Carlo Menotti's *La Loca* at the San Diego Opera, which had commissioned the work for her. And in October of 1980 she plans to return to the San Diego Opera to appear in *Die Fledermaus*, alternating with Joan Sutherland in the roles of Rosalinde and Adele. In 1979 her recording *Up in Central Park* was a classical best-seller, as was her *Don Pasquale*. She won the Recording Industry Association of America's eleventh annual cultural award for her role at the Metropolitan and New York City operas and in opera houses around the world. All this hardly sounds like a woman who's winding down her career.

For Brooklyn-born Belle Silverman, music was an early assumption. When she was only nine she sang such arias as "Cara nome" and "The Bell Song" on radio's "Major Bowes Capitol Family Hour." After high school she sang with the New York City Opera for eleven years, not becoming a prima donna until she shivered her audience's spines in a bravo-raising performance of Cleopatra in Handel's *Julius Caesar.*

She followed that triumph with one invigorating performance after another, winning critical and audience cheers in the Donizetti trilogy, *Roberto Devereux, Maria Stuarda,* and *Anna Bolena.* She amazed audiences with her mastery of the difficult lead role in *Lucia di Lammermoor.* Not limited to heavy drama, she revealed an artful comedic style as Marie in *The Daughter of the Regiment* and Rosina in *The Barber of Seville.*

In 1970 Sills debuted at Covent Garden as Lucia and in Paris at an orchestral concert early in 1971. Her eagerly anticipated debut at New York's Metropolitan Opera took place in April 1975 in a brilliant performance of Rossini's *The Siege of Corinth.* Throughout her professional career she has recorded fifteen full-length operas and several solo recital albums. Her still-increasing repertoire includes more than seventy roles. Her 1976 album, *Music of Victor Herbert,* won her a Grammy for best classical vocal soloist performance.

In addition to her vast operatic credits, Miss Sills is also author of a best-selling autobiography, *Bubbles,* has had her own weekly television program, was hostess/commentator with the New York Philharmonic on the 1977/78 season of CBS's "Young People's Concerts," and has been a frequent guest on many talk shows. The BBC production "Beverly Sills—A Profile" won an Emmy in 1975, and her TV special with Carol Burnett, "Sills and Burnett at the Met," was nominated for an Emmy.

1978/79 Discography: *Don Pasquale*
Up in Central Park

CARLY SIMON

The famous Carly Simon grin gleams from beneath her sinister chapeau on the cover of her 1979 album, *Spy.* From all reports, despite a single called "Vengeance," the grin is still there, shared mainly these days with hubby James Taylor and children Benjamin and Sarah, the three most important persons in her life. She and James enjoyed a joint hit song when their version of "Devoted to You" climbed to number three on the easy-listening charts in October of 1978.

That was not the first time Carly has been one half of a singing duo. When she and sister Lucy attended Sarah Lawrence College, the two performed together as the Simon Sisters, an experience that has left Carly with perennial stage fright, notwithstanding the overjoyed reaction she always gets from audiences. Throughout her career, Carly has concentrated on recording rather than performing live. Her records themselves have been astonishingly successful, especially considering that she doesn't tour to promote them.

Her hits have always been critically acclaimed as well as commercially successful. They include "That's the Way I've Always Heard it Should Be," which won her a Grammy as best new artist of 1971; "Anticipation," now doing double duty as background for an attention-getting catsup ad; the instant classic "You're So Vain"; 1977's James Bond theme, "Nobody Does It Better"; and 1978's "You Belong to Me," from her gold-winning album *Boys in the Trees.*

She broke her self-injunction against touring with a single brilliant performance at New York's Other End in 1977 and a month-long tour of the East Coast in 1978. The word in 1979 was that she was getting ready to try again.

1978/79 Discography: *Spy*

SISTER SLEDGE

Debbie—Vocals, guitar
Joni—Vocals, flute
Kim—Vocals
Kathie—Vocals, guitar, piano

The exuberant energy of the talented family Sledge blossomed in 1979, but beneath their first platinum LP seethes a lifetime of music. A true family, the sisters grew up with the dedication and support of their loving parents, both successful entertainers who encouraged the girls to develop their talents. While mother Flo currently acts as go-between with agents and managers and triples as road manager, it was grandmother Viola Williams, a former opera singer, who first put the girls onstage. When they were two, three, four and six, they performed with their grandmother at banquets, teas, parties, and other social events in their native Philadelphia.

The four high-spirited teenagers grew up performing session work as back-up vocalists for songwriters/producers Gamble and Huff, somehow managing to squeeze in a college education at Temple University. When Henry Allen, then of Atlantic Records, heard the girls, he signed them to Atlantic. Their early albums, although they never made the mass-market breakthrough, are now prized collector's items. The girls enjoyed other performing treats as well. They sang at Muhammad Ali's title bout in Zaire in 1974; in 1975 they won the silver prize in the Fourth Annual Tokyo Music Festival International Contest in Japan.

The Pointer Sisters   Jim Shea/Courtesy Planet Records

Jean-Luc Ponty   Courtesy Atlantic Records

Courtesy RCA Records

Charley Pride

Queen   Christopher Hopper/Courtesy Elektra Records

Lynn Goldsmith/Courtesy Elektra Records

Eddie Rabbitt

144

Their major breakthrough came when they were introduced to Chic's Bernard Edwards and Nile Rodgers, who wrote, arranged, produced, and performed on *We Are Family*. The combination produced the infectious "He's the Greatest Dancer," a number-one soul single, and the potent "We Are Family," both of which helped drive the album to its million sales.

In 1979 they temporarily lost sister Debbie, who took time off to give birth to a baby girl.

1978/79 Discography: *We Are Family*

SPYRO GYRA

Jay Beckenstein—Saxophones

Jim Kurzdorfer—Bass

Tom Schuman—Piano, oberheim

Gerardo Velez—Caliente congas, timbalis

Chet Catallo—Guitar

Eli Konikoff—Drums

Their belief in their own melodic, intense music was so great that Spyro Gyra and producer Richard Calandra paid for their first album out of their own pockets and put it out on their own label, Crosseyed Bear Records, in the fall of 1977. By March of 1978 the disk had sold so well around their hometown of Buffalo, New York, that Amherst Records, their distributor, released the LP. On a small label with a tiny promotional budget, Amherst sold more than 100,000 copies. In 1979 the authoritative band signed with Infinity and produced their latest, *Morning Dance*, a top-five jazz LP.

The core of the band is sax master Jay Beckenstein, bass player Jim Kurzdorfer, and pianist Tom Schuman. They came together in late 1975 and played in local bars, inviting other musicians to join in. "This is what we did for fun on Tuesdays and Thursdays," said Beckenstein. "We worked for very little money just to do it, and we got real good; because it was the only honest thing we were doing. I mean we were really getting off on the music." They soon caught the eye of producer Richard Calandra and composer/producer Jeremy Wall, who eagerly devoted their talents to the mix. All of the band and the two producers were working elsewhere to make money. Calandra and Beckenstein were producing other projects, and in their spare hours in the studio sneaked in work on Spyro Gyra. For a year they put together that first album in bits and pieces.

By this time the band was beginning to be self-supporting in those rowdy bars, where, surprisingly, people would quiet down and listen. Spyro Gyra began to take themselves seriously, let other assignments drop away, and pushed their first album as hard as they could. In 1978 they were voted the most promising new pop instrumental group by *Record World* and hit the charts with their rousing instrumental single "Shaker Song."

By the time they signed with Infinity, they had brought in musicians Gerardo Velez, Chet Catallo, and Eli Konikoff, completing today's lineup. Although they are consistent winners on the jazz charts, their music is wide-ranging. As Beckenstein says, summing up the reason for Spyro Gyra's success, "Whether it's salsa or R & B, classical, rock, or jazz, or 'music from Mars,' if it's got a nice melody . . . it appeals. I like beautiful melodies and easy to understand rhythms. And I'm a happy person, so the music is easy and happy."

1978/79 Discography: *Morning Dance*

STATLER BROTHERS

Harold Reid—Vocals

Lew DeWitt—Vocals

Don Reid—Vocals

Phil Balsey—Vocals

None of them are Statlers—they got the name from a box of Statler facial tissues ("We could just as easily be known as the Kleenex Brothers," Don Reid wisecracked to *People* reporter Jim Jerome)—and only two of them, Harold and Don Reid, are brothers. Their fans probably wouldn't care much if they called themselves the Dolly Sisters, for the country quartet known as the Statler Brothers present their audiences with a truckload of genuine, dyed-in-the-wool country and western music from a group of fellows as pure and all-American as apple pie. To relax after concerts, they show vintage Roy Rogers and Gene Autry films in their tour bus.

Although they failed to capture the Country Music Association's award as best vocal group in 1978, they had pulled in that coveted honor for each of the six prior years. At the end of 1978 their album *Entertainers . . . On and Off the Record* sold gold, and in 1979 that LP won them the National Association of Record Merchandisers award for best-selling country group. They closed 1978 with a number-three country single, "Who Am I to Say," and in 1979 "The Official Historian on Shirley Jean Berrell" was a number-five country winner. North Carolina made each of them honorary attorney generals in 1979.

The beloved Statler Brothers began in 1955, when Harold and Don Reid, Lew DeWitt, and Phil Balsey joined voices for the first time in the Lynhurst Methodist Church in their hometown of Staunton, Virginia. Their harmonies were sweet, pleasing both singers and listeners, and the boys sang together as a gospel group until 1958, when they broke apart.

In 1960 they re-formed as the Kingsmen and sang gospel songs in Staunton's churches, at banquets, and on local television. Still wary of becoming professional singers, they cautiously held on to their nine-to-five jobs until 1963, when they met Johnny Cash at a show in Roanoke, Virginia. Cash asked them to open a show for him, and Harold Reid spent the next four months trying to reach Cash on the phone and parlay Cash's enthusiasm into concrete assignments. Reid finally cornered Cash, who hired the group to tour with him. The band changed its name to the Statler Brothers and for the next eight years toured the world with Johnny. In 1966 they had their first country smash, "Flowers on the Wall," which also won them their first two Grammy awards. They won another Grammy for their 1972 hit "The Class of '57" and through the years have scored with such winning singles as "Bed of Rose's," "Do You Remember These," "I'll Go to My Grave Loving You," "Thank God I've Got You," "I Was There," and "Do You Know You Are My Sunshine." In 1977, in addition to their fifth Country Music Association award as vocal group of the year, they won that honor from the Academy of Country Music as well and earned a platinum album with *Best of the Statler Brothers*, still a landmark as the only pure country album to sell a million copies.

1978/79 Discography: *The Originals*

AL STEWART

Glasgow-born, London-polished, American-honored, singer/guitarist/songwriter Al Stewart is an unlikely pop star, his songwriting talents complex and his onstage manner reserved, almost shy. He has always believed there was an audience for intelligent songs, telling an interviewer, "My philosophy was always that there was a proven market for lyrically oriented music. The public is much more clever than the media assume them to be."

With his roots and early experience in British folk music, in the late sixties and early seventies he released a string of albums in

Britain that dealt intimately and autobiographically with problems of lost love. Although they won some critical notice, they didn't attract a large audience. It wasn't until 1974 and *Past, Present and Future*, a panoramic view of the history of Europe, that Stewart's popularity began to build. Backed by an electric band, he toured the States for the first time in 1974 and won a large number of American fans. His album *Modern Times* was another hard rocker, and his American audiences continued to grow.

In 1977 Stewart broke through with his first platinum album, *Year of the Cat*, whose chart-topping title song was a mysterious epic of love and adventure. Touring, performing, and entrancing audiences throughout 1978, Stewart scored again at the end of the year when "Time Passages," the title song of his 1978 album, reached the top of the easy-listening charts and the album itself sold gold.

1978/79 Discography: *Time Passages*

AMII STEWART

With a blinding flash, Amii Stewart's fireball version of Eddie Floyd's "Knock on Wood" flamed to number one on the pop charts, winning gold certification and pulling her debut album of the same name to gold. Although a newcomer to the recording scene, sizzling Amii is a seasoned entertainer, having been a professional dancer from the time she was sixteen. Her movie credits include *King Kong, The Greatest*, and *The Return of the Pink Panther*. She has brought her dynamic presence to such television shows as "Dinah!," "The Soap Factory," "Merv Griffin," "Soul Train," and "Midnight Special."

She was starring in the London version of the hit show *Bubbling Brown Sugar* when producers/songwriters Barry Leng and Simon May tapped her to record their songs, "You Really Touched My Heart" and "Closest Thing to Heaven." The recordings created a stir in Britain and attracted the attention of Ariola/Hansa Records, which released her first album.

1978/79 Discography: *Knock On Wood*

ROD STEWART

Every picture indeed tells a story, and the 1979 photos of Rod Stewart tell a happy tale. They all show him fat and sassy, his smile as deep-down satisfied as the cat that got *all* the cream. For former bad boy Rod, who just as recently as 1978 was making headlines with all manner of raunchy goings-on, his new glow is not just a result of the dizzying success of his 1979 pop, soul, and disco platinum-winner "Do You Think I'm Sexy?" or the number-one platinum kudos won by *Blondes Have More Fun*, with ten million copies sold worldwide. Platinum-sellers have been the norm for the gravel-voiced singer since 1976, when he scooped up his first million-seller with *A Night on the Town* and its mammoth single, "Tonight's the Night," followed without a pause for breath by 1977's *Foot Loose and Fancy Free* and its winning single "You're in My Heart." Nor was his grin the result of sold-out tours nor even his controversial sexy dancing on the Bee Gees' "A Gift of Song" television benefit for UNICEF. No, his blissful expression is undoubtedly due to domesticity, for in 1979 rock's most skittish bachelor was captured by Alana Hamilton, herself beaming in every photo, both no doubt anticipating the birth of their first child.

One of rock's long-time survivors, London-born Rod's been in the business since 1964, when he returned to London after two adolescent years of hitchhiking throughout Europe. On the continent he frequently sang British folk songs for his dinner. Back in London he combined that white folk music with black blues under the tutelage of British bluesman Long John Baldry, with whom Rod sang in Baldry's Hoochie Coochie Men and later in Steampacket. After Steampacket split up, Stewart joined with Jeff Beck's band and struck up a friendship with Ron Wood; when Wood was fired from that band, Rod followed him out. Stewart had made his mark on two Beck albums, however, *Truth* and *Beck-Ola*, and on the strength of those performances was signed to Mercury Records as a solo performer in 1969. That same year he, Wood, Kenny Jones, Ronnie Lane, and Ian McLagan joined their raucous talents to form Faces.

In 1970 and 1971 his output was prodigious, including three albums with Faces: *First Step, Long Player*, and *A Nod's as Good as a Wink to a Blind Horse* and his own *The Rod Stewart Album* and *Gasoline Alley*. In 1971 came his breakthrough album, *Every Picture Tells a Story*, with the ravishingly beautiful ballad "Maggie May." Both the album and the single dominated the charts, and Rod's career began to fulfill its early promise. In 1972 *Never a Dull Moment* and the hit single "You Wear it Well" both sold gold.

The energetic singer continued to tour and record both as a solo act and with Faces through 1975, but his albums *Smiler* and *Atlantic Crossing* were not so successful. His growing fame, however, began to eclipse that of Faces, causing tensions within the group. In 1975 he announced his departure from Faces and his intention to perform only as a solo act from then on, beginning a new era in his fabulous career.

1978/79 Discography: *Blondes Have More Fun*

BARBRA STREISAND

Theater critic Walter Kerr summed up Barbra Streisand's explosive appeal in his review of the original Broadway version of *Funny Girl*: "Everybody knew that Barbra Streisand would be a star, and so she is." The little girl from Brooklyn with the awe-inspiring voice has racked up a boatload of honors, awards, historic performances, and gold and platinum records in the sensational course of her seventeen-year career. From her first acclaimed performances in such nightclubs as New York's Bon Soir and Detroit's Caucus Club and her Broadway debut as Miss Marmelstein in *I Can Get it for You Wholesale*, she's brought the same immense talent and inspired intelligence to everything she's attempted. She has recorded thirty-four albums of which twenty-two are gold or platinum, including the extraordinarily successful soundtrack from *A Star Is Born*. Her *Greatest Hits, Volume II* was a number-one charter for weeks at the beginning of 1979 and a platinum-winner on its release. She's starred in theater, on television, and in films.

Always years ahead of fashion, she's twice been elected to the international best-dressed list. She has performed at the White House for presidents Kennedy and Johnson, and her June 1967 outdoor concert in Central Park drew 135,000 people, a record that stood for twelve years. During the five years she appeared at the Las Vegas International Hotel she was the highest-paid café performer in history. She's won six Grammies, one Emmy, four Golden Globes and, although her films have not always been treated kindly by the critics, has pulled in two Oscars, one for best actress for her performance as Fanny Brice in *Funny Girl*, the other for best song, "Evergreen," written with Paul Williams.

In addition, Barbra won the New York Drama Critics Poll for *I Can Get it for You Wholesale;* among other honors, she has been chosen star of the year or entertainer of the year by *Cue* magazine, the National Association of Theatre Owners, the Friar's Club, the American Guild of Variety Artists, and the Hollywood Women's Press Club.

At the end of 1978 Barbra scored a number-one pop hit with Neil Diamond, a duet called "You Don't Bring Me Flowers." In 1979 she wisecracked through the movie *Main Event* and hit with the title song.

1978/79 Discography: *Greatest Hits, Volume II*

Main Event

Jean-Pierre Rampal

Charlie Rich   Courtesy United Artists Records

Linda Ronstadt

Kenny Rogers   Courtesy United Artists Records

Rose Royce   Courtesy Whitfield Records

The Rolling Stones   Courtesy Atlantic Records

Diana Ross   Courtesy Motown Records

Devadip Carlos Santana   Courtesy Columbia Records

Christian Steiner

Christian Steiner/Courtesy Angel/EMI Limited

Beverly Sills

Renata Scotto

Courtesy Cotillion Records

Sister Sledge

Pam Frank/Courtesy Elektra Records

Carly Simon

Robin Platzer

Roz Levin Perlmutter

Roz Levin Perlmutter

Preceding page: *The energetic Billy Joel writes Grammy-winnng
ballads and hard rock with equal skill. Opposite, top: Veteran
performer Barry Manilow got his first driving license in 1979.
Opposite, bottom: Cheap Trick's Rick Nielsen often plays three guitars.
Above: Meat Loaf's eagerly awaited second album arrived in October.*

Courtesy Columbia Records

Michael Putland/Retna

Courtesy Jim Halsey

Pictorial Parade/Photographers International copyright

Opposite, top to bottom: *Pianist Claude Bolling and flutist Jean-Pierre Rampal enjoyed a monster crossover hit with Bolling's* Suite for Flute and Jazz Piano. *The beloved Statler Brothers held their tenth annual Happy Birthday U.S.A. celebration in 1979. Linda Ronstadt talks to the animals on her 1979 African jaunt.* Above: *When Earth, Wind & Fire takes over a stage, audiences come alive. Here they sparkle in the Bee Gees' UNICEF benefit 'A Gift of Song.'*

Opposite, top: *Weather Report's Mr. Gone was an effortless jazz winner for the ace band.* Opposite, bottom: *Singer/guitarist George Benson won a Grammy for his performance of "On Broadway."* Left: *Full of fire, top performer Ann-Margret wowed a New York audience at Billboard's Disco Forum VI.* Following page: *Disco helped propel Blondie to the top, but "Heart of Glass" was not the only pop sparkler from the LP Parallel Lines.*

Tracy Frankel/Neal Peters

STYX

Dennis DeYoung—Keyboards	
John Panozzo—Drums	
Tommy Shaw—Guitars	
James Young—Guitar	
Chuck Panozzo—Bass	

After years of hard playing, hard touring, and hard luck, Styx found the gods smiling at a particularly fortunate confluence of sevens: on 7/7/77 they released their seventh album, *The Grand Illusion*—and the first dramatic breakthrough came for the Chicago-born band. *The Grand Illusion*, with its exuberant hit single "Come Sail Away," has now sold nearly three million copies. Their next LP, *Pieces of Eight*, also won platinum, and its success inspired an earlier LP, *Crystal Ball*, to finally climb to gold sales. Although their 1978 tour, dubbed The Main Event, included every chic special effect, the band kept firm musical control. As Dennis DeYoung points out, "We always make sure that the effects don't overshadow the music—we don't want to become a circus!"

The music is what drove them from the beginning in 1963, when brothers Chuck and John Panozzo and neighbor Dennis DeYoung played accordion, bass guitar, and drums. The trio performed throughout Chicago; in 1968 guitarists John Curulewski and James Young joined the group, which they called the Tradewinds. They played noisy clubs and small concerts, where audiences clamored for Beatles songs. "The real test," Dennis recalls, "was to perform original material and have it accepted."

In 1970 they won their first record contract with a local RCA subsidiary called Wooden Nickel Records and renamed themselves Styx. As James Young remembers, "It was one of a hundred names we tried and it turned out to be the only one that none of us hated." During the next three years they released *Styx II*, *The Serpent Is Rising*, and *Man of Miracles*. Each sold minimally and the band kept itself going with gruelling, nonstop touring throughout the Midwest. Despite a growing sweat equity, their careers didn't seem to be going anywhere until Chicago radio station WLS began getting requests for "Lady," a song from the album *Styx II*. The more the station played the song, the more requests they got. "Lady" was reissued as a single, became a huge national hit, and pushed *Styx II* to gold.

Observing that their songs were successful when people got to hear them, the band decided that they might do better with a different label, and signed with A & M, where they self-produced the album *Equinox*. Just as they were about to begin a national promotion tour, John Curulewski dropped out, and the band did some fast scrabbling to find Tommy Shaw, an Alabaman with prodigious musical talents. Within a week he had learned their music and was on the road with them, providing a luminous melodic counterpoint to the unleashed rock of James Young. *Equinox* soon won platinum in Canada, and in 1976 they released *Crystal Ball*, the first LP to include Tommy Shaw's playing.

DONNA SUMMER

Her red bee-stung lips, bedroom eyes, mane of black curls, and voluptuous body have made Donna Summer an exotic sex goddess. But it's her shimmering talent, keen intelligence, and the self-assuredness she's had since she was a child that have made her a staggering musical success. In 1979 the glorious Miss Summer surpassed all her previous achievements. She won a Grammy for top R & B female vocal performance for her recording of "Last Dance," Paul Jabara's Oscar-winning song from *Thank God it's Friday*. She became the first woman to simultaneously have a number-one album and single on

Billboard's pop charts on two different occasions. She scored first in November 1978, when her ecstatic version of "MacArthur Park Suite" and her platinum-winning album *Alive and More* occupied those top spots. In June 1979 she achieved that rare combination a second time, when her gold single "Hot Stuff" and her platinum LP *Bad Girls* were both number one at the same time. To cap her triumph, she had a simultaneous top-five hit with the title single from *Bad Girls*. In addition to these recording pinnacles, Donna appeared on the Bee Gees' UNICEF benefit, "A Gift of Song," and was special guest star at the eighth annual Tokyo Song Festival.

This prodigious output came from the woman cynics dismissed as a one-hit singer after the sensational success of her sixteen-minute disco smash "Love to Love You Baby." But the skeptics obviously never knew Donna when she was a determined little girl, daughter of a hard-working, often poor Boston family who, even in those lean days, was certain she was destined to be a star. She made her singing debut as a substitute for an ailing church soloist, and from that time on singing was her life. She took the first steps on her meteoric career when she left school during the twelfth grade to perform in the European touring company of *Hair*, then playing in Munich, Germany. After *Hair* closed, she stayed in Munich, singing in the Vienna folk Opera, performing in German stage versions of American Broadway musicals, and singing back-up vocals on European disco records. When producer Peter Bellotte and his partner in Oasis Records, Giorgio Moroder, heard her voice, they excitedly recorded three of her songs and took them to the MIDEM record business convention in Cannes. Bellotte easily sold the three, and "Hostage" became a hit, making Donna a major star in Europe. After cutting several pop hits, she, Bellotte, and Moroder wrote a three-minute version of "Love to Love You Baby." Although it was released twice in Europe, it never really caught fire. However, when Casablanca president Neil Bogart played it at West Coast parties, guests invariably wanted him to play it again. Shrewd Bogart persuaded Moroder to record a longer version and the song became a smash in America, and, on its third release, in Europe as well.

Donna has since recorded four gold albums for Casablanca: *Love Trilogy*, *Four Seasons of Love*, *I Remember Yesterday*, and *Once Upon a Time*. At the end of 1978 "Heaven Knows," a song she recorded with Brooklyn Dreams, became a gold-winning number-five pop single. Donna's next career goal is to break out of the restrictive disco mold and allow her voice to shine on a wide range of material. 1978/79 Discography: *Bad Girls*

SUPERTRAMP

Roger Hodgson—Vocals, keyboards, guitars	
Richard Davies—Vocals, keyboards	
Dougie Thomson—Bass	
John Anthony Helliwell—Woodwinds, vocals	
Bob C. Benberg—Drums, percussion	

With *Breakfast in America* a platinum smash and "Logical Song" a top-ten pop winner, Supertramp, the British band relocated on American soil, has broken through with a free, breezy sound. As singer Rick Davies says, the album is "very much more open and flowing" than their earlier, more elegantly constructed art/rock disks.

Supertramp began in London in 1970, when singer/songwriters Richard Davies and Roger Hodgson were brought together with three other musicians by a fast-talking Dutch millionaire. They cut the album *Supertramp*, originally released only in Europe; it won good reviews, but the band fragmented and the millionaire disappeared. Undaunted, Roger and Rick gathered together three new sidemen and made *Indelibly Stamped*, a less distinctive album than their first, and the band fell apart again. Roger and Rick were determined, however. They stuck together at the urging of bass player Dougie

Thomson and gathered to them California drummer Bob C. Benberg and woodwind player John Anthony Helliwell.

Roger and Rick had enough songs for a third album, and the five musicians made *Crime of the Century,* a sophisticated, tuneful musical excursion that became their first number-one smash in England. Thanks to America's FM rock stations, who couldn't play enough of it, the album remained for more than eight months on the American charts. *Crisis? What Crisis?,* in the band's crisp, lucid style, followed, and fans cheered Supertramp lustily when the band set out on a mammoth ten-month tour of Europe, the United States, Canada, Australia, New Zealand, and Japan. In 1977 *Even in the Quietest Moments* became their first platinum disk, and they attracted sell-out crowds on their 1977–78 worldwide tour. The American and Canadian tour that began in March of 1979 was the first in which they played large arenas, and they and their fans were grateful for the opportunity to raise a rocking ruckus.

1978/79 Discography: *Breakfast in America*

SYLVESTER

The outrageous creature who leaps onstage trailing gleaming caftans and batting flirtatious, mascaraed eyelashes has somewhere inside him the eight-year-old, upper-middle-class black boy who was a star singer on the gospel circuit. Guided by his grandmother, 1930s blues singer Julia Morgan, Sylvester had a striking vocal style and flamboyant manner even as a child. As he grew, he moved away from the church, became fascinated by the recording stars of the twenties and thirties, stopped singing for a while, and then moved from Los Angeles to San Francisco. There, he says, he found himself suddenly freed from former constraints. "All of a sudden there was absolutely no pressure. I could be any kind of person at all and no one cared." Sylvester blossomed with the outrageous transvestite group the Cockettes, his piercing falsetto the perfect sound for their campy body English.

America was not ready for this spectacle, and Sylvester's three albums for Blue Thumb Records vanished quickly. He was stuck in local gigs until Motown producer Harvey Fuqua found him in 1977. The first album, *Sylvester,* was not a huge success in America, although one song, "Over and Over," was a substantial disco winner, especially in England In June 1978 Fantasy released *Step II,* declared gold in the beginning of 1979 partly because of the excitement generated by the disco hits "Dance (Disco Heat)" and "Mighty Real." Sylvester followed that up in mid-1979 with *Stars,* a bold album consisting of only four long songs, including the powerful Lieber Stoller R & B classic "I (Who Have Nothing)." Because of his fabulous disco success Sylvester won three major awards at the 1979 Disco Forum: best male singer, disco dj favorite single, and best heavy disco single. He will be seen in the Bette Midler film *The Rose* as a nightclub rock singer who performs Bob Seger's "The Fire Down Below" with Bette. And he was honored in his adopted city of San Francisco when March 11, 1979, was proclaimed Sylvester Day in celebration of his gala sold-out concert at the San Francisco War Memorial Opera House.

Although his stage show has toned down some since his Cockette days, Sylvester still sometimes sports outrageous duds, and he's always surrounded by two very large ladies known as "Two Tons o' Fun." Sylvester describes how he chose hefty singers Martha Wash and Izora Rhodes: "We were having auditions and I was tired of all these beautiful skinny girls who couldn't sing. When Martha came in, I took one look at her and *knew* she could sing. I hired her instantly and asked if she knew any other girls like her—big, black, and beautiful. She brought Izora along and that was it. The girls will be with me forever."

1978/79 Discography: *Stars*

A TASTE OF HONEY

Janice Johnson—Lead vocals, bass

Hazel Payne—Lead vocals, guitar

Perry Kibble—Piano

Don Johnson—Drums

At the end of 1978 the sweet, smooth, danceable "Boogie, Oogie, Oogie," swept to platinum sales, as did a first album by a new group. Both album and group were called A Taste of Honey; the group's unique lineup featured two fetching ladies on lead vocals, bass, and guitar. The lovely femininity of Janice Johnson and Hazel Payne helped lead A Taste of Honey to an unprecedented year. Not only did that first album sell platinum, but the group won a Grammy as new artists of the year.

Of course, the band did not spring full-blown out of nowhere just in time to make the Grammy nominations. In 1972, Janice Johnson, Perry Kibble, a guitarist who was later replaced by Hazel Payne, and drummer Don Johnson formed a band in Los Angeles. They performed on the predictable small-club circuit and toured the world with the USO. International audiences loved them, and they represented the United States at the Fifth World Popular Song Festival in Japan in 1974.

When they returned to the United States they soon learned that the performing life could mean bouncing from club to club indefinitely. They got themselves booked into the Etc, a popular Hollywood club, however, and they were so well liked that they stayed as house band for almost a year. There they were spotted by Jackson Five producers Fonce and Larry Mizell who thought the band, with its female lead guitar and bass, were dynamite. They signed to Capitol Records and their first album was the magnificent *A Taste Of Honey.*

In 1979 the band competed in the Tokyo Music Festival at Budokan, where they won gold prize for their song "Do It."

1978/79 Discography: *Another Taste*

JAMES TAYLOR

With his late-1978 version of "Devoted to You" (a duet with wife Carly Simon) both a reflection of his domestic tranquility and a top easy-listening hit, and with his new album, *Flag,* declared gold on shipping, James Taylor has traveled light years from 1970 when he was a frightened young boy, trembling at the astonishing three-million sales of his second album, *Sweet Baby James.* Two sobering songs, "Fire and Rain" and "Country Road," clearly marked the end of the turbulent sixties, capturing the pensive mood that began the 1970s.

Today James can take his success in stride—as evidenced by the cool ease with which he faced the record-breaking crowd of 250,000 who came to hear him in New York's Central Park in August 1979. But in 1970, as he describes it: "My picture on the cover of *Time* was really a jinx. That kind of exposure is a publicity wallop that very few people can handle. Elton John and David Bowie seemed to be able to, but it really froze me. It made me overconscious about trying to keep doing what I did to get there. I was reeling, everything was happening so fast. Nothing seemed all that real to me."

With a background that included stays in two mental hospitals to help him battle an addiction to hard drugs, it was no wonder that James was unprepared for this smashing success. His first album,

Spyro Gyra
Courtesy Infinity Records

Al Stewart
Courtesy Arista Records

The Statler Brothers
Courtesy Mercury Records

Amii Stewart
Courtesy Ariola Records

Courtesy Warner/Reprise

Rod Stewart

Courtesy Columbia Records

Barbra Streisand

159

Styx   Courtesy A&M Records

Donna Summer

Sylvester   Courtesy Fantasy Records

Supertramp   Courtesy A&M Records

A Taste of Honey   Courtesy Capitol Records

James Taylor   Courtesy Columbia Records

James Taylor, had emerged with an enormous amount of fanfare, as James was one of the few artists signed by the Beatles to their label, Apple. But despite critical acclaim and the weight of the Beatles, the album was a commercial failure. All the more reason for James to be a little staggered by the fabulous greeting won by his second LP.

Because of his fear, James withdrew from the public. He guested on the LPs of pals Carole King and Joni Mitchell, and Elvis Presley had a hit with James's song "Steamroller Blues." But it wasn't until early in 1972 that James reluctantly entered the limelight again, this time with the mellow, poignant "You've Got a Friend," his first gold single, from the album *Mud Slide Slim and the Blue Horizon.* This was followed by *One Man Dog* and *Walking Man,* and James's creditable performance in the film *Two Lane Blacktop,* which also featured Dennis Wilson.

In 1972 James married Carly Simon, and the happiness of this union is celebrated on his gold albums *Gorilla*—with its two hit singles, "How Sweet it Is" and "Mexico"—*In the Pocket,* and *J.T.* In 1977 James won a Grammy for best pop vocal performance, for the honeyed single "Handy Man."
1978/79 Discography: *Flag*

GEORGE THOROGOOD AND THE DESTROYERS

George Thorogood—Guitar, vocals

Jeff Simon—Drums

Bill Blough—Bass

Onstage, George Thorogood is a tempest, a hard-as-nails rocker who wields a lightning-fast guitar and sings with a growl. His whirlwind performances of good-time R & B and early rock and roll—songs by Chuck Berry, Bo Diddley, Elmore James, John Lee Hooker, Johnny Cash, and Hank Williams—raise his audiences right into his own frenzy, always fulfilling Thorogood's unquenchable desire to have fun and to give his audiences that same priceless commodity. In a business where the big buck all too often becomes a musician's sole motivation, George is that rarity: a performer who plays, sings, and dances with passion because he loves every minute of it. His uninhibited all-stops-out performances have won astonished critical praise from every reviewer fortunate enough to see him. With no publicity other than gasping word of mouth and limited FM radio play, his first album, a blistering powerhouse called *George Thorogood and the Destroyers,* sold more than 100,000 copies. His second, *Move it on Over,* which made inroads on the pop album charts in 1979, to date has sold more than 150,000 copies and is still climbing.

Born in Baton Rouge, Louisiana, raised in Wilmington, Delaware, Thorogood first encountered the guts of rock and roll on a 1964 edition of television's "Shindig" that featured the Rolling Stones and Howlin' Wolf. Transfixed, he rushed out to buy *Chuck Berry's Golden Decade* and followed that with hundreds of classic rockers. He learned them all, gathered sidemen Jeff Simon and Ron Smith (later replaced by Billy Blough), and then went out and played local clubs and bars with freewheeling flash. A genuine renegade, Thorogood sticks with his tiny Boston company, Rounder Records, despite offers from major labels. He disdains the rock star trip many musicians crave and is eager to have time to do all the things he enjoys. In addition to music his obsessions include playing hardball with the Delaware Destroyers in the Roberto Clemente League in Wilmington.

The only critical cavil directed at this near-perfect neorocker is that he does no original material. He responded to this charge, telling *Rolling Stone* reporter Charles M. Young: "Why should I write songs when Chuck Berry already wrote them all?"
1978/79 Discography: *Move it on Over*

MEL TILLIS

One of country's most appealing stars, Mel Tillis swings through some two hundred annual bookings on an arduous 120,000-mile tour route. That gruelling schedule is only part of the year's work for Mel, who is a frequent guest on network television shows, a top recording artist, head of Sawgrass Music Publishing company, and author of nearly a thousand songs. The famous Tillis stutter, the result of an early childhood bout with malaria, doesn't slow him down one bit but rather enhances his charm. It took Mel years to make his peace with it, however. The stammer made his Florida childhood miserable until he decided one day that it was part of him and he might as well make good use of it. Shrewdly understanding that a stammer makes listeners feel protective, Mel will come onstage and joke, "I wrote a talking part in 'Detroit City,' which was a stupid thing on my part. If *I* had to record it, I'd still be in the studio."

Mel didn't have to record "Detroit City" because, like so many of his songs, it became a gold-winner for another artist. "Detroit City" did it for Bobby Bare; "Ruby, Don't Take Your Love to Town" was a million-seller for Kenny Rogers and the First Edition. The success of these and hundreds of others won Mel his place in the Songwriter's Hall of Fame in 1976. Because of his own smashes, such top country singles as "What Did I Promise Her Last Night" and "I Believe in You," in 1976 he was named country music entertainer of the year by the Country Music Association. His most recent hits include 1978's "Ain't No California" and 1979's number-one country winners "Send Me Down to Tucson/Charlie's Angels" and "Coca Cola Cowboy."

TOTO

David Paich—Keyboards

Jeff Porcaro—Drums

David Hungate—Bass

Steve Porcaro—Keyboards

Steve Lukather—Guitar

Bobby Kimball—Vocals

Blasting out of L.A. on a wave of power-chord rock, Toto's first self-titled album zoomed to platinum, winning them the National Association of Record Manufacturers' award for the best-selling album by a new group. Its first single, "Hold the Line," was a fast million-seller. Their first tour, at the end of 1978, found them playing to packed houses, often as headliners. These impressive achievements grow naturally out of the equally impressive credentials of the six red-hot musicians who make up the band.

David Paich and Jeff Porcaro have known each other since they were Hollywood thirteen-year-olds and for ten years have been close friends and comusicians. Jeff's brother, Steve, and Steve Lukather were smashing out high-decibel guitar/keyboard combinations at San Fernando Valley's Grant High School when they met David Hungate. Individually and collectively the five were called on for studio work by giant pop stars. Paich was cowriter and arranger with Boz Scaggs on *Silk Degrees* and arranged the Doobie Brothers' *Minute by Minute.* Jeff Porcaro's crisp backbeat sizzled on the records of Boz Scaggs and Steely Dan, among others. Texas bass player David Hungate recorded with such glittering stars as Barbra Streisand, Leo Sayer, and the Pointer Sisters. Steve Porcaro toured with Boz Scaggs and played with Gary Wright and Leo Sayer. Steve Lukather's guitar credits include road time with Boz Scaggs and recording with Hall & Oates and Alice Cooper. Bobby Kimball, a warm, personable singer from Vinton, Louisiana, is a veteran of several New Orleans bands and had come to L.A. to sing with another group but was immediately snapped up by Toto as their lead vocalist.
1978/79 Discography: *Toto*

TANYA TUCKER

The sweet-faced teenager whose bold voice belted out 1974's astounding country and pop smash "Delta Dawn" has grown up. Today Tanya Tucker is sporting an explosive, sexy new image, typified by the title of her gold-winning 1979 album, *TNT*, and the skin-tight red jumpsuit she wears on an eyepopping poster that accompanies the record. Aiming for the pop bull's-eye in an all-out crossover attempt, Tanya has pushed her voice and stage presence into a dynamic new range, retaining her country twang while she rocks with the hottest. The new image is a winner. Not only has *TNT* sold gold, but 1978's *Tanya Tucker's Greatest Hits* has also sold a gold-winning half a million copies.

By the time the Wilcox, Arizona girl was a mere nine years old, she had set her heart on a singing career. Luckily, she had the wholehearted support of her father, Beau, who became her manager. Tanya's parents drove her to every local fair for miles around so the aspiring singer could watch country greats and learn as much as she could. Young Tanya's determination to perform was so intense that she would often manage to talk her idols into letting her appear onstage with them. She also managed to talk reluctant producer Mike Motors into giving her a cameo role in the movie *Jeremiah Johnson*.

When Tanya was barely twelve her father invested $400, a lot of money to the Tuckers in those days, in a demo tape. He sent out the tapes only to have his high hopes dashed time and again by rejection letters. Finally, however, songwriter Dolores Fuller heard the potential in Tanya's full-throttle delivery and played the tapes for Nashville producer Billy Sherrill. Sherrill immediately called Tanya into a Nashville recording studio, and the two of them pored over material until they found the song "Delta Dawn," Tanya's skyrocket to stardom.
1978/79 Discography: *Tanya Tucker's Greatest Hits*
TNT

CONWAY TWITTY

"If you do right, it'll come back to you," says Conway Twitty, known to his millions of fans as the beloved Twitty Bird. Conway, who has the reputation of being one of the music world's most decent people, has always lived by this belief. As he told John Pugh in *Country Music* magazine, the only way to communicate "is to be *sincerely* interested in other people, to get past surface appearances and really interreact with them."

His communication is legendary, including more than thirty number-one country singles in a row and more than forty awards, including a Grammy, four Country Music Association awards, six Academy of Country Music awards, fourteen *Music City News* awards, four American Music awards, thirteen *Billboard* awards and two hard-won Truckers' awards. Twitty's phenomenal country-music success is even more startling when you remember that Conway, born Harold Lloyd Jenkins in Helena, Arkansas, began his career as a rock-and-roll star.

Actually, the Twitty music saga goes back to when he was a little boy sitting in the pilothouse of his father's Mississippi riverboat, where he sang and accompanied himself on the guitar. Although by the age of ten he had formed his own band, the Phillips County Ramblers, a group professional and accomplished enough to have a radio show in Helena, Harold was undecided about what he wanted to do in life. After high school, the active and athletic teen was offered a baseball contract with the Philadelphia Phillies, but before he could toss out his first ball he was drafted by the army.

During his tour of duty he formed the Cimarrons, a band that toured the Japanese club circuit. That thrilling experience made him realize that it was music he wanted to pursue. When he returned to civilian life and the Phillies again offered him a baseball contract, he turned them down. He changed his name to Conway Twitty (after Conway, Arkansas, and Twitty, Texas), and wrote and recorded "It's Only Make Believe," 1958's smash million-selling love song.

During the next eight years Conway wrote and recorded many more rock 'n' roll stompers, including three that were million-sellers, but rock and roll started to wear thin for him and he found himself tugged by his roots. Almost overnight he changed his image and became a country singer, recording his first country album in 1965 and his first monster hit, "Hello Darlin'," in 1970.

At the beginning of the 1970s Conway teamed up with Loretta Lynn for a recording session. The duet was so successful they picked up the Country Music Association's duo-of-the-year award for four years in a row as well as a Truckers' award in 1974 and a Grammy in 1971, to say nothing of enchanting millions of fans throughout the years with their firecracker performances.

One of the busiest men in country music, a field not noted for slackers, Conway manages to squeeze into his year more than two hundred concert dates, hundreds of hours of songwriting—more than two hundred songs to date—managing the several music publishing companies he owns, managing the United Talent Agency he and Loretta co-own, and helping direct the Nashville Sounds baseball team, which he also co-owns.

In 1979 Conway scored with the top-five country single "Your Love Has Taken Me That High," the number-one "Take it Away," and "I May Never Get to Heaven."
1978/79 Discography: *Cross Winds*

V

VAN HALEN

| David Roth—Vocals |
| Edward Van Halen—Guitar |
| Michael Anthony—Bass |
| Alex Van Halen—Drums |

Take your basic rock quartet—the pared-down blend of guitar, bass, drums, and vocals—laser strop it to a wicked 1980's glitter, overlay it with a stratospheric electric rush, and you've got an inkling of the sound that jet-propelled Van Halen's self-titled first album to double platinum sales and kept it on the charts throughout 1978 and into 1979, the sound that blasted *Van Halen II* into a million homes. Not only is their studio sound a twenty-first century charge, but their fiery onstage presence pounds with a relentless energy, the same energy that detonated their explosive rise to the top.

Van Halen began with Dutch brothers Alex and Edward Van Halen. Both trained as concert pianists but traded in their keyboards for guitar and drum when they moved to America and flipped for American rock and roll. They met Michael Anthony and David Roth, two transplanted midwesterners, in Los Angeles, and the foursome caught fire wherever they appeared. And for four arduous years they appeared everywhere—in endless rounds of small clubs, beer bars, outdoor parties, and dance concerts. The band and their friends gathered crowds of thousands by passing out fliers and through breathless word of mouth. No manager, agent, or record company could have built a sturdier or more fiercely loyal base of fans. So tight and aggressive was their music that when Warner Brothers Records Chairman Mo Ostin and Executive Producer Ted Templeman spotted them performing in Los Angeles's Starwood Club one rainy February 1977 night they signed the band the next day.

Before you could say "Dance the Night Away," (the band's hot top-twenty 1979 hit), Van Halen was in the studio with Templeman, producer of the Doobie Brothers, welding a towering album of pure

George Thorogood and the Destroyers

Mel Tillis   Courtesy MCA Records

Tanya Tucker   Courtesy MCA Records

Van Halen   Courtesy Warner/Reprise

Toto   Courtesy Columbia Records

Conway Twitty   Courtesy MCA Records

electric rock. Raring to go, the tireless band set out for ten months on the road, treating glazed fans to their spectacular stage show, the climax of the tour a heart-stopping parachute jump before 62,000 screaming fans at Anaheim Stadium.
1978/79 Discography: *Van Halen II*

GINO VANNELLI

When Gino Vannelli steps into the spotlight it's never just another performance. "I really don't think of it as a job. I see it as partaking in the realization of a dream, the sharing of my dream with a room full of people who want to share it with me." More than one million people shared the dream Gino expressed on his 1978 album, *Brother to Brother,* the first platinum-winner for this intense, black-haired singer/songwriter/arranger/producer/bandleader who's been honing and developing his musical vision since he was a child.

Born in Montreal, Gino grew up listening both to the sounds of the 1950s' big bands and to early rock and roll. By the time he was twelve he was playing drums with a band called the Cobras, and a year later, with brother Joe, he formed the Jacksonville Five, a band with a Memphis-Motown sound. When he was sixteen he cut his first single, a top-ten Canadian hit. Gino spent the next two years writing songs in New York City and then returned to Montreal, where he gained experience performing in night clubs with his own band.

On a 1973 trip to Los Angeles, Gino was heard by A & M Records, who immediately signed the twenty-year-old. His first album, *Crazy Life,* featured him on drums and his brother Joe on keyboards. His second, *Powerful People,* spawned the international hit single "People Gotta Move." By his third album, 1975's *Storm at Sunup,* Gino had begun to develop a new emphasis on synthesizers.

The Gist of Gemini and *A Pauper in Paradise* followed in 1976 and 1977, with *A Pauper in Paradise* featuring a symphony performed by Vannelli's band accompanied by the Royal Philharmonic Orchestra.

His platinum-winning *Brother to Brother* featured Gino, Joe, and younger brother Ross, who wrote "I Just Wanna Stop," the album's top-five single.
1978/79 Discography: *Brother to Brother*

VILLAGE PEOPLE

Randy Jones (Cowboy)—Vocals

David Hodo (Construction worker)—Vocals

Victor Willis (Naval commander/policeman)—Lead Vocals

Alexander Briley (GI/sailor)—Vocals

Glenn Hughs (Biker)—Vocals

Felipe Rose (Indian chief)—Vocals

Their bouncy, exuberant music and irrepressible, costumed images are everywhere. In the space of two short years, the Village People have jetted from being six unknown young men to the hottest disco/pop group in the world today. They hit in 1977 with the gold-winning *Village People* and its number-one disco monster, "San Francisco/Hollywood," followed that with the gold-winning "Macho Man" from the platinum album of the same name, followed that with the double platinum *Cruisin'* and its platinum single, the irresistibly buoyant "Y.M.C.A.," and followed *that* in dizzyingly short order with *Go West,* a swift platinum, and the million-copy single "In the Navy," reputedly being eyed by the U.S. Navy as a recruiting jingle. They are enormously successful in Germany and Japan, have graced the covers of magazines from *Us* to *Rolling Stone,* and have stripped down for a four-color photo feature in the February 1979 *Playgirl.* Their spring tour appearances were *the* chic event in cities across the country.

The spirited band with its nonstop, razzle-dazzle, tightly choreographed stage show is the brainchild·of composer/producer Jacques Morali, who was inspired by the sight of Felipe Rose dancing at a New York disco in a feathered headdress and loincloth. Morali became obsessed with the idea of an all-male singing group, each member dressed in a stereotyped male costume and singing ironic macho songs. He hired studio musicians to create the first album and models to pose for the album photo, but when the LP succeeded in discos, Morali had to gather performers who could dance and sing as well as model. Three of Morali's original choices were Rose, Victor Willis, and Alex Briley, each of whom had some performing experience. Morali then auditioned more than two hundred men for the other three group members, finally choosing David (Scar) Hodo, an out-of-work chorus boy; Randy Jones, who was an Agnes De Mille dancer; and Glenn Hughes, who was a toll collector in the Brooklyn Battery Tunnel with no singing or dancing experience but plenty of chutzpah. Morali brought the six together, fashioned a manic, hellzapoppin' show, and let them loose with their tongue-in-cheek macho fantasies, appealing to a universal spectrum of tastes.

In August, ten days before shooting of their highly publicized first movie was scheduled to begin, lead singer Willis shocked the music world by announcing he was leaving the group to pursue a solo career. Several days later, Ray Simpson was named to replace him.
1978/79 Discography: *Cruisin'*
Go West

W

ANITA WARD

Like a long sigh, a song called "Ring My Bell" caressed the ears as it jetted from nowhere to number one, a gold-winning pop, soul, and disco rocket that drove its parent album, *Songs of Love,* to an equally swift gold. The high, tremulous, sugar-sweet voice of the singer was the perfect vehicle for the song's cheerily suggestive lyrics, and with it, twenty-two-year-old Anita Ward achieved international success.

Born in Memphis, Tennessee, on December 20, 1957, Anita first sang publicly when she was nine and won her first recording contract when she was fourteen. While attending Rust College in Holly Springs, Mississippi, she appeared in a local version of *Godspell* and sang with the school's choir. She was chosen Miss A Cappella Choir for the world famous Rust Singers and starred as a soloist for the Rust College Female Quartet, with whom she traveled around the world. It was at Rust that she met Chuck Holmes, her current manager. While she developed her professional style in the school's singing groups, he sent out demo tapes until he matched Anita up with an enthusiastic Juana Records, distributed by Hialeah's T.K. Productions. They released an unsuccessful single from the album and then "Ring My Bell," Anita's hot ticket.

A gracious and charming performer, Anita has appeared on all the top television music shows in America as well as England's "Top of the Pops," Canada's "First Annual Disco Awards Show," and Puerto Rico's "Latin Disco." In 1979 she performed with Con Funk Shun, McFadden and Whitehead, and Lenny Williams and the Gap Band. In July of 1979 she enchanted a cynical audience of music-business pros at *Billboard's* Disco Forum VI at New York's Roseland.
1978/79 Discography: *Songs of Love*

GROVER WASHINGTON, JR.

Bursting with new musical and business ideas, premier saxophone player Grover Washington, Jr., relishes his continually blossoming success, a popularity that grows out of the man's dedication to his music, his warm, modest personality, and his inimitable artistry. In 1979 Washington moved to Elektra/Asylum Records, where his first album, *Paradise*, was a major jazz contender, its songs a rich blend of Latin rhythms, spiritual melodies, and up-front funk. It marked Washington's debut as a pianist, contained one cut where he plays flute, and continued his exciting development as a musician.

He was born in Buffalo, New York, on December 12, 1943, into a musical family—his mother sang in church choirs, and his father played saxophone. Grover got his first saxophone when he was ten years old, by which time he was already sneaking into clubs to hear such players as Jack McDuff, Harold Vick, and Charles Lloyd. By age twelve he had begun his professional career, playing R & B with a vocal group and gut-bucket blues with a funky blues band. The energetic Washington would play in clubs until three in the morning and be in school at a quarter to eight. During the day he played classical music, practicing constantly.

Grover left Buffalo to play with the Four Clefs when he was just sixteen, traveling with them around the country. He spent his two army years at Fort Dix, New Jersey, playing saxophone in the army band and moonlighting in New York and Philadelphia, making connections with many major New York musicians. When a spot opened in organist Charles Earland's band, Grover stepped in, recorded an album with Earland, and began to develop his reputation. The album that established him as a vital new saxophone voice was the best-selling *Breakout*, with Johnny Hammond.

When Hammond's producer, record-company owner Creed Taylor, heard Grover play, he signed him to record as a lead. *Inner City Blues*, Washington's first album for Taylor, was so successful that Washington put together his own group. He went on to record *All the King's Horses*, *Soul Box*, and the fabulous gold-winner *Mr. Magic*. He made eight albums for Taylor, including *Feels So Good*, *A Secret Place*, *Live at the Bijou*, and 1978's *Reed Seed*. In addition, he has recorded with such top jazz musicians as Bob James, Randy Weston, Eric Gale, Ralph McDonald, and Dave Grusin.

Continually growing, Grover currently plans to institute a scholarship program, form his own production company, and record with such artists as McCoy Tyner, Stevie Wonder, Joni Mitchell, and Marvin Gaye.
1978/79 Discography: *Paradise*

WEATHER REPORT

Josef Zawinul—Keyboards

Wayne Shorter—Saxophones

Jaco Pastorius—Bass

Peter Erskine—Drums

Their free and breezy jazz-rock fusion sound, swung out with seemingly effortless ease, has won them the highest international awards. For seven years in a row *Downbeat's* readers have voted them band of the year; five of their seven albums were voted album of the year. Perhaps their eighth, 1978's top-three jazz charter *Mr. Gone*, will make that six out of eight. Weather Report swept the 1978 People's Poll held by the noted European jazz periodical *Jazz Forum*; they were also voted group of the year, and *Heavy Weather* was voted record of the year. In 1977 they won band- and record-of-the-year awards from *Playboy*; record of the year from *Cash Box*, instrumental group of the year from *Record World*, and Zawinul's "Birdland," from *Heavy Weather*, won a Grammy nomination for best instrumental composition. Pastorius received a Grammy nomination for best jazz soloist for his work on *Heavy Weather*.

With *Mr. Gone* a top jazz LP and their 1979 concerts occasions for joyously uncontrolled audience response, Weather Report continues to dominate the jazz fusion scene, drawing on the impressive experience of its members to create its winning music. Austrian-born Josef Zawinul began playing piano when he was twelve, studying for years at the Conservatory of Vienna. When he arrived in the United States in 1959, he had won a scholarship to Boston's Berklee College but dropped out of school to play in Maynard Ferguson's big band, where he first met Wayne Shorter.

During the following years, Zawinul played with such top jazz artists as Dinah Washington, Harry "Sweets" Edison, Joe Williams, Jusef Lateef, Cannonball Adderley, and the legendary Miles Davis. During the 1960s he recorded three solo albums as well.

During this time Wayne Shorter played with Art Blakey and Miles Davis and performed on several solo albums. Jaco Pastorius, an award-winning bass player, was featured on two of Joni Mitchell's albums and won raves for his own debut solo LP. Newest member of Weather Report, drummer Peter Erskine, began playing drums professionally when he was fourteen and by the time he was eighteen was a member of Stan Kenton's band. He moved from there to Maynard Ferguson's orchestra and then, in 1978, to Weather Report.
1978/79 Discography: *8:30*

BOB WELCH

Bob Welch explains his success simply. "I think I broke through with *French Kiss*," he says, "because I relaxed and did what I could do best, which is write songs that I, myself, would like to hear on the radio, rather than songs that would impress my friends with my obscure and moody brilliance." *French Kiss*, the singer/guitarist/songwriter's 1977 million-and-a-half-seller was a necessary hit for Welch at a late stage in a career that began in the late sixties. He worked then with a showband, the Seven Souls, playing night clubs around the country, lesser Las Vegas lounges, and chic European resorts.

While living in Europe in 1971 he was tapped to fill Jeremy Spencer's guitar spot in Fleetwood Mac, then a distinctive if as yet little-known band. Welch's association with Fleetwood lasted happily until 1975.

He loved playing with the band and, because of their acceptance, flourished with them as a songwriter. But at the end of 1974, Bob left, exhausted by tour after gruelling tour, the demands of completing a new album, and the attack Fleetwood was forced to mount against a ruthless ex-manager who toured another band using their name. To everyone's astonishment, soon after Bob left, Fleetwood Mac, with newly added Stevie Nicks and Lindsey Buckingham, scored its first titanic successes. Bob, in the meantime, was struggling once again to find his own musical identity. He began a band called Paris, a grating hard-rock trio whose two albums failed. Bob then heeded the encouragement and advice of Mick Fleetwood and Capitol Records' Director of Artist Acquisition John Carter, now his manager and producer, respectively. "They told me to do what I do best—just to be myself." On *French Kiss*, playing every instrument but drums, he did just that. In 1979 he followed that winning pattern with *Three Hearts*, a gold-winner, and fabulously successful tours of Japan and North America.
1978/79 Discography: *Three Hearts*

DOTTIE WEST

For youthful country-music veteran Dottie West, 1979 has been another year of duo triumph, as her 1978 smash with Kenny Rogers, "Every Time Two Fools Collide," won them a Country Music Association award as duo of the year. In 1979 their song "All I Ever Need Is You" was a number-one country winner; *Classics*, their duo album, was a top country LP.

From the beginning, Dottie's music career has been highlighted with very special awards and honors. She opened the 1973 season for

Gino Vannelli Courtesy A&M Records

The Village People Courtesy Casablanca Records and Filmworks

Anita Ward Courtesy TK Productions

Weather Report Courtesy Columbia Records

Bob Welch Olivier Ferrand/Courtesy Capitol Records

Grover Washington, Jr. Paul S. Wilson/Courtesy Elektra / Asylum Records

166

the Memphis Symphony Orchestra and performed with the Kansas City Symphony for a week. She won a B.M.I. Writer's award in 1961 for "This Is Me," a song made famous by Jim Reeves, the first of a roomful of songwriting and performing awards. She also wrote and performed two very successful commercials for Coca Cola. The second, containing the line "I was raised on country sunshine," won a Cleo, the advertising industry's top award, and the song "Country Sunshine" won her two Grammy nominations. That song came from her childhood experiences: "I was born and raised on a farm," Dottie says "I think the way you were raised never really leaves you. All of those roots are still there."

Since her early days as the oldest of ten children on a farm near McMinnville, Tennessee, Dottie always knew she would be a songwriter and a singer. She majored in music at Tennessee Tech, and during summer vacations she'd work in northern night clubs. In 1962 she signed with RCA; during her years with that label she wrote the top country song "Here Comes My Baby." Today Dottie is a hard-working country performer, putting in more than two hundred days a year on the road.
1978/79 Discography; *Classics* (with Kenny Rogers)

BARRY WHITE

Barry White calls his orchestra Love Unlimited, and the message of that name is the message of White's music. In the six short years since his single "I'm Gonna Love You Just a Little More Baby" shot to number one on the charts, followed by his first gold album, *I've Got So Much to Give*, he has won sixty gold and fifteen platinum records in the United States and abroad. The latest gold-winner for this sensitive and vibrant composer/arranger/producer/pianist and singer is 1979's *The Message Is Love*, following closely his 1978 platinum-winner *The Man*.

Known as The Maestro, Barry's love affair with music began in East Los Angeles, where he played piano at the age of five. When he was ten he was not only a singer in his church's choir but its organist and director as well. He quit high school at seventeen and struck out for Hollywood, where he paid dues for the next ten years. White's first job was in the artists and repertoire department at Bronco Records, and it was there that he was given his first opportunity to produce, turning out Felice Taylor's "I Feel Love Comin' On." He followed this with other hits, and then his own songs began to skyrocket to fame. "Love's Theme," the first hit for the Love Unlimited Orchestra, first zinged in discos. Although Barry won a special award from *Billboard* magazine as "The Man Who Started It All," he never followed the disco trend, but continued to make the music he loved to hear. When he recorded "It's Ecstasy (When You Lay Down Next to Me)," experts believed it was too mellow for disco success—but dancers felt differently. They loved it so much that they demanded its play and even developed a dance—the Spank—just for that song.

Today, Barry White is head of his own Unlimited Gold Records, distributed by CBS. With his label he can continue to do what he loves almost as much as he loves to perform: nurture new talent and turn it into tomorrow's stars.
1978/79 Discography: *The Message is Love*

THE WHO

Roger Daltrey—Vocals

Peter Townshend—Guitar

John Entwistle—Bass

Kenny Jones—Drums

In their heyday their rambunctious onstage antics were unforgettable and unsurpassed: Keith Moon fiendishly beating his drums; angelic Roger Daltrey swinging his microphone around his head like a twenty-first century lasso; improbably tall, long-faced Peter Townshend leaping high in the air and landing squarely on his knees as his audiences gasped, then cheered. At the end of their shows they smashed their instruments in a joyful frenzy, filling auditoriums with the earsplitting wails of tortured strings and crackling wood. They turned out a series of monster rock-and-roll albums and the first only-rock opera, the staggeringly successful *Tommy*. Throughout their sixteen-year career their classic songs have made rock history: "My Generation," "The Kids Are Alright," "I Can See for Miles," "Magic Bus," "Pinball Wizard," "I'm Free," "We're Not Gonna Take it," "Won't Get Fooled Again," and, 1978's smash surprise, "Who Are You," a hit all the more welcome after their two year absence from the recording studio. In 1979 they released their concert movie, *The Kids Are Alright*, a bonanza featuring some of their best performances between 1965 and 1978. Despite the devastating death of Keith Moon in 1978, the band continues.

Daltrey, Entwistle, and Townshend began making music with drummer Doug Sanden and singer Colin Dawson in 1963. Calling themselves the Detours, they floundered formlessly for a while. When their original singer left, Daltrey took over that role and they began to vary their mostly Beatles repertoire with R & B songs. Late in 1964, after Keith Moon had joined the group, they became the Who; in 1965 they released *The Who Sings My Generation*. The albums that followed—*Happy Jack, The Who Sell Out* (its satire on Radio London is generally considered rock's first concept album), and *Magic Bus*—all combined their lighter-than-air touch with ferocious rock and roll. By this time they were touring America, including appearances as headliners at the opening of the Fillmore West and at the Monterey Pop Festival. Their 1967 tour also saw them as opening act for Herman's Hermits.

In 1969 came the breathtakingly audacious *Tommy*, a brilliant success. After a mesmerizing performance at Woodstock, they returned to America later in the year to perform *Tommy* in concert halls throughout the United States. Although *Tommy* won them new respect, it also obscured their original reputation as a hard-rocking band. In 1970 they gave a final performance of *Tommy* at the Metropolitan Opera House in New York and released *Live at Leeds* to remind people of their rocking roots.

In the years that followed the Who released *Who's Next, Meaty, Beaty, Big and Bouncy, Quadrophenia, Odds & Sods, The Who By Numbers, Who Are You*, and, in 1979, the soundtrack of *The Kids Are Alright*.
1978/79 Discography: *The Kids Are Alright*

DON WILLIAMS

If country music stars are traditionally hard-drinking, rambling, gambling men, then in his own quiet way Don Williams Is a rebel, because he is none of those things. In a business where the outrageous is the norm, Williams is a serious, private, family man who says of himself, "I'm just not a big hanger-outer—never have been. I'd just rather be at home with my wife and sons." Affectionately known as the "gentle giant," Don relies on his awesome talent to win him fame and success. In 1978 and 1979 he continued to pull in honors, winning the Country Music Association's male vocalist award in 1978 and seeing his 1978 song "Tulsa Time" voted the single record of the year by the Academy of Country Music. In 1979 he had a top-five country single with "Lay Down Beside Me."

The Texas born singer/guitarist/songwriter, who has more than five hundred songs to his credit, including the memorable "Amanda," "Come Early Morning," "Atta Way to Go," "The Ties that Bind," and "Till the Rivers Run Dry," played his first guitar when he was twelve. He fell in love with it immediately and would rush home after school to listen to the radio and pick out the melodies he heard. During high school and the army he played with a number of different small groups. In 1964 he formed the Pozo Seco Singers with two other country singers; the trio hit big with the classic song "Time."

The Pozo Seco Singers broke up in 1970, and Don began writing country songs that were recorded by such stars as Charley Pride, Sonny James, Johnny Cash, and Lefty Frizzell. Producers who had heard Williams sing urged him to record his own songs, and when he finally did they all turned into hits.

Y

WINGS with Paul McCartney

Paul McCartney—Bass, guitars, synthesizer, vocals

Linda McCartney—Synthesizers, organ, piano, vocals

Denny Laine—Guitars, bass, piano

Laurence Juber—Guitar

Steve Holly—Drums

In 1979 it was a new Paul McCartney—head thrust forward, mouth open wide, wailing his heart out, his music supercharged with deep emotion. The irresistible melodic hooks were still there, but such songs as the insistent "Goodnight Tonight," the driving "Getting Closer," and "Daytime, Nighttime Suffering," were uncensored outpourings from the soul. Did his fans respond? With fervor. McCartney in 1979 added new luster to his already gleaming reputation as a high prince of pop rock. According to the *Guinness Book of World Records* McCartney has earned a total of fifty-nine gold disks, more than any other performer. Forty-three date from his Beatle days and sixteen were earned with his ace band Wings. In 1979 he and Wings won another gold with "Goodnight Tonight" and flaunted two more platinum feathers, one for the bountiful *Wings Greatest*, the other for *Back to the Egg*, an album of occasional oddities, sweet jazzy moments, and hard rockers.

Billed as a concept album by McCartney, *Back to the Egg* features Paul's own rock symphony, "Rockestra Theme," boasting such stellar musicians as John Bonham on drums, Ronnie Lane on bass, J.P. Jones and Gary Brooker on keyboards, David Gilmore and Peter Townshend on guitar. That historic session had been planned to take place in the celebrated Abbey Road Studio Two, but it was unavailable. Undaunted Paul created an uncanny facsimile in the basement of McCartney Productions headquarters in Soho Square. The portable setup was correct to the last detail, even including curtains on the walls where the windows were in the actual studio.

Recognizing McCartney's stunning success today, it's hard to believe that after the Beatles split he struggled for several years to find his own voice. Critics trashed his first two solo disks, *McCartney* and *Ram*, while *Wild Life* and *Red Rose Speedway*, his first tentative efforts with an embryonic Wings, were far from chart burners. Those largely disappointing disks, however, contained gleams of the old McCartney magic in such melodic smashes as "Uncle Albert/Admiral Halsey," "My Love," "Hi Hi Hi," and "Live and Let Die." His next three albums found Paul spinning music with his old fire, creating such classic songs as "Band on the Run," "Listen to What the Man Said," "Letting Go," and "Silly Love Songs," from the albums *Band on the Run*, *Venus and Mars*, and *Wings at the Speed of Sound*. In 1976 Wings toured America and delivered an unequalled show, captured on the live LP *Wings Over America*. *London Town*, his 1978 million-seller, contained the hit single "With a Little Luck," winning for Paul his sixth number-one single since the beginning of the 1970s. He also recorded the loving celebration of his Scottish home, "The Mull of Kintyre," Britain's most popular single of all time.
1978/79 Discography: *Back to the Egg*

NEIL YOUNG

For a brief, bright moment between 1966 and 1968 a brilliant American band called the Buffalo Springfield flashed across the music scene. The core of the group was singer/songwriter/guitarists Neil Young and Stephen Stills, and their achingly beautiful songs—including Stills's moving anthem "For What it's Worth" and Young's distinctive "Broken Arrow," "Mr. Soul," and "Nowadays Clancy Can't Even Sing"—marked the band as an instant legend. Stills and Young consistently squabbled, however, leading to the band's early demise.

Before the Springfield, Toronto-born Young had formed a pop band, Neil Young and the Squires, in Winnipeg. He broke away from them to work as a folk singer in Canadian and border clubs. It was in one of those clubs that he met Stills. Young liked Stills and his musical ideas and in 1966 drove to Los Angeles in his 1953 Pontiac hearse to find him. When the Springfield broke up, Young again began to play on his own in small clubs. He released his first solo album, *Neil Young*, in January 1969. This disappointing LP was followed by his first disk with the band he named Crazy Horse. *Everybody Knows This Is Nowhere*, featuring the mournful keening of Young's voice and his impressive guitar work, contained the outstanding songs "Cowgirl in the Sand" and "Down by the River."

In June 1969 he joined with David Crosby, Stephen Stills, and Graham Nash, forming the supergroup Crosby, Stills, Nash and Young. To their first album, 1970's *Deja Vu*, he contributed the powerful "Helpless" and "Country Girl." His next solo album was the haunting *After the Goldrush*, considered Young's best album to date. Young's fame was at a peak and his creative and performing abilities never seemed greater, yet his next album, *Harvest*, was dismal. For the next few years his work declined, accentuated by his stricken reaction to the overdose deaths of Crazy Horse guitarist and vocalist Danny Whitten and roadie Bruce Berry.

Near the end of 1975, however, Young released the album *Zuma*, a return to less painful music. It was followed by the Stills and Young collaboration *Long May You Run*, the solo *American Stars 'n Bars*, the massive retrospective *Decade*, 1978's gold-winning *Comes a Time*, and 1979's *Rust Never Sleeps*, the soundtrack from the movie of the same name, a documentary of Young's last tour.
1978/79 Discography: *Rust Never Sleeps*

Dottie West   Courtesy United Artists Records

Barry White

Don Williams   Courtesy MCA Records

The Who   Courtesy MCA Records

Wings with Paul McCartney   Courtesy Columbia Records

Neil Young

169

NEWCOMERS

DIRE STRAITS

Mark Knopfler—Lead guitar, vocals

David Knopfler—Rhythm guitar

John Illsley—Bass

Pick Withers—Drums

No, it wasn't Bob Dylan, although there was a quality in the baritone of the singer that made you look up and ask, "Dylan?" And it wasn't Lou Reed, although there was a flavor of Reed lurking in the music. However, as you listened, pulled easily in by the shimmering guitar work and the haunting melody, you realized with growing excitement that this unknown band made music like you'd never heard before. Dire Straits' first single, "Sultans of Swing," announced itself with such unquestionable authority and such melodic élan that it commanded instant attention. Slicing cleanly through 1979's universal disco throb and pounding punk rhythms, their first album, *Dire Straits*, sold a million copies at the speed of sound.

The typical overnight success story is one in which "overnight" means heartbreaking years of grinding work and one-night stands, the struggle to become good and to be heard. But Dire Straits seems to have been born full blown, an instantly polished merger of vocals and instrumentals. The band was formed in 1977 by former journalist and English teacher Mark Knopfler, his brother David, and David's roommate, John Illsley. Pick Withers, a drummer living in London, joined the band, and the four began to play together seriously, finally scraping up enough pounds sterling to cut a demo tape.

They sent the tape to Charlie Gillett because the foursome admired his Sunday morning music show on Radio London and agreed with the rock reviews he wrote as well. All they hoped for was that Gillett would listen to the tape and give them some advice; but when Gillett heard Dire Straits' music he went wild for their sound and played tracks on his show. Offers from record companies and tour promoters began to pour in. The band signed with Warner Brothers Records in America and toured to superlative reviews. Their second LP, *Communiqué*, also sold a million copies, and Mark Knopfler and Pick Withers were chosen by Bob Dylan to play on his 1979 album.
1978/79 Discography: *Dire Straits*
Communiqué

RICKIE LEE JONES

With her debut album and her winsome single "Chuck E's in Love" both gold-winning, top-five hits, the very relaxed, sensual Rickie Lee Jones shines out as a radiant major artist.

Born in Chicago twenty-four years ago, her father was a songwriter and musician who wrote a lullaby titled "The Moon Is Made of Gold" to celebrate the birth of his daughter. She moved to Los Angeles in her early twenties, began writing songs and performing them wherever she could play. As she explains, with her straightforward grin, she'd play "in dives and little bars that pay about ten dollars per four sets. If I could get one, I'd use a jazz trio; if not, I'd go solo." Her solo career was only five performances old when her manager took her tape to Warner Brothers Records, who recognized a future star.

Warner was so impressed by her original material that Lenny Waronker, Warner's A & R chief, and producer Russ Titelman were eager to coproduce her debut album. They picked the cream of the crop when they chose her musicians, selecting such stellar names as Jeff Porcaro on drums, Willie Weeks on fender bass, Red Callender on acoustic bass, Mac Rebennack on keyboards, Randy Newman on synthesizer. Despite her youth and inexperience Rickie Lee blended skillfully with the veterans to produce songs that burst with vitality, some with an R & B throb, some with a jazz base, all deft, complex, yet direct. With her soaring vocal range, distinctive singing style, and intimate stage presence, Rickie Lee Jones is a new star who's here to stay.
1978/79 Discography: *Rickie Lee Jones*

THE KNACK

Doug Fieger—Lead vocals, guitar

Berton Averre—Lead Guitar

Bruce Gary—Drums

Prescott Niles—Bass

With an infectious single called "My Sharona" and a debut album called *Get the Knack*, the fresh, young, energetic band called the Knack zoomed onto the music scene in mid-1979, knocked audiences out of their seats, won breathless praise from *Rolling Stone* and, according to Doug Weston, owner of Hollywood's starmaker club the Troubadour, "The band has created the most excitement I've seen at my club since Elton John debuted in the U.S. in 1970." They were barely a year old when "My Sharona" slammed into the top of the charts, led by the already gold-winning *Get the Knack*.

After a few short months of honing their powerhouse performances, the band signed with Capitol and swiftly pulled in ace producer Mike Chapman to produce their album. That disk flowed out of them in less than two weeks, its combination of steaming rockers and hook-laden pop confections an instant winner. Tours of Europe and the United States showed off their full-tilt live energy, winning new fans everywhere for this dynamic new band.
1978/79 Discography: *Get the Knack*

Dire Straits

Rickie Lee Jones

The Knack

TOP SELLERS

(From October 1978 through August 1979)

Platinum Record Awards

Albums (Indicates sales of more than 1 million copies)

Briefcase Full of Blues, Blues Brothers
Elan, Firefall
Brother to Brother, Gino Vannelli
Toto, Toto
Octave, Moody Blues
Spirits Having Flown, Bee Gees
The Gambler, Kenny Rogers
Minute by Minute, Doobie Brothers
Two for the Show, Kansas
Time Passages, Al Stewart
Love Tracks, Gloria Gaynor
Dire Straits, Dire Straits
2 Hot, Peaches and Herb
Go West, Village People
Desolation Angels, Bad Company
Bad Girls, Donna Summer
Destiny, The Jacksons
Van Halen II, Van Halen
Breakfast in America, Supertramp
Sleeper Catcher, Little River Band
Live At Budokan, Cheap Trick
We Are Family, Sister Sledge
Parallel Lines, Blondie
I Am, Earth, Wind & Fire
Back To The Egg, Wings
Discovery, Electric Light Orchestra
Dynasty, Kiss
Teddy, Teddy Pendergrass
Get the Knack, The Knack
Candy-O, The Cars
Rickie Lee Jones, Rickie Lee Jones
Million Mile Reflections, The Charlie Daniels Band

Singles (Indicates sales of more than 2 million copies)

"Hot Child in the City," Nick Gilder
"Y.M.C.A.," Village People
"Too Much Heaven," Bee Gees
"Do Ya Think I'm Sexy," Rod Stewart
"I Will Survive," Gloria Gaynor
"Reunited," Peaches and Herb
"Tragedy," Bee Gees
"Shake Your Body," The Jacksons
"Ain't No Stoppin' Us Now," McFadden and Whitehead
"Hot Stuff," Donna Summer
"Knock on Wood," Amii Stewart

Gold Record Awards

Albums (Indicates sales of more than 500,000 copies)

Heaven Tonight, Cheap Trick
Spark of Love, Lenny Williams
10th Anniversary of Golden Piano Hits,
   Ferrante and Teicher
John Denver, John Denver
Life for the Taking, Eddie Money
Love Beach, Emerson, Lake and Palmer
New Kind of Feeling, Anne Murray
Sanctuary, J. Geils Band
Gold, Jefferson Starship
Willie and Family Live, Willie Nelson
Step II, Sylvester
Energy, Pointer Sisters
Armed Forces, Elvis Costello
Cheryl Lynn, Cheryl Lynn
TNT, Tanya Tucker
Three Hearts, Bob Welch
Knock on Wood, Amii Stewart
Crosswinds, Peabo Bryson
Nicolette, Nicolette Larson
Enlightened Rogues, The Allman Brothers Band
Wanted Live in Concert, Richard Pryor
Livin' Inside Your Love, George Benson
I Love You So, Natalie Cole
Evolution, Journey
Legend, Poco
Music Box Dancer, Frank Mills
Instant Funk, Instant Funk
Music Box, Evelyn "Champagne" King
Inspiration, Maze featuring Frankie Beverly
Disco Nights, G Q
George Harrison, George Harrison
Flag, James Taylor
Hair, Various Artists
Greatest Hits, Waylon Jennings
Take Me Home, Cher
The Message Is Love, Barry White
Sooner or Later, Rex Smith
Night Owl, Gerry Rafferty
Winner Takes All, Isley Brothers
State Of Shock, Ted Nugent
Underdog, Atlanta Rhythm Section
Monolith, Kansas

Annie, Original Cast Album
The Kids Are Alright, The Who
Communiqué, Dire Straits
Best Of Nat King Cole, Nat King Cole
Molly Hatchet, Molly Hatchet
Classics, Kenny Rogers and Dottie West
Where I Should Be, Peter Frampton
The Music Band, War
Waiting for Columbus, Little Feat
Hot Property, Heatwave
Queen Live Killers, Queen
Reality…What a Concept, Robin Williams
One for the Road, Willie Nelson and Leon Russell
Decade, Neil Young
Bustin' Loose, Chuck Brown and the Soul Searchers
Rock On, Raydio
In Color, Cheap Trick
McFadden and Whitehead, McFadden and Whitehead
Street Life, The Crusaders
What Cha Gonna Do With My Lovin', Stephanie Mills
A Night At Studio 54, Various Artists
Candy, Con Funk Shun
Rust Never Sleeps, Neil Young

Gold Record Awards

Singles (Indicates sales of more than 1 million copies)

"(Our Love) Don't Throw it All Away," Andy Gibb
"Got To Be Real," Cheryl Lynn
"My Life," Billy Joel
"Instant Replay," Dan Hartman
"September," Earth, Wind & Fire
"Every 1's A Winner," Hot Chocolate
"Fire," Pointer Sisters
"A Little More Love," Olivia Newton-John
"Hold The Line," Toto

"Shake Your Groove Thing," Peaches and Herb
"I Don't Know if It's Right," Evelyn "Champagne" King
"I Want Your Love," Chic
"Heaven Knows," Donna Summer with Brooklyn Dreams
"Bustin' Loose," Chuck Brown and the Soul Searchers
"In the Navy," Village People
"Music Box Dancer," Frank Mills
"I Got My Mind Made Up (You Can Get it Girl)," Instant Funk
"What A Fool Believes," Doobie Brothers
"Heart of Glass," Blondie
"Livin' it Up," Bell and James
"Love You Inside Out," Bee Gees
"Disco Nights (Rock-Freak)," G Q
"Take Me Home," Chér
"Good Night Tonight," Wings
"Boogie Wonderland," Earth, Wind & Fire with the Emotions
"Stumblin' In," Suzi Quatro with Chris Norman
"We Are Family," Sister Sledge
"Bad Girls," Donna Summer
"Good Times," Chic
"You Take My Breath Away," Rex Smith
"Makin' It," David Naughton
"Just When I Needed You Most," Randy Vanwarmer
"She Believes in Me," Kenny Rogers
"I Want You to Want Me," Cheap Trick
"My Sharona," The Knack
"I Was Made for Lovin' You," Kiss
"Mama Can't Buy You Love," Elton John
"The Devil Went Down to Georgia," The Charlie Daniels Band
"When You're in Love with a Beautiful Woman," Dr. Hook
"Main Event," Barbra Streisand
"You Gonna Make Me Love Somebody Else," The Jones Girls

MAJOR AWARDS

Billboard's #1 Music Award Winners

(Presented December 23, 1978, by Billboard magazine)

Album of the Year: *Saturday Night Fever*, Bee Gees
Female Artist of the Year: Linda Ronstadt
Male Artist of the Year: Andy Gibb
Single of the Year: "Shadow Dancing," Andy Gibb
Group of the Year: Bee Gees
Soul Artist of the Year: Earth, Wind & Fire
Country Artist of the Year: Dolly Parton
Disco Artist of the Year: Donna Summer
Jazz Artist of the Year: Chuck Mangione
Easy Listening Artist of the Year: Barry Manilow
New Artist of the Year: Meat Loaf
Soundtrack of the Year: *Saturday Night Fever*

Dick Clark's American Music Award Winners

(Presented January 12, 1979, by Dick Clark)

Favorite Pop/Rock Male Vocalist: Barry Manilow
Favorite Pop/Rock Female Vocalist: Linda Ronstadt
Favorite Pop/Rock Duo or Group: Bee Gees
Favorite Pop/Rock Album: *Grease*, movie soundtrack
Favorite Pop/Rock Single: "Three Times a Lady," Commodores
Favorite Country Male Vocalist: Kenny Rogers
Favorite Country Female Vocalist: Crystal Gayle
Favorite Country Duo or Group: The Statler Brothers
Favorite Country Album: *10 Years of Gold*, Kenny Rogers
Favorite Country Single: "Blue Bayou," Linda Ronstadt
Favorite Soul Male Vocalist: Teddy Pendergrass and Lou Rawls (dual award)
Favorite Soul Female Vocalist: Natalie Cole
Favorite Soul Group: Earth, Wind & Fire
Favorite Soul Single: "Too Much, Too Little, Too Late," Johnny Mathis and Deniece Williams
Favorite Soul Album: *Saturday Night Fever*
Favorite Disco Male Vocalist: Isaac Hayes
Favorite Disco Female Vocalist: Donna Summer
Favorite Disco Group: Village People
Favorite Disco Single: "Last Dance," Donna Summer
Favorite Disco Album: *Live and More*, Donna Summer

Golden Globe Award Winners

(Presented January 27, 1979, by the Hollywood Foreign Press Association)

Best Original Score for a Motion Picture: Midnight Express, Giorgio Moroder

Best Original Motion Picture Song: "Last Dance," by Paul Jabara

Grammy Award Winners

(Presented February 15, 1979, by the National Academy of Recording Arts and Sciences)

Record of the Year: "Just the Way You Are," Billy Joel; Columbia; producer: Phil Ramone

Album of the Year: *Saturday Night Fever*, Bee Gees, David Shire, Yvonne Elliman, Tavares, Kool and the Gang, K.C. and the Sunshine Band, MFSB, Trammps, Walter Murphy, Ralph MacDonald; RSO; producers: Bee Gees, Karl Richardson, Albhy Galuten, Freddie Perren, Bill Oakes, David Shire, Arif Mardin, Thomas J. Valentino, Ralph MacDonald, W. Walter, K.G. Productions, H. W. Casey, Richard Finch, Bobby Martin, Broadway Eddie, Ron Kersey

Song of the Year: "Just the Way You Are," Billy Joel; publisher: Joelsongs

New Artist of the Year: A Taste of Honey; Capitol

Producer of the Year: Bee Gees, Albhy Galuten, Karl Richardson

Pop Female Vocal Performance: "You Needed Me," Anne Murray; Capitol

Pop Male Vocal Performance: "Copacabana (At the Copa)," Barry Manilow; Arista

Pop Vocal Performance, Duo, Group or Chorus: *Saturday Night Fever*, Bee Gees; RSO

Pop Instrumental Performance: "Children of Sanchez," Chuck Mangione Group; A&M

R&B Female Vocal Performance: "Last Dance," Donna Summer; Casablanca

R&B Male Vocal Performance: "On Broadway," George Benson; Warner Brothers

R&B Vocal Performance, Duo, Group or Chorus: "All 'N' All," Earth, Wind & Fire; Columbia

R&B Instrumental Performance: "Runnin'," Earth, Wind & Fire; Columbia

R&B Song: "Last Dance," Paul Jabara; publisher: Primus Artists/Olga

Contemporary Soul Gospel Performance: "Live in London," Andraé Crouch and the Disciples; Light

Traditional Soul Gospel Performance: "Live and Direct," Mighty Clouds of Joy; ABC

Jazz Vocal Performance: "All Fly Home," Al Jarreau; Warner Brothers

Jazz Solo Instrumental Performance: "Montreux '77—Oscar Peterson Jam," Oscar Peterson; Pablo

Jazz Group Instrumental Performance: "Friends," Chick Corea; Polydor

Jazz Big Band Instrumental Performance: "Live in Munich," Thad Jones, Mel Lewis; Horizon/A&M

Country Female Vocal Performance: "Here You Come Again," Dolly Parton; RCA

Country Male Vocal Performance: "Georgia On My Mind," Willie Nelson; Columbia

Country Vocal Performance by a Duo or Group: "Mamas Don't Let Your Babies Grow Up to be Cowboys," Waylon Jennings and Willie Nelson; RCA

Country Instrumental Performance: "One O'Clock Jump," Asleep at the Wheel; Capitol

Country Song: "The Gambler," Don Schlitz; publisher: Writer's Night.

Instrumental Composition: "Theme From 'Close Encounters of the Third Kind,'" John Williams

Album of Original Score Written for a Motion Picture or a Television Special: "Close Encounters of the Third Kind," John Williams; Arista

Instrumental Arrangement: "Main Title (Overture Part One)—'The Wiz,'" original soundtrack, Quincy Jones and Robert Freedman; MCA

Arrangement Accompanying Vocalists: "Got To Get You Into My Life," Maurice White; RSO

Arrangement for Voices: "Stayin' Alive," Bee Gees; RSO

Inspirational Performance: "Happy Man," B. J. Thomas; Myrrh

Contemporary or Inspirational Gospel Performance: "What A Friend," Larry Hart; Genesis

Traditional Gospel Performance: "Refreshing," The Happy Goodman Family; Canaan

Ethnic or Traditional: "I'm Ready," Muddy Waters; Blue Sky

Latin: "Homenaje A Beny More," Tito Puente; Tico

Children's: "The Muppet Show," Jim Henson; Arista

Comedy: "A Wild and Crazy Guy," Steve Martin ; Warner Brothers

Non-Musical Spoken Word: "Citizen Kane," Orson Welles; Mark 56

Cast Album: *Ain't Misbehavin'*, Thomas Fats Waller and other composers; Thomas Z. Shepard producer; RCA Red Seal

Classical Album of the Year: *Brahms: Concerto for Violin in D Major*, Itzhak Perlman with Carlo Maria Giulini, Chicago Symphony; Christopher Bishop producer; Angel

Classical Orchestra Performance: *Beethoven: Symphonies (9) Complete*, Herbert von Karajan, Berlin Philharmonic, Michel Glotz producer; DG

Opera Recording: *Lehár: The Merry Widow*, Julius Rudel, George Sponhaltz and John Coveney producers; Angel

Choral Performance Other Than Opera: *Beethoven: Missa Solemnis*, Sir Georg Solti, Chicago Symphony; Margaret Hillis choral director; London

Chamber Music Performance: *Beethoven: Sonatas for Violin and Piano*, Itzhak Perlman and Vladimir Ashkenazy; London

Classical Instrumental Soloist with Orchestra: "Rachmaninoff: Concerto No. 3 in D Minor for Piano" *(Horowitz Golden Jubilee)*, Vladimir Horowitz; RCA

Classical Instrumental Soloist without Orchestra: *The Horowitz Concerts 1977/78*, Vladimir Horowitz; RCA

Classical Solo Vocal Performance: *Luciano Pavarotti—Hits From Lincoln Center*, Luciano Pavarotti; London

Classical Engineering: "Varèse: Amériques/Arcana/Ionisation" *(Boulez Conducts Varèse)*, New York Philharmonic; Bud Graham, Arthur Kendy, and Ray Moore engineers; Columbia

Award Winners for Best-Selling Records

(Presented March 27, 1979, by the National Association of Recording Merchandisers)

Movie Soundtrack Album: *Saturday Night Fever*, Bee Gees
Broadway Cast Album: *Annie*
Album by a Group: *Double Vision*, Foreigner
Album by a Male Artist: *The Stranger*, Billy Joel
Album by a Female Artist: *Greatest Hits, Volume II*, Barbra Streisand; *Live and More*, Donna Summer (dual award)
Album by a Country Group: *Best of the Statler Brothers*, The Statler Brothers
Album by a Male Country Artist: *Stardust*, Willie Nelson
Album by a Female Country Artist: *Let's Keep It That Way*, Anne Murray
Album by a Black Group: *Natural High*, Commodores
Album by a Black Male Artist: *Weekend in L.A.*, George Benson
Album by a Black Female Artist: *Live and More*, Donna Summer
Jazz Album: *Feels So Good*, Chuck Mangione
Comedy Album: *A Wild and Crazy Guy*, Steve Martin
Classical Album: *Suite for Flute and Jazz Piano*, Jean-Pierre Rampal and Claude Bolling
Children's Album: *Sesame Street Fever*, the Muppets and Robin Gibb
Album by a New Artist: *Bat Out of Hell*, Meat Loaf; *City to City*, Gerry Rafferty; *The Cars*, the Cars; *Toto*, Toto
Single Record: "Stayin' Alive," Bee Gees

Academy Award Winners

(Presented April 9, 1979, by the Academy of Motion Picture Arts and Sciences)

Best Original Music Score: *Midnight Express*, Giorgio Moroder
Best Original Score Adaptation: *The Buddy Holly Story*, adapted by Joe Renzetti
Best Original Song: "Last Dance," music and lyrics by Paul Jabara

Academy of Country Music Award Winners

(Presented May 2, 1979, by the Academy of Country Music)

Bass: Rod Culpepper
Fiddle: Johnny Gimble
Drums: Archie Francis
Guitar: James Burton
Keyboard: Jimmy Pruitt
Steel Guitar: Buddy Emmons
Specialty Instrument: Charlie McCoy (harmonica)
Band of the Year (Touring): Original Texas Playboys (Leon McAuliffe)
Band of the Year (Non-Touring): Rebel Playboys (Danny Michaels)
Radio Station of the Year: KVOO, Tulsa, Oklahoma
Disk Jockey of the Year: Billy Parker, KVOO, Tulsa, Oklahoma

Country Night Club of the Year: Palomino, North Hollywood, California
Top New Female Vocalist: Christy Lane
Top New Male Vocalist: John Conlee
Top Vocal Group: The Oak Ridge Boys
Album of the Year: *Ya'll Come Back Saloon*, The Oak Ridge Boys
Top Male Vocalist: Kenny Rogers
Top Female Vocalist: Barbara Mandrell
Single Record of the Year: "Tulsa Time," Don Williams
Entertainer of the Year: Kenny Rogers
Song of the Year: "You Needed Me," Anne Murray
Jim Reeves Memorial Award: Joe Cates
Pioneer Award: Eddie Dean

Tony Award Winners

(Antoinette Perry Awards presented June 3, 1979, by the American Theatre Wing and the League of N.Y. Theatres and Producers)

Best Musical: *Sweeney Todd*, music by Stephen Sondheim
Best Musical Book: *Sweeney Todd*, book by Hugh Wheeler
Best Musical Score: *Sweeney Todd*, music by Stephen Sondheim
Best Actor in a Musical: Len Cariou, *Sweeney Todd*
Best Actress in a Musical: Angela Lansbury, *Sweeney Todd*
Best Featured Actor in a Musical: Henderson Forsythe, *The Best Little Whorehouse in Texas*
Best Featured Actress in a Musical: Carlin Glynn, *The Best Little Whorehouse in Texas*
Best Director of a Musical: Harold Prince, *Sweeney Todd*
Best Choreographer: Michael Bennett and Bob Avian, *Ballroom*
Best Scenic Designer: Eugene Lee, *Sweeney Todd*
Best Costume Designer: Franne Lee, *Sweeney Todd*
Lawrence Langner Award: Richard Rodgers

Billboard's Disco Forum VI Awards

(Presented July 15, 1979 by Billboard magazine)

Best Overall Disco Performer: Donna Summer
Best Female Disco Artist: Donna Summer
Best Male Disco Artist: Sylvester
Best Female Disco Group: Sister Sledge
Best Male Disco Group: Village People
Most Promising New Female Disco Artist: Anita Ward
Most Promising New Male Disco Artist: Gino Soccio
Most Promising New Disco Group: GQ
Best Album: *Live and More*, Donna Summer, and *C'est Chic*, Chic (dual award)
Best Single: "Le Freak," Chic
Best Live Group: Village People
Best Studio Group: Voyage
International Grand Prix Award: "I Will Survive," Gloria Gaynor

Emmy Award Winners

(Presented September 9, 1979, by the Academy of Television Arts and Sciences)

Comedy-Variety or Music Special: "Steve and Eydie Celebrate Irving Berlin," Steve Lawrence and Eydie Gormé

Classical Program in the Performing Arts: George Balanchine for "Dance in America, Great Performances"

Outstanding Musical Composition for a Series (Dramatic Underscore): David Rose for "Little House on the Prairie"

Outstanding Achievement in Musical Composition for a Special (Dramatic Underscore): Leonard Rosenman for "Friendly Fire"

Outstanding Achievement in Choreography for a Music-Variety Special: Kevin Carlisle for "The Third Barry Manilow Special"

Outstanding Achievement in Cinematography for a Limited Series or a Special: Howard Schwartz for "Rainbow"

Country Music Association Awards

(Presented October 8, 1979, by the Country Music Association)

Entertainer of the Year: Willie Nelson

Single of the Year: "The Devil Went Down to Georgia," the Charlie Daniels Band

Album of the Year: *The Gambler,* Kenny Rogers

Song of the Year: "The Gambler," by Don Schlitz

Female Vocalist of the Year: Barbara Mandrell

Male Vocalist of the Year: Kenny Rogers

Vocal Group of the Year: the Statler Brothers

Vocal Duo of the Year: Kenny Rogers and Dottie West

Instrumental Group of the Year: the Charlie Daniels Band

Instrumentalist of the Year: Charlie Daniels

UPDATE

Rock

After years of tantalizing promises, ABBA brought its shining sound to America, beginning September 13 in Canada and winging throughout the country until the first week in October. Grace Slick and Marty Balin officially stopped performing with the Jefferson Starship, which was joined by Mickey Thomas.

Hot rockers late in 1979 were "Don't Bring Me Down" by the Electric Light Orchestra, "Lonesome Loser" by the Little River Band, "Pop Muzik" by M, "Cruel to Be Kind" by Nick Lowe, and "Bad Case of Loving You" by Robert Palmer. The albums that rocked were Led Zeppelin's explosive *In Through the Out Door,* Cheap Trick's *In Color,* Fleetwood Mac's *Tusk,* the Eagles' *Long Run.*

R & B

The top soul singles in the fall and early winter included "Found a Cure" by Ashford and Simpson, "Don't Stop Til You Get Enough" by Michael Jackson, "I Just Want to Be" by Cameo, "Firecracker" by Mass Production, "Sing a Happy Song" by the O'Jays, "Sail On" by the Commodores, "Dim All the Lights" by Donna Summer, and "Break My Heart" by David Ruffin.

LPs that climbed to the top of the soul charts were *Midnight Magic* by the Commodores, *Minnie* by Minnie Riperton, *Risqué* by Chic, *Secret Omen* by Cameo, *Off the Wall* by Michael Jackson, *Stay Free* by Ashford and Simpson, *Identify Yourself* by the O'Jays, and *Take it Home* by B. B. King.

Country

Autumn 1979's hottest country singles included Conway Twitty's "I May Never Get to Heaven," Kenny Rogers and Dottie West's "Til I Can Make it On My Own," Charley Pride's "You're My Jamaica," Moe Bandy and Joe Stampley's "Just Good Ol' Boys," Don Williams's "It Must Be Love," Jim Ed Brown and Helen Cornelius's "Fools," and T. G. Sheppard's "Last Cheater's Waltz." Top albums were Dolly Parton's *Great Balls of Fire* and Hank Williams, Jr.'s *Family Tradition.*

The Silver Spurz Orchestra cut disco versions of such western chestnuts as "Happy Trails" and "Tumblin' Tumbleweeds."

Disco

On September 8 disco fans flocked to Buffalo, New York, for the World's Largest Disco, with performances by Gloria Gaynor, the Trammps, and the Raes.

Among disco's hottest numbers in the fall were Freddie James's "Get Up and Boogie," Ashford and Simpson's "Found a Cure/Stay Free/Nobody Knows," France Joli's "Come to Me/Don't Stop Dancing/Playboy," Kat Mandu's "The Break," Cory Daye's "Pow Wow/Green Light," Michael Jackson's "Don't Stop Til You Get Enough," and M's "Pop Muzik."

Jazz

Top jazz albums through the end of the year included Bob James's *Lucky Seven,* Joni Mitchell's *Mingus,* and Stanley Clarke's *I Wanna Play for You.*

Jazz Festivals were strong, including the Jazz Institute of Chicago's seven days of top music, with Benny Goodman, Mel Tormé, the Billy Taylor Trio, and McCoy Tyner. Tributes to Charlie Parker, John Coltrane and Wes Montgomery, Duke Ellington, and Benny Goodman and Mel Tormé were successful features of the event. In France, Ray Charles, Count Basie, and Keith Jarrett highlighted the 20th Festival International de Jazz at Juan Les Pins. Basie celebrated his seventy-fifth birthday on the "Today" show on August 22.

The month of September was proclaimed Jazz Month in Atlanta in honor of the Atlanta Free Jazz Festival held between September 28 and 30 and featuring such stars as Woody Shaw, Bobby Hutcherson, the Jimmy Owens band featuring Bill Hart, Lester Bowie, and Eddie Henderson.

Easy Listening

Top fall 1979 MOR songs included Herb Alpert's "Rise," Maureen McGovern's "Different Worlds," Lobo's "Where Were You When I Was Falling in Love," and Earth, Wind & Fire's "After the Love Has Gone."

Claiming top-forty radio resistance to their name, performers Steve Lawrence and Eydie Gormé released "Hallelujah" under the pseudonym Parker and Penny.

Classical

The San Francisco Symphony adopted the format of New York's successful Mostly Mozart Festival and performed six weeks of baroque and classical selections beginning September 24. The West Coast version, as in New York, featured one low price for all seats, an informal atmosphere, and such promotional items as T-shirts and Frisbees, all aimed at attracting a younger audience to the classics.

Top classical records in the fall of 1979 were *New Year's in Vienna,* performed by the Vienna Philharmonic; *Pipa Concerto, the Boston Symphony China Tour;* Zubin Mehta and the Israel Philharmonic's version of Mahler's Fourth Symphony; Itzhak Perlman's *Virtuoso Violinist;* and *More Rampal's Greatest Hits.*

Movies

French Postcards, with music by John Sebastian, was released on September 28. In November audiences welcomed Bette Midler's long-awaited *The Rose,* with Bette starring as a hard-living, hard-singing Janis Joplinesque 1960s rock singer. In December came Steve Martin's loony *The Jerk* and the eagerly anticipated *All That Jazz,* Bob Fosse's big musical.

The Electric Horseman, featuring Willie Nelson in a non-singing role, starred Robert Redford and Jane Fonda and opened in December.

Stage

Undaunted by the failures of the 1978–79 Broadway season, musical theater popped in late 1979. Several musicals recaptured the big-band era. *The 1940's Radio Hour* opened at the St. James on October 7. The recreation of a live radio broadcast featured music by Duke Ellington, George Gershwin, Richard Rodgers, Harold Arlen, and Johnny Mercer. *All Night Strut,* with music by Irving Berlin, Johnny Mercer, Fats Waller, Duke Ellington, and Charlie Parker, opened off-Broadway in New York in October after playing since 1975 in Cleveland, San Francisco, Toronto, and Boston.

Revivals were popular in 1979, including *The Most Happy Fella,* Frank Loesser's 1956 smash. Starring Giorgio Tozzi and Sharon Daniels, this version opened on October 11.

Burlesque made a smash return in Mickey Rooney's *Sugar Babies,* also starring Ann Miller, which opened at the Mark Hellinger on October 8 after playing to packed houses around the country. Early in September *Big Bad Burlesque* opened at the Orpheum to excellent reviews for the verve of its cast, particularly Susan Orem as the Soubrette and Steve Liebman as Top Banana.

Television

Stars appearing in their own specials on ABC included John Davidson, Cheryl Ladd, Barry Manilow, Ann-Margret, Olivia Newton-John, John Travolta, and Donna Summer. Christmas shows were gifts from Pat Boone, the Carpenters, Perry Como, John Davidson and Donny and Marie, with "Christmas at the Grand Ole Opry" as well.

NBC's fall season of music specials began on September 16 at 8 P.M. with "Bob Hope on the Road to China," a broadcast taped entirely in the People's Republic of China and including such music stars as Crystal Gayle, Peaches and Herb, and Big Bird.

On October 16, NBC presented "The 1970's—The Explosion of Country Music," starring Dolly Parton, Eddie Rabbitt, Glen Campbell, Johnny Cash, Roy Clark, Loretta Lynn, Larry Gatlin, Ronnie Milsap, Dottie West, Tammy Wynette, Mel Tillis, Ray Stevens, Freddy Fender, Tom T. Hall, Charlie Rich, the Statler Brothers, and the Oak Ridge Boys.

Other NBC music offerings included "The Bee Gees Special," a record of their 1979 concert tour from Oakland to New York City, aired November 15; "The Rod Stewart Special," on November 23; "A Country Christmas Carol," based on Charles Dickens's *A Christmas Carol* and starring Hoyt Axton, Barbara Mandrell, Lynn Anderson, Larry Gatlin, Mel Tillis, the Statler Brothers, Danny Davis, and Tennessee Ernie Ford, was shown on December 18; the 1979 edition of "Mac Davis's Christmas Special" aired December 21.

Some of CBS's musical shows included a Crystal Gayle special, codirected by Russ Petranto and fashion photographer Francesco Scavullo and featuring the Statler Brothers, B. B. King, and Judy Collins. The Country Music Association awards show, hosted by Kenny Rogers, was telecast October 8. Kenny Rogers's second television special guested Dottie West, the Charlie Daniels Band, and Mac Davis, while Johnny Cash's twenty-five years in show business were honored in the winter. Christmas shows on CBS included "A Country Christmas," starring Eddie Rabbitt and a Johnny Cash special.

CBS also aired a tribute to Maybelle Carter, called "The Lynn Anderson, Carter Family, Johnny Cash, Ray Charles, Larry Gatlin, Emmylou Harris, Waylon Jennings, Kris Kristofferson, Willie Nelson, Linda Ronstadt Tribute....The Unbroken Circle: A Country Celebration of the Music of Mother Maybelle Carter."

On September 16, PBS broadcast via satellite to Europe and the United States the San Francisco Opera's performance of *La Gioconda,* with Renata Scotto as La Gioconda and Luciano Pavarotti as Enco. On September 24 "Live from the Met" kicked off with *Otello,* starring Placido Domingo in the title role. A show called "Musical Comedy Tonight," written, produced, and hosted by Sylvia Fine Kaye featured such stars as Ethel Merman, Carol Burnett, Sandy Duncan, Bernadette Peters, Richard Chamberlain, Rock Hudson, Gemze de Lappe, and John Davidson in a history of musical comedy. Included in the show was a sparkling appearance by Agnes de Mille, who recounted priceless *Oklahoma!* anecdotes. "Song by Song" was a seven-part series of hour-long tributes to lyricists. Beginning October 22 with Alan Jay Lerner, each segment concentrated on great contemporary lyricist, including such names as E. Y. Harburg, Lorenz Hart, Howard Dietz, Oscar Hammerstein, II, Dorothy Fields, and Sheldon Harnick. "Soundstage" began its sixth season on October 30 with such contemporary greats as Gordon Lightfoot, the Doobie Brothers, Elvin Bishop, Joan Armatrading, and the Temptations. On October 27 "Live from Lincoln Center" kicked off with the New York City Opera's production of *Streetscene,* Kurt Weill's 1947 English-language opera based on Elmer Rice's play.

Musical Lifelines

NOVEMBER 1978

Married:

11/13 Mary Costa (opera singer) to George Brent.

Died:

11/1 Larry Hiller (55), CBS recording engineer whose work included restoration of rare recordings by Bessie Smith and Louis Armstrong.

11/9 Miguelito Valdez (62), singer who introduced "Babalu," a song later popularized by Desi Arnaz.

11/10 Linda Scott (28), country-and-western singer who recorded under the name Charlee.

11/12 George Owen, trumpet sideman with the bands of Paul Whiteman and Les Brown.

11/14 Lou Preager, one of England's major big-band leaders; performed extensively on British television.

11/15 Grace Nelson Byrne, soprano during early radio days.

11/16 Theodore Fishberg, former viola player with New York Philharmonic.

11/18 Lennie Tristano (59), jazz pianist and instructor.

11/21 Bill Bates, composer, arranger, and producer.

11/21 Berry Gordy, Sr. (90), father of Berry Gordy, founder of Motown Records; remained active as corporate consultant to the label until his death.

11/26 Frank Rosolino, jazz trombonist of the be-bop era with Stan Kenton and Merv Griffin's television band.

DECEMBER

Married:

12/15 Don Bowles (lyricist/musician) to Lahoma Kaiser.

Died:

12/3 William Grant Still, black American composer, conductor, and arranger whose works include "Afro American Symphony" and "To You America"; played with W. C. Handy, Paul Whiteman, and Artie Shaw.

12/5 Ira D. (Pop) Nelson, father of "outlaw" singer Willie Nelson and a western swing musician in his own right.

12/8 Norman Lee (57), leader of the Eddy Howard Big Band in the Midwest.

12/15 Nat Debin, general manager of Long Island's Westbury Music Fair.

12/16 Blanche Calloway Jones, sister of bandleader Cab Calloway; one of the first women to lead a major U.S. dixieland band; sang with the bands of Earl Hines, Louis Armstrong, and Duke Ellington.

12/17 Don Ellis (44), musician/composer who wrote the score for The French Connection.

12/25 Lawrence (Ronnie) Blackwell, musician and vocalist on country-and-western circuit.

12/26 Reverend John M. Positano, former jazz clarinetist turned priest.

12/27 Chris Bell (27), guitarist/producer of Memphis group Big Star.

12/29 Janet A. Page, singer with opera troupes in the United States and abroad.

JANUARY 1979

Born:

1/27 To Cerrone (disco artist/producer) and wife Florence, a boy, Gregory, in Los Angeles.

Married:

1/7 David Amram (composer/conductor) to Loralee Ecobelli.

Died:

1/1 Ralph Cherry, big-band era trumpeter.

1/5 Charles Mingus (56), seminal jazz bass player whose innovations spotlighted the solo capabilities of the instrument.

1/7 James Pappoutsakis, flutist with the Boston Symphony for forty years.

1/8 Sarah Carter Bayes (80), last member of the original Carter Family Singers.

1/13 Donny Hathaway (33), renowned soul singer/composer/arranger and Grammy-winner.
Marjorie Lawrence (71), Australian-born dramatic soprano; her life was the subject of the Hollywood film Interrupted Melody.

1/15 Euphemia G. Gregory, lyric soprano.

1/18 Cyril J. Mockridge (82), composer with 20th Century-Fox for more than thirty years.

1/26 Jesus Sanches Erazo (78), considered Puerto Rico's finest troubadour; made many recordings as Chuito el de Bayamon.

1/27 Wayne J. (Sean) Koonce (27), jazz musician/composer.

1/28 Robin Reynold (25), singer/songwriter.

1/29 Sonny (Percival) Payne (52), jazz drummer who played with Count Basie and Harry James, among others.

FEBRUARY

Married:

2/25 Lydia O'Connor (pop singer) to Al Fisher (comedian).

Died:

2/2 Sid Vicious (John Simon Ritchie) (21), bassist with punk band the Sex Pistols, and solo artist.

2/7 Herbert L. (Peanuts) Holland, big-band era trumpeter and vocalist.

Charles Seeger (92), father of folk singer Pete Seeger; musicologist who taught the first such course in the United States.

2/11 Cecelia Thompson Ott, soprano with the Philadelphia Orchestra.

2/15 Zbigniew Siefert (33), promising Polish-born jazz violinist.

2/17 Albert Stillman (73), top pop lyricist who cowrote "Chances Are" and "It's Not for Me to Say," among others; music consultant to Radio City Music Hall.

2/21 Ray Whitley (77), singer/composer of western music, including "Back in the Saddle Again."

2/22 Henry H. Joseph, credited with helping establish American Federation of Musicians, Local 809, as major union local.

2/26 Jerry Davis (41), North Carolina-based guitarist.

2/27 Hugo Kolberg (80), former concertmaster of Berlin Philharmonic and several U.S. orchestras.

MARCH

Born:

3/11 To George Johnson (one half of the Brothers Johnson) and wife Barbara, a girl, in Los Angeles.

3/22 To Chaka Khan (singer) and Richard Holland, a boy, Damien Milton Patrick, in Los Angeles.

Married:

3/2 Robert Taylor (guitarist with Australian rock group Dragon) to Sue Lindsay.

3/21 Mel Tillis (county singer) to Julia Ann Edwards, in Gallatin, Tennessee.

3/27 Eric Clapton (rock guitarist) to Patti Boyd Harrison (former wife of George Harrison), in Tucson, Arizona.

Died:

3/1 Stefan Frankel, former concertmaster of Metropolitan Opera.

3/3 James S. Rull (82), composer/pianist/vocalist, public affairs consultant for ASCAP.

3/5 Alan Crofoot (49), Metropolitan Opera tenor.

3/6 Ethel von Povlich West, soprano, concert pianist, and voice coach.

3/7 Guiomar Novaes (83), Brazilian pianist.

3/9 Albert Yves Bernard (75), retired violinist of Boston Symphony Orchestra.

3/17 Giacomo Lauri-Volpi (86), tenor who specialized in Verdi.

3/22 Walter Legge (72), founder of London's Philharmonia Orchestra and classical record producer; husband of singer Elisabeth Schwarzkopf.

3/23 Jack Mills (87), founder of Mills Music, a leading pop music publisher; one of the first pop publishers to enter the educational and international publishing fields.

3/29 Zillah S. Young (33), conductor of the Honolulu Symphony Chorus and Hawaii Opera Theater Chorus.

3/31 Ernest Goldstein, first violinist of Philadelphia Orchestra.

APRIL

Born:

4/6 To Gerald Rothberg (publisher and editor-in-chief of *Circus Magazine*) and wife, a daughter.

4/16 To Anne Murray (top Canadian singer) and husband, a daughter.

4/19 To Goldie Hawn (film star) and Bill Hudson (member of the Hudson Brothers pop group), a daughter.

4/24 To Ted Feinman (musician with State Street) and wife, a son.

4/27 To Nesuhi Ertegun (president of WEA International) and wife Selma, a girl, Leyla, in New York.

Married:

4/2 Jim Carter (folk singer) to Amanda Arnold, in Texas.

Heinz (German singer) to Princess Hannelore Auersperg, in West Germany.

4/6 Rod Stewart (rock performer) to Alana Collins Hamilton, in Beverly Hills, California.

4/26 Terry Slezak (tenor) to Ruth Fry, in Houston.

Died:

4/1 Bruno Coquatrix, director of the Olympia, top Paris music hall.

4/2 Willie Rice, Jr. (58), jazz musician.

4/6 Leonard Whitcup (75), composer/lyricist/publisher.

4/8 Frank Coughlan, bandleader of Trocadero Ballroom.

4/9 Paul H. Curry, jazz pianist.

4/10 Malcolm Johnson (80), orchestra leader.

Nino Rota (68), Academy award-winning composer of music for *The Godfather;* composed music for many Fellini films; classical composer.

4/11 Lydia Johnson, singer with Johnson Family.

4/13 Margo Henderson (33), blues singer.

4/25 Leopold Ludwig (71), musical director of the Hamburg Opera for nineteen years.

4/26 Charles (Chic) Jensen (64), lead trumpet for Top Hatters in 1930s and 1940s.

4/27 Sammy Madden, Milwaukee-based orchestra leader for many years.

4/29 Werner Singer, concert pianist/accompanist/voice teacher.

4/30 Peg Tisdall, vaudeville pianist and singer.

MAY

Born:
5/9 To Riccardo Muti (Eugene Ormandy's successor as musical director/conductor of Philadelphia Orchestra) and wife, a son.
5/19 To Waylon Jennings (country singer) and Jessi Colter (country singer), a son, Waylon Albright Jennings, in Nashville.
5/25 To Joan Coplan (mezzo-soprano with Salzburg Orchestra) and Christian Merritt (lead tenor with Salzburg Orchestra), a daughter.
5/27 To Molly Bee (country singer) and Ira Allen (singing country bandleader), a son, Michael Jackson Allen, in Los Angeles.

Died:
5/1 Betty Cherie Harvey (54), big-band era vocalist.
5/6 Milton Ager (85), beloved composer of "Happy Days Are Here Again," "I'm Nobody's Baby," "Ain't She Sweet," and many other timeless song classics throughout a half-century career; father of author/television personality Shana Alexander.
5/8 George Redman, retired musical conductor and leader of big bands.
5/9 Eddie Jefferson (60), jazz lyricist.
5/11 Lester Flatt (64), one of the major popularizers of bluegrass guitar; member of the Flatt & Scruggs duo for twenty-one years.
5/14 Thomas Scherman (61), founder of the Little Orchestra Society and its conductor for twenty-seven years.
5/16 Roy Montrell (51), guitarist in Fats Domino's band.
5/19 Vernon Brown (72), trombonist with several big bands.
5/21 Richard A. (Blue) Mitchell (49), jazz trumpeter with a thirty-year musical career.
5/22 Alvin Thomas, Jr. (49), jazz pianist and accompanist for Sarah Vaughan.
5/23 Ralph Mendelson (62), violinist with the New York Philharmonic for twenty-six years.
5/25 Leonard Stogel, rock promoter who coproduced the California Jams and Canada Jam.

JUNE

Born:
6/1 To Jimmy Buffett (singer/songwriter) and wife Jane (noted skier), a daughter, Savannah Jane, in Aspen, Colorado.
6/2 To Lynn Anderson (country singer/composer) and husband Harold Stream, a son, in Lake Charles, Louisiana.

6/14 To Margaret Keller (singer) and Andrew Urban (publisher of *Encore* Magazine), a daughter, in Australia.
6/18 To David Hungate (bass player with Toto) and wife Deborah, a son, Noah, in Los Angeles.
6/25 To Merrill Osmond (singer/entertainer) and wife Mary, a son, Shane George, in Provo, Utah.

Married:
6/9 Muddy Waters (celebrated bluesman) to Marva Jean Brooks, in Chicago.

Died:
6/7 Alton Redd (75), veteran jazz drummer.
6/21 Raymond Allard (81), Boston Symphony French bassoonist.
6/22 Jeffrey Sam Guercio (26), brother of producer James Guercio; a recording engineer.
     Walter (Pee Wee) Hunt, trombonist and singer in big-band era.
6/26 Vernon Presley (62), father of Elvis Presley.
6/28 Paul Dessau (84), German composer, believed to be the last of Bertolt Brecht's collaborators in musical theater.
6/29 Lowell George (34), leading West Coast rock performer and composer, who had embarked on a successful solo career following the breakup of his band, Little Feat.

JULY

Born:
7/3 To Paul Gemignani (musical director of *Sweeney Todd*) and wife, a son.
7/16 To Gerry Beckley (member of pop group America) and wife, a son.
7/17 To Paul Katz (cellist with Cleveland Quartet) and wife Martha (violinist), a daughter.
7/30 To Frank Zappa (recording artist and record label head) and wife Gail, a daughter, Diva, in Los Angeles.
7/31 To Donny Osmond (singer/entertainer) and wife Debra, a son, Donald Clark, in Provo, Utah.

Died:
7/6 Van McCoy (35), singer/composer/arranger, who had enormous hit with "The Hustle."
7/8 Billie Haywood (75), blues singer.
7/10 Arthur Fiedler (83), beloved American conductor of the Boston Pops for almost half a century. His treatments of classical and semiclassical music popularized this music for generations of concertgoers and record buyers, beginning in 1935, when his version of "Jalousie" became the first million-selling record for RCA's Red Seal. Since that time his singles and albums have sold more than 40 million copies, including record-

ings made with such pop and jazz performers as Peter Nero, Henry Mancini, Al Hirt, Chet Atkins, and others. His love for charismatic performers was so great that he once even invited Elvis Presley to appear with the Boston Pops, but was turned down regretfully because the orchestra could not pay Presley's fee.

7/12 Minnie Riperton (31), highly acclaimed singer whose reputed 5½-octave coloratura voice led the mid-1960's band Rotary Connection. When she became a soloist in the early seventies, with Stevie Wonder as her producer, she recorded the international smash "Loving You."

7/16 Alfred Deller (67), British countertenor.

7/29 Phil Boutelje (84), pianist/conductor/composer of such songs as "China Boy," "Little Doll," and "Lonesome."

AUGUST

Born:
8/20 To Rod Stewart (rock singer) and wife Alana, a girl, Alana Kimberly, in Los Angeles

Married:
8/20 Vicki Carr (singer) to Michael Nilsson.

8/24 Tanya Welk (singer) to Kenny Roberts.

Died:
8/7 Jimmy Eaton (73), veteran lyricist whose songs include "Dance With a Dolly With a Hole in Her Stocking" and "Turn Back the Hands of Time."

8/13 Dick Foran (69), well-known star of Broadway musicals and singing cowboy in films.

8/14 Anna Turkel (mid-70s), American soprano.

8/17 Vivian Vance (66), beloved comedienne, who in addition to her fourteen years working with Lucille Ball on "Lucy" and "The Lucy Show" was a singer in clubs and appeared in several Broadway musicals, including *Skylark* and *Let's Face It.*

8/19 Dorsey Burnette (46), singer/composer who wrote "Tall Oak Tree," "Hey, Little One," and "Big Rock Candy Mountain."

8/22 Urias LeFevre (69), gospel singer with the family group the LeFevre Trio, later the LeFevre Family.
Sean Nolan (39), actor/singer/dancer/restaurateur who appeared in both the Broadway and the touring companies of Hello Dolly.

8/24 Paul Dumont (90), one of the first radio singers.

8/25 Stan Kenton (67), bandleader/composer/pianist/arranger who was a major and controversial force in the 1940s' development of progressive jazz. An experimenter whose personal flamboyance was an integral part of his music, Mr.

Kenton's sound was characterized by blaring brass which enchanted some listeners and enraged others. His big band was popular for its wide range of music and featured many fine vocalists, including June Christy and Anita O'Day. During the past twenty years, in addition to spending most of the year on the road, Kenton formed the Stan Kenton Clinic, teaching summer courses to musicians, and his own record company, Creative World Records.

8/25 Ray Eberle (60), pop singer during the 1930s and 1940s who sang with the Glenn Miller Orchestra for five years.

8/26 Ben Oakland (71), songwriter/director/producer/pianist whose songs include "Twinkle, Twinkle Little Star" and "I'll Dance at Your Wedding."

SEPTEMBER

MARRIED:
9/1 Debby Boone (singer) to Gabriel Ferrer, in Los Angeles.

DIED:
9/5 Nat Simon (79), conductor, lyricist, pianist, and composer of many hit songs, including "Poinciana."
Guy Bolton (96), writer of books for musicals with scores by such composers as Jerome Kern, Cole Porter, and George and Ira Gershwin.

9/15 Tommy Leonetti (50), night club singer who sang on television's "Your Hit Parade" in 1957–58, and who was enormously popular in Australia.

9/27 Gracie Fields (81), beloved star of music halls, stage, and screen and who for decades was known as "our Gracie" to millions of adoring British fans.
Jimmy McCulloch, guitarist with the Dukes group, formerly with Wings and Small Faces.

OCTOBER

Died:
10/1 Roy Harris (81), renowned American composer; often referred to as the Walt Whitman of American music, he was best known for his Third Symphony.

INDEX

183

184